The

BOOK-
MAKERS

The

BOOK-
MAKERS

A HISTORY OF THE BOOK
IN EIGHTEEN LIVES

ADAM SMYTH

BASIC BOOKS

New York

Basic Books
Hachette Book Group
1290 Avenue of the Americas, New York, NY 10104
www.basicbooks.com

Printed in the United States of America

Originally published in 2024 by The Bodley Head in Great Britain
First US Hardcover Edition: May 2024

Published by Basic Books, an imprint of Hachette Book Group, Inc. The Basic Books name and logo is a registered trademark of the Hachette Book Group.

The Hachette Speakers Bureau provides a wide range of authors for speaking events. To find out more, go to hachettespeakersbureau.com or email HachetteSpeakers@hbgusa.com.

Basic books may be purchased in bulk for business, educational, or promotional use. For more information, please contact your local bookseller or the Hachette Book Group Special Markets Department at special.markets@hbgusa.com.

The publisher is not responsible for websites (or their content) that are not owned by the publisher.

Typeset in 12/14.75pt Baskerville MT Pro by Jouve (UK), Milton Keynes

Library of Congress Control Number: 2023951481

ISBNs: 9781541605640 (hardcover), 9781541605657 (ebook)

LSC-C

Printing 1, 2024

Meanwhile the blades of the scissors do not snap but glide.

Tom Phillips (1937–2022), 'Henri Matisse: The Cut-Outs'

Contents

List of Images

Introduction

This is a book about books, and the people who made them. It's about grand, two-volume folio Bibles, and quickly Xeroxed 2020s zines, and the many books in between. It's about the lives that brought these forms – forms variously wondrous, strange, familiar, new – into being. It's about fragments of the earliest fifteenth-century books that only barely survive, and eighteenth-century volumes of such typographical elegance and calm that they sailed forth serenely (as one observing historian put it) 'to astonish all the librarians of Europe'. It's about books whose perfection makes us approach them with reverential care – *look at the inking! look at the binding! feel the paper!* – and books covered with the scribbled doodlings of readers heckling from the long-ago past.

Here is a moment when the history of a book came alive. I am in the Bodleian Library in Oxford, working my way through a pile of big folio volumes written by the magnificently singular Margaret Cavendish, Duchess of Newcastle (1623–73). Cavendish is fascinating for all kinds of reasons, not least as a scientist (the first woman to attend a Royal Society meeting), and as the inventor of something like science fiction – her *Blazing World* (1666) describes a young woman invading the world with an army of talking animals and submarines pulled by 'fish men'. Cavendish was also what we'd call an early modern celebrity: 'The whole story of this lady is a romance,' wrote Samuel Pepys in 1667, after spending a fruitless day trying to catch a glimpse of her coach. On title pages, she styled herself 'Thrice Noble, Illustrious, And Excellent Princess'. Pepys imagined 'her footmen in velvet coats, and herself in an antique dress', and he fixated on the image of Cavendish bowing from her box in the theatre after a performance of her play *The Humorous Lovers*.

(183)

As if they kept wife Counfels for their Lives ;
For when they Fly away they feek new Hives :
So Men, when they have any great Defign,
Their Thoughts do gather, and in heaps Combine,
But when they are Refolv'd, each one takes Flight,
And ftriveth which firft on *Defire* fhall Light ;
And thus Thoughts meet and fly about, till they
For their Subfiftence can find out a way :
But Doubting Thoughts, like Droans, live on the reft
Of Hoping Thoughts, which Honey bring to Neft ;
For like as Bees, by their Stings induftry
Get Honey, which the ftinglefs Drones live by ;
So Men without Ambition's Stings do live
Upon th' Induftrious Stock their Fathers give ;
And fome do Steal another Poets VVit,
And Drefs it up in their own Language fit :
But Fancy into every Garden flies,
And fucks the Flowers fweet from Lips and Eyes ;
Sometimes it Lights on thofe that are not Fair,
Like Bees on Herbs, that Dry and VVither'd are ;
As pureft Honey on fweet Flowers lies,
So fineft Fancies from young Beauties rife.

The Prey of Thoughts.

IF Thoughts be the Mind's Creatures, as fome fay,
Then, like the reft, they on each other Prey ;
Ambitious Thoughts, like to a Hawk, fly high,
In Circles of Defires mount to the Sky,
And when a Covy of young *Hopes* up Springs,
They ftrive to Catch them with their fwifteft Wings :
Thus, as the Hawk on Patridges doth Eat,
So Hopefull Thoughts are for Ambition's Meat :

Thoughts

A printer's fingerprint in Margaret Cavendish's Poems,
and Phancies *(1664), p. 183.*

I am midway through Cavendish's *Poems, and Phancies* (1664) when in the margins of a page I see a dark smudge. I look closer. It is ink. Closer still. A blurred fingerprint – at least I think that's what it is – parts of the swirling lines just about visible.

This is a fingerprint of the man who printed the book in 1664: an accidental, left-behind signature. And for a moment, as if by lightning, the process of this book's production is lit up: the print shop of William Wilson in 1664, the noise and the paper windows and the stink, a pressman plucking sheets still wet with ink from

2

the press and, before hanging them to dry on high strings running across the room, touching mistakenly an inky finger to the margin of the sheet, the sheet which, after drying, folding, stitching, and binding, was acquired by the Bodleian, and which, after a gap of 359 years, I am peering at now. That fingerprint doesn't summon into being the nameless print-shop worker who held the page I am looking at, but it does let me see Cavendish's book for what it is: a physical object, made by a little group of individuals at a particular time. Books tell all kinds of stories – romances, tragedies, comedies – but if we learn to read the material signs correctly, books can tell us the story of their own making, too.

The Book-Makers is a story of how books have been made by individuals across a period of about 530 years: from the very early printed books made by the Dutch immigrant Wynkyn de Worde working in London in the 1490s, to the zines of Black-Mass Publishing in New York in 2024. In between, we'll explore paper-making and binding, typography and cut-and-paste Bibles, libraries and small presses, huge books and ephemeral ballads, collectors who couldn't stop and publishers who produce a new book every week. The story has an English, French, and North American spine, but any history of the book is sprawlingly international, and we'll take in China from the second century, and the Islamic world from the eighth.

The Book-Makers is a history of the book told through biographical portraits of eighteen men and women, each of whom made, or is making, vital contributions to the development of the book as a physical form. Some of these names will be familiar, but many will not: this is not quite the roll call we might expect.

Many of these lives are richly documented, and loom out at us from the past in something like 3D, like Nancy Cunard, printing in rural France in the 1920s and 1930s. Some, like Sarah Eaves, partner and wife of John Baskerville in eighteenth-century Birmingham, were always there in the archive, but historians have been blind to, or uninterested in, their presence. Others, far back in time, like William Wildgoose, binding books in 1620s Oxford,

3

are harder to grasp: we see fragments, glimpses. We arrive in the room just after they have left – but their books stand in a pile on the desk.

The Book-Makers is a history of the book with people put back in: not a techno-determinist account where abstract mechanical forces drive change, not a chronology of inventions, but a narrative teeming with lives, and a history that is full of the contingencies and quirks, the successes and failures, the routes forward and the paths not taken, of these eighteen book-makers. People make books, and this is a history of the ways they have done so. *The Book-Makers* is a history that is also a celebration: a celebration of both the printed book as a technology at the heart of human culture, and a celebration of the rich and unpredictable particularity of the lives that put it there.

One crucial coupling in this volume is that of books and people. Another is that of books and time. One of the refrains running through *The Book-Makers* is that books have a complicated, deeply layered, often looping relationship to temporality. The book in my hands has existed at all moments between 1664 and today, and will continue to endure long after I have gone. The marks on books – the readers' annotations, the ticks or crosses, the heckling commentaries, the signs of damage and use, the scribbled records of ownership – describe this journey.

The Book-Makers is organised chronologically, from Wynkyn de Worde to Yusuf Hassan, but it doesn't argue for a linear narrative of improvement. It isn't the case that books, as objects, get better as the years tick by: a Whiggish version of history as improvement or a process of refining doesn't work. The paper used by Gutenberg in the first printed Bible, with its brilliantly clear bunch-of-grapes watermark, is of a time-defeating quality unsurpassed by modern industrial processes. The pages look today as they did on a summer's morning in 1455. At William Morris's Kelmscott Press in the 1890s, books were made to the specifications of medieval manuscripts, even though that age had long passed. Morris's books flicker between historical periods, belonging to several, not one. At Thomas Cobden-Sanderson's Doves Press in the early twentieth century, type was designed to resemble Nicolas Jenson's letters from 1470s Venice: Doves Press books were purposeful anachronisms, books that didn't fit, ways of refusing the drift of technology at a time when industrial book production was developing fast. And chronological adjacency – the sense that an object is explained by the thing next to it in time – is not always the best basis for comparison: Laura Grace Ford's cut-and-paste *Savage Messiah*, written in the early 2000s and battling the gentrification of London, finds a natural interlocutor in Mary and Anna Collett's collaged, cut-and-paste Bibles from the 1630s.

The Book-Makers is a history of the physical printed book that has been written in a contemporary culture which is increasingly online. I have chosen not to devote a whole chapter to e-books or online publications, although the book-makers of the final chapter have lots to say about these. One way of understanding the relationship between the digital and print in the 2020s is to look back to history at other moments of media change, like the relationship between manuscript and print in the fifteenth and sixteenth centuries. Printing didn't wipe out a culture of handwritten texts: the relationship was a kind of mutuality. Early printed books – including the first of them, Gutenberg's Latin Bible of 1455 – tried very hard to look like handwritten texts, in part because, like all new media scrambling for credibility, print disguised its own novelty, but also more generally because handwritten texts were the only available models. What else could print look like apart from manuscript? The idea that the new media form (print) replaced the old (handwriting) just isn't right, any more than digital has replaced print today. The most popular kind of early printed text, the almanac, actively encouraged handwritten interventions: one almanac from 1566 offers itself as a space for anyone 'that will make & keepe notes of any actes, deedes, or thinges that passeth from time to time, worthy of memory, to be registered'. Far from killing off scribal activity, early printing functioned, in the words of the book historian Peter Stallybrass, as 'a revolutionary incitement to writing by hand'. One way to think about digital culture and print is to see a similar kind of mutuality – not a Darwinian struggle, or a 'death', but a catalyst sparking new developments in the book. As sales of printed titles increase, and as the academic study of physical books and the history of print grows, we can see a correlation between our increasingly online lives and a rising sense of wonder at what the material text can do.

Digital culture affects print in the simple but profound sense that printing is altered by the possibility of another medium. It is a choice to print a book in a way it was not before online publishing, and the printed book acquires new connotations by the presence of digital culture as a kind of shadow, or pair, or other: these bookish connotations vary, but they might include endurance, slowness, quality, cost, history, time, depth. The older medium is changed by the presence of the new. To publish a punk zine in the 1970s was one thing; to publish a punk zine in 2009, when online blogging was increasingly popular and easy, is a different statement of intent. In his essay 'Tradition and the Individual Talent' (1919), T. S. Eliot argued that the canon of literature is altered by new work which modifies the tradition to make room for itself; in a similar way, the printed book has become a different object with the belated arrival of the digital. Contemporary zine makers like Craig Atkinson and Yusuf Hassan are producing books in a digital age but the staples-and-paper of their nimble publications recalls a pre-digital culture of purposefully low-fi publishing that stretches back through the twentieth century. The word 'radical' comes from the Latin *radix*, 'root': it suggests a concern with what came before, as well as (our more familiar sense) a growing towards something new. Printed books – the books I describe in *The Book-Makers* – are radical in this double sense.

And it is to print that we now turn – specifically, to a noisy, teeming, multi-lingual London in 1492. A Dutchman called Wynkyn walks into a tavern. It sounds like the start of a joke, but in fact it's the start of this history of the book.

I. PRINTING
Wynkyn de Worde (d.1534/5)

I Wynkyn de worde citizen and stacionner of London . . .

He is dead – long dead; his bones buried in a church on Fleet Street. Nearly five hundred years have passed. But his books – some of them – survive.

The book I have on the desk in front of me was printed at a shop called the Red Pale in Westminster, 531 years ago, in 1492: the year Columbus sails to the New World; the year the Jews are expelled from Spain; the year the Spanish monarchs Ferdinand and Isabella complete the Reconquista against Muslims. In fact, 'book' is the wrong word: it's a fragment of a book, two leaves, printed on one side each, the pages stained, battered, torn, imperfectly patched, and, more than anything else, fragile. This book has seen a lot. Each lift of the paper feels a risk. The fragment comes from a work titled *A Lytyll Treatyse Called the Booke of Curtesye*: a guide for children in verse, addressed to a universal 'John', and intended to steer its reader towards virtuous conduct. Avoid rough games and violent sports. Eat moderately. Say your prayers. Look people in the eye. Play the lute. And more than anything: read – and again, and again. Read John Gower, read Geoffrey Chaucer, read Thomas Hoccleve, read John Lydgate – fourteenth- and fifteenth-century writers, working in English, suggesting our reader 'John' is more Everychild than aristocrat, and conveying also the beginnings of a sense of a tradition of literature in English, rather than Latin or French.

The fragment has on one leaf three verses from a longer section on reading, celebrating Hoccleve (endearingly called 'Ocklyf'),

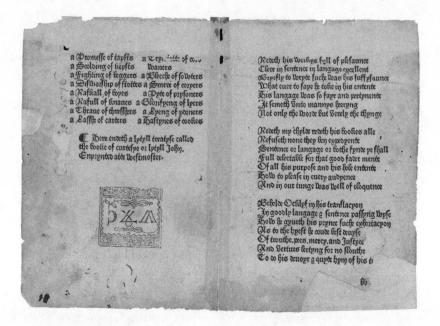

A fragment of A Lytyll Treatyse Called the Booke of Curtesye *(1492).*
The glue stains suggest these pages were once glued into another
book as binding supports – hence their survival.

and prescribing 'Redeth my chylde redeth his bookes alle'. On the other leaf, which would have come at the very end of the book, there's the colophon: the bit of text recording 'Here endeth a lytyll treatyse called the booke of curtesye or lytyll John. Enprynted atte Westmoster.' (Colophons, from the Greek for 'summit', or 'finishing touch', migrated from final page to title page around the start of the sixteenth century.) There's also the symbol of the printer, an elegant 'W' and 'C', but this emblem or 'device' is printed upside down. Something went wrong. This is a printer's proof, a trial print produced to spot errors. Once it had been scanned and this rather howling mistake noted – *I can't believe you've printed his emblem upside down!* – these pages would have been discarded as scrap. And this is why it survives today: a binder working on another book reached for these unwanted pages and used them as waste paper to line the inside covers. Lots of pages of torn-up, discarded books ended up being recycled in this way, and the backs of the leaves are still stained with the glue that once stuck them into a now-lost host. The survival of this fragment – which, apart from a single leaf in the British Library, is the only extant evidence of this edition of *The Booke of Curtesye* – is a happy accident of this unknown binder's work. In a paradox of popularity, all other copies of this guide for children from 1492 were read to pieces, and this mistaken, misshapen fragment is the thread that remembers this publishing hit.

The printer's emblem has a 'W' and a 'C', but William Caxton was dead by 1492. This book was printed by a former junior who had learnt his skills under Caxton and who, in a gesture of affection, admiration, and savvy marketing, persisted in using his master's sign. We know that printer, if we've heard of him at all, as Wynkyn de Worde, but in records he is called Winandum van Worden, Wynand van Worden, Windanus van Worden, Wynkyn Vort, William Wykyn, Wynken de Vorde, even Johannes or Jan or John Wynkyn. 'De Worde' suggests a birthplace, which might well be Woerden in Holland, making him Dutch, although for many years scholars thought it meant Woerth-sur-Sauer in Alsace, or Wörth am Rhein close to the French-German border, meaning he was German. This far back, the most fundamental aspects of identity become uncertain. *What is your name? Where were you born?*

De Worde was a printer, publisher, and bookseller in the earliest years of European printing, working for forty years with unflagging dynamism to make books, and his significance was to unlock the printing press's potential in England.

He was born as the technology that would change communication, and the world, was in its European infancy. In around 1450, Johannes Gutenberg in Mainz, a prosperous town on the Rhine, took what he knew about metalwork and about the screw presses used to produce wine and paper, and turned this knowledge into the mechanical movable-type printing press. Printing from movable type meant arranging or setting individually cast metal characters, made from lead alloy, into the page shape required, applying ink and then pressure via a press, producing as many copies as needed, before returning or 'distributing' the type back into compartments ready for the next setting. East Asian forms of printing certainly preceded Gutenberg by many centuries. Woodblock printing, in which paper is pressed to inked wooden blocks carved with text and image, was widespread across Asia after its introduction in China, probably some time before the eighth century CE – a 5-metre scroll made from paper strips printed from carved wooden blocks, known as the Diamond Sutra, was published in China in 868. Movable type, at first with clay characters, and later using wood and sometimes metal as well, was also developed from the eleventh century, although the number of characters needed for languages in China and Korea meant movable type did not dislodge the carved woodblock as the dominant printing form. It seems possible to the point of plausibility – although it's not at present provable – that Gutenberg learnt from China and Korea and that the history of printing is a joined-up story of the movement of knowledge from east to west. As Chapter 6 explores, the spread of paper-making technology from Asia through the Arab world from the eighth century, to North Africa and eventually Spain in the twelfth, provides a compelling model for knowledge as something on the move, and printing may have followed a comparable path.

Gutenberg's invention – the diversion of existing metalwork and screw-press technologies to a new end – had a power that ensured its quick distribution across Europe. In Cologne in 1471–2, Kentishman William Caxton acquired the skills to print, and by the time he moved back to England in 1476, he had de Worde as an assistant. De Worde matters for the history of the book as the worldly, vernacular successor to courtly William Caxton, whose speciality had been English translations of French chivalric works that had been hits at the Burgundian courts. De Worde was a pioneer who had a new kind of skill that the emerging business of printing made necessary: the ability to understand the desires and aspirations of readers he had never met. He grasped the disseminating potential of print, its capacity to reach readers beyond the coteries of manuscript (from the Latin, 'handwriting') circulation.

He knew, too, the advantages of aristocratic and royal connections, cultural amphibian that he was, and he could swim in that water; but his achievement was to reach a newly broad audience with bestselling books in English. He published more than 800 titles which constitutes, by one scholar's estimate, about 15 per cent of the entire known printed output in England before 1550. These Wordean titles included perennially popular grammar guides (about a third of de Worde's surviving output – how times change); religious works in English, handbooks to devotion, and biographies of the exemplary, like the *Lyf of Saynt Vrsula* (1510); translations of Latin works into English that appealed to would-be humanists with rusty Latin – helpful leg-ups, if you will, into the classical world, like the compact little volume of Cicero's *De Officiis*, on the best way to live, printed with facing pages of Latin and English and often (to judge from the 1534 copy I read) covered with handwritten scribbles and notes from eager readers; chronicles or outlines of history for those who could never quite remember whether Egbert came before or after Æthelwulf; books about husbandry and guides to caring for animals like *Proprytees & Medicynes of Hors[es]* (1497); jest books and ballads and almanacs, almost all of them now lost or surviving only as recycled waste in the bindings of later books; works of poetry and imaginative writing and medieval romances and what we'd call today (but not then) 'literature'; and travel writing, like Mandeville's *Travels* in 1499, an account of a knight from St Albans journeying to Constantinople, Jerusalem, and China – we should probably call it a story, a mixing of existing tales and fantasies and armchair dreaming.

De Worde's printing of Mandeville's travel narrative shows two traits that are key to his reaching success. First, de Worde's decision to publish a work that had already proved hugely popular, pre-Gutenberg. Mandeville's fantasy travel text had been a big pre-print hit since the later fourteenth century in England and northern France, and de Worde's task was to transfer this material across media, from manuscript to print. In this sense, he's less a revolutionary than a great redirector – flinging open a new channel for information to flow through. And that second de Wordean trait: pictures. De Worde loved images and his books express this: his thinking was more instinctively visual than verbal, and, more than any of his rivals, he learnt from the sophisticated visual presentation of text by Continental printers. More than half of de Worde's books have illustrations and these come from more than 1,100 separate cuts or blocks. Lots are rough and ready – de Worde worked fast – but as a whole they reveal the arrival of the English printed book as an illustrated object. For his 1499 Mandeville, De Worde employed a cutter – nameless to us now, but their handwork appears everywhere across de Worde's output – to make copies of woodcuts from a German translation of Mandeville from 1482. Only two surviving copies of de Worde's book survive. Each has seventy-two pictures or 'cuts', and there's one of Samson in Gaza I particularly like: Samson as 'he slewes the king in his palays [palace] & many a thousande more with hym', the woodcut showing tiny faces at the windows staring out as the building tumbles, the landscape itself contorting at the violence.

This man at the heart of English printing's origin moment was a foreigner. Internationalism isn't a quality we expect to find in English culture at this time, so loud have been the various fictions of national exceptionalism that historians have told us, but English printed culture was and remains profoundly indebted to immigrants from other lands. We can name-check some of the more prominent figures, but these are only the brightest lights dotting a much wider field. Alongside de Worde, crucial early figures were Theodoric Rood, the first, or maybe second, printer in Oxford, *c.*1481, who lugged his type and press from Cologne; John Siberch – Johann Lair von Siegburg – who also left Cologne to set up in Cambridge around 1520, working at a printing house on the site of present-day Gonville and Caius College; and Richard Pynson from Normandy, who became in 1506 the official King's Printer, first to Henry VII and then Henry VIII. Even Kentish-born William Caxton, England's first printer, travelled as a merchant overseas where he spoke French and Dutch. Surviving documents place Caxton regularly in Bruges and Ghent, which means Caxton was in northern Europe just as 'this specifically teutonic invention' (bibliographer David Rundle's nice phrase), developed by Gutenberg in Mainz, was making its mark. It was in Cologne in 1471–2 that Caxton learnt to print, probably working in partnership with type-cutter and printer Johannes Veldener from Flanders. And it was here that he acquired a printing press before moving to Bruges in 1472, and then back to England in 1476 with, probably, a team of European print-shop workers, including de Worde, who served as typesetters, pressmen, proofreaders, and binders.

Caxton rented property in Westminster Abbey at the sign of the Red Pale: close to the court and at the centre of a pool of affluent potential book-buyers. To hold in one's hand the first book Caxton printed in England, *The Canterbury Tales* (1476), is to hold an object made of paper imported from France, printed with type cut and supplied from Louvain, bound in ornamented brown calf by highly skilled (but largely nameless) immigrant bookbinders, the whole produced with the skill and patience and care acquired in Cologne. Early books may now sit still on shelves or behind glass or on book rests on a desk in hushed libraries, but they are pan-European objects, the product of movement, a gathering together of materials and labour and knowledge from across the Continent.

Government legislation recognised the need for these foreign skills. When, in 1484, acts were passed restricting foreign (or alien) traders, an exemption was made for foreign workers connected with the book trade who could live and work in England. De Worde didn't take out letters of denization (a denizen was a foreigner allowed to live in the country) until 1496 because of this latitude. But this legal openness was always in tension with life on the ground. Native workers in the book trade reacted jealously, and sometimes violently, to immigrant workers: Pynson, from Normandy, the future King's Printer, was assaulted with his servants on 21 April 1500. The nationalist grip was already tightening by 1523, when aliens were banned from having non-English apprentices, and in 1529, when aliens were prevented from setting up print shops. Any lingering tolerance was fully repealed in 1534, when it was made unlawful to buy printed books from any 'stranger'. The act justified this change by claiming, with considerable exaggeration, that printing skills had been diffused through the realm, and a reliance on imported skill was no longer required:

> many of this realme beinge the Kinges natural subjectes, have given them so diligently to lerne and exercise the saide craft of printing that at this day there be within this realme a great number of connyng [cunning, skilful] and expert in the said science or craft of printing, as able to exercise the saide crafte in all pointes as any stranger in any other realme or country.

We know where de Worde lived and worked, and we have a sense of his neighbourhood. Today numbers 130 and 131 Fleet Street are occupied by fast-food chain itsu, purveying 'health & happiness', but in late 1500 this was Wynkyn de Worde's home and printing house. He lived and worked there until his death in 1534/5, renting a former inn for £3 6s 8d per year from a priory in Buckinghamshire. The property, just to the west of Shoe Lane, was big: three or perhaps four storeys, with garrets at the top. The books de Worde printed around the time carried variations of the

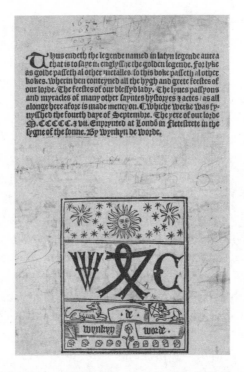

De Worde's device, in Legenda aurea, *printed 'In Fletestrete in the signe of the Sonne, by Wynkyn de Worde', 1507.*

declaration, 'Enprynted in fleete strete at the sygne of the sone. By me Wynkyn de Worde', so the building – which as an inn had been called the Falcon – was probably hung with the sign of a sun like the one that appears at the top of his emblem in books, where de Worde's identity is layered over his former master's. De Worde used Caxton's device at the start of his career, and even when he did change to his own device it was still a revised version of Caxton's. The puns must have occurred to him: the prolific printer who dealt in words; the professional son of Caxton whose shop logo was a sun.

Let's imagine a bright morning in 1501. De Worde is looking out from his home on a busy Fleet Street. The smaller houses, crammed close to the street, are the homes of tradesmen like the cap-makers and the tavern keepers and the bookbinders along

Shoe Lane; the larger homes, set back with gardens, belong mostly to members of the clergy, to abbots and bishops with ecclesiastical posts far away in distant parts of the country. In 1509, a youthful Henry VIII and his Queen Catherine would process past this spot where, now, on this morning in 1501, a servant collects water from the conduit outside de Worde's shop. To the left, high above the other buildings, is St Paul's, whose churchyard is the centre of bookselling. The smell of the tanneries is bad. Boats selling oysters and herring row up the Fleet River. Bustle is everywhere. Raised voices. Shouts. When de Worde walks to the right up Fleet Street, pushing against a tide of people, in three minutes he is at St Dunstan-in-the-West. Standing outside this 500-year-old church, as the street traders cry out, over and over again, de Worde thinks about being alive right now, and about the people who walked this street centuries ago. St Bride's Church, where de Worde prays and where he knows he will be buried, is less than a minute's walk from his shop, tucked back from Fleet Street, built on the remains of seven previous churches and once, far back in time, the site of a Roman villa. For us in the twenty-first century, the church is doubly removed, by Wren's rebuilding after the fire in 1666, and by the restoration after a bomb in December 1940. But on a crisp September morning in 1501, the bells have just started ringing.

De Worde was working in the middle of printing's new locale: this was the start of Fleet Street's invention as an international centre of the printed word. A little further up Fleet Street is number 188, to the west of St Dunstan's Church, opposite Ye Olde Cock Tavern, where de Worde's main rival, Norman-born printer Richard Pynson, had his print shop. De Worde had moved the two miles east from Westminster where he'd run his business in the Abbey's shadows at the print shop of his master, Caxton, for nine years after Caxton's death in 1492. *The myracles of oure blessyd lady* (1496) was, the printed text declares, 'Enprynted at Westmynster: In Caxtons house. by me Wynkyn de Worde' – which probably means one of the tenements rented by Caxton in the almonry. De Worde also took over Caxton's small print shop next to the Abbey's chapter house. So eager was he to remember and honour his master that the move to Fleet Street, to the different culture it represented, must have been difficult. The move was a shift away from proximity to court to a printing world more popular and vernacular and market-driven. Perhaps de Worde worried he was letting Caxton down; perhaps he sensed he was at the start of something huge. It was a move into a marketplace of print that we can recognise today.

The earliest image we have of a print shop at work is, to modern eyes, a wonderfully strange mixture of the documentary and the allegorical, contained in a work about the imminence of death, published in Lyon in 1499, around the time de Worde was establishing his reputation post-Caxton (see plate section). Death reaches everyone, this French book declares, and quickly – no matter your rank or wealth, no matter your trade, no matter your effort and virtuous toil.

One of the many scenes where the dance of death occurs is the printer's shop. Here is grinning Death, with a touch to the arm as gentle as it is inevitable, summoning the compositor setting type with his composing stick and copy text, pointing to the life to come for the puller and the beater with his raised inking ball. Death touches the printers, but it does not touch the printed books, and if this is an allegory of human mortality, it is also an early statement of the capacity of print to live on, a recognition that a printed book is the work of hands lost to history, a kind of residue, an object that endures through time, across generations.

What did de Worde's print shop look like? What was it like to push open the doors of the converted tavern and walk inside? We don't have a first-person account, but we can get a long way through typicality: many smaller printing shops across the sixteenth and seventeenth centuries followed similar forms. Print shops were both workshops and homes. In one room there might be three or four printing presses, with a probably bulky man called a 'puller' yanking the bar to turn the screw which presses paper against a 'forme' of metal type, holding for a second or two a moment of 'dwell' when the pressure was at its maximum; and a second man called a 'beater' applying ink with inking balls made from animal skin to the type, and inspecting the printed sheet when the press rose back up. The Sun wasn't purpose-built so there would almost certainly have been a sense of machinery and bodies squeezed in; of repurposing and spatial improvisation. The place is surely cramped, and probably dark; too hot in summer. Candles flicker. Just-printed sheets hang from high ropes like drying laundry. The windows are paper, not glass, a cheap way to block sunlight from the printed pages. But – in winter – so cold. Scraps of paper lie around – old proof pages, torn sheets – ready for reuse as improvised window covers, or wrappers, or to fill a thin space between wobbly letters: there is a thriftiness to everything, a spirit of maximal extraction. And the place stinks: from bodies printing 250 sheets an hour for twelve-hour days; from the strongly alkali lye, bubbling in a tub, used to clean the lead type; from the beer spilt on the floor, brought in every couple of hours by the young apprentice; from the linseed oil boiling in a cauldron over logs, nearly ready to be mixed with carbon and amber resin to make ink; and from the buckets of urine in which the inking balls' leather covers soak and soften overnight.

If we pass through the press room, we reach a second chamber, this one for composition: the space for the setting of type, with frames of type-cases, and a large flat imposing stone where formes of set type were placed. Bigger venues might have a third room for storing paper – maybe de Worde's roomy tavern did – and there would be benches with stacks of paper next to the presses.

We can get a bit more speculative detail from an inventory of a printer's shop called the George, owned by William Powell, who seems to have offered the contents as collateral for a loan in 1553. It's not the Sun, but it's probably close. The inventory is written in a mix of Latin, English and French that is tricky today but that catches London in its multi-lingual sixteenth-century richness. The document was probably compiled by foreign workmen and only later transcribed by a lawyer's clerk. It's organised room by room: what at first seems a piled-up confusion has a walking-through logic, and the effect is as if time has been paused in a busy print shop on a day in the mid-sixteenth century.

The inventory is extremely detailed and conveys the book in process, caught at each stage of its movement towards printed completion. There are texts handwritten on parchment which serve as copy for the compositors to follow as they pick out letter after letter: the pages held in place on a visorum, a wooden frame attached to a type-case. There are loose letters: 'basketts' and 'cases wythe letters to prynt wythe', including 'grete Roman', and also 'grete woodden letters' for headings and ornamental printing. There is a box 'full of stykes for the presses': compositors' sticks, the handheld narrow trays in which compositors placed individual letters, one by one, to make words and lines. There are lead letters laid out or set as page units, locked up and held in place in a metal 'chase', with wooden sticks and blocks or 'furniture' filling out the gaps and held tight in place with wedges or 'quoins' – this whole 'forme' awaiting transfer to the press for printing. There are four printing presses ('quatuor lez pryntyng presses') and shelves with 'pyftures [pictures] & historiis . . . par del wood', which probably means woodblocks for printing pictures and scenes or stories. There are three 'pottes for pryntynge Inke': two black, and one red. There are various binding tools ('Tolis') or 'instruments' – in the macaronic language of the inventory, 'diuers Instrument cum Tolis too bynde Wyth'. There are also references that suggest the in-shop casting of metal type, with two tubs, a ladle, an old cup, and some lead ('le ladell et certum parvum metallum' and 'le trowghe plumbeis'): the printer would pour the liquid metal into a hand mould. And then there are the piles and piles of finished books, awaiting distribution or sale, including lots printed, or perhaps printed, by de Worde: sixty-four copies of *The boke of hawkynge, and huntynge, and fysshynge* (1518); fifty copies of one of many editions of John Stanbridge grammar guides, *Accidence* (first printed in 1495); twelve copies of Chaucer's

Canterbury Tales (1498). The value of the whole is put at £280, which means about £160,000 in today's money.

De Worde's book-making existed between two overlapping cultures: on the one hand, what we might call the emerging market of popular print, where books were bought by unknown readers and de Worde operated with an acute and savvy sense of popular taste; on the other, a late-medieval culture of aristocratic and royal patronage, where the preferences of powerful single individuals shaped books. The marketplace of print, where anonymous hands turned over books on a stall, weighing up what was on offer, is recognisably a version of our own book world today, and de Worde was operating within, and to some extent creating, this version of modernity. We can see his instincts for the book that would sell in huge numbers – and his acute sense of what people wanted – in the Latin grammar guides he published (a 'cash crop', in the words of print historian Lotte Hellinga): more than 150 editions by Robert Whittington, and more than 75 by John Stanbridge. We see this too in the many volumes of English poetry he published. If you wanted to read the best-known recent poems, like Stephen Hawes's wonderful allegorical account of the pilgrimage through life of the knight Graunde Amoure, *The pastyme of pleasure* (1509), then de Worde was your man. (The battered fragment of Hawes's poem in the Bodleian Library is pocked with wormholes, and has the name 'Nycolas' – some distant reader-doodler – written in red pencil in the gutter between the second and third pages.) De Worde's rival Pynson was only occasionally invested in English poetry, and his characteristic caution sets off de Worde's boldness. We might even argue that de Worde invented the idea of the contemporary printed poet: his 1499 publication of John Skelton's satire of court life, *The Bowge of courte* (1499), was the first appearance in print of a long poem by a living

English author, and reframed printed poetry as something that occurred in the present tense. ('Bowge' is from *bouche*, or 'mouth' in French, and means here court rations.) But if allegory and satire sound a bit demanding, then drop down a rung or two on the literary ladder, and de Worde is there for you, too – not judging, just selling – with hit medieval English romances like *Sir Bevis of Hampton* (1500), and comic tales like *A mery Jest of the Mylner of Abyngdon* (1532–34), a reworking of Chaucer's 'Reeve's Tale'.

But even as de Worde marketed these bestsellers, he was operating in the more rarefied culture of royal commission. Neither two-faced nor hypocritical, this Dutchman in London could slide easily between different worlds, wiping the ink from his fingers as he walked up the steps to court. Here the crucial figure is Lady Margaret Beaufort (1443–1509), Countess of Richmond and Derby, and mother of King Henry VII. Beaufort is perhaps best known as the woman who coordinated the overthrow of Richard III that brought Henry to the throne, but she is also a powerful figure in the world of books, someone who had close relations with the three pre-eminent printers of her time, Caxton, Pynson, and de Worde. Beaufort understood the religious books she commissioned and perhaps funded – sermons, copies of prayers, a saint's life, service books, guides to good spiritual living – as external expressions of an inner piety, and de Worde, in the process of establishing a profitable market in devotional print, was delighted to collaborate with such an eminent figure whose money helped with production costs. We can see this flowering relationship in Beaufort's financial accounts, which record tips being frequently paid to de Worde, or associated servants, for the delivery of books: on 6 July 1508, a shilling 'in reward the vj [6th] day of the said moneth to Wynkyn de Worde printer for bringing vnto my ladys grace of certan Bokes'. When Beaufort died, the summary of accounts after her death recorded £20 advanced to de Worde. We also see this collaboration in de Worde's colophons, so punctually dated that we can imagine de Worde inspecting the wet sheets hanging from strings: 'Thus endeth Nychodemus gospell. Enprynted at London in Fletestrete at the sygne of the sonne by Wynkyn de Worde prynter unto the moost excellent pryncesse my lady the kynges moder [mother]. In the yere of our lorde god. M. CCCCC. ix. the. xxiii. daye of Marche.'

There is a more extended articulation of de Worde's collaborations in his edition of *Scala Perfeccionis* of 1494. Written by Walter Hylton (*c*.1340–96), a member of the Augustinian Priory in the small village of Thurgarton, Nottinghamshire, it is an English handbook for the good spiritual life: a 'Scale of Perfection', a kind of devotional ladder for purifying the soul on the climb to a spiritual Jerusalem. Hylton's guide had circulated widely in manuscript – de Worde knew he was on to a hit – and while de Worde's *editio princeps* (the bibliographer's way of saying 'first edition') is a relatively plain production, later editions add in de Wordean charms to nudge the flagging reader, like historiated (or decorated) capitals with little faces peeping out from within the letters. The book was widely read and, it seems, studied and enacted, and as copies of it made their way out from de Worde's print shop 'in fletestret at the sygne of the Sonne' to meet their readers, travelling through time, they accumulated the scars of reading and use: a 1533 copy in the British Library is covered in handwritten doodles and notes from the sixteenth century, many of them in turn crossed out by a later, disagreeing reader, and suggesting a text moving through the world.

This sense of books carrying their own histories, whether through marks by readers or their own printed descriptions of how they came into being, is a particular feature of de Worde's output. The book historian D. F. McKenzie put this nicely when, thinking about a later period, he wrote that 'every book tells a story quite apart from that recounted by its text'. McKenzie meant that the story of a book's production is carried in its material form, alongside the text we more quickly and easily read. We see versions of this self-reflexivity all over de Worde's publications, but here's one example, from *De Proprietatibus Rerum* (1495) – a vast reference guide on the properties of things. De Worde's was the first printed edition of the English translation of this influential thirteenth-century work of science that had been a huge hit in manuscript: typically, de Worde was following the contours of popularity already created by late-medieval manuscript culture. In the epilogue we are offered a vignette of the book's history.

> And also of your charyte call to remembraunce
> The soule of William Caxton, first prynter of this boke
> In Laten tonge at Coleyn [Cologne] hysself to avaunce,
> That every well-disposed man may theron loke:
> And JOHN TATE the younger joye mote [may] he broke,
> Which late hathe in Englond doo make this paper thynne,
> That now in our Englysshe this boke is printed inne.

The book remembers the soul of the departed Caxton, who printed a Latin version in Cologne, and records also that this is a book printed on paper made in England by John Tate the Younger. Tate was a former merchant dealing in fine cloth who converted a water-powered mill upstream from Hertford into England's first paper mill, the exception to English reliance on imported Dutch, French, or Italian paper, which ran from about 1480 for some twenty years. De Worde's book is one of the very first books printed on paper made in England. Hold the pages up to the light and you can see Tate's watermark, an elegant eight-pointed star or petal set in a double circle.

Margart Beaufort catalysed several important books, including English translations of the *Imitatio Christi*, but by far the most significant of these is *The Ship of Fools*. This is a book still quite widely known today, and it's easy to see why: it's hilarious in the way most books from 1494 really are not – a mix of humanist learning and backslapping guffaws, the kind of book that makes you say, 'Oh, here's another bit' as you read it to your friends. The original was Sebastian Brant's *Narrenschiff* (1494), written in German

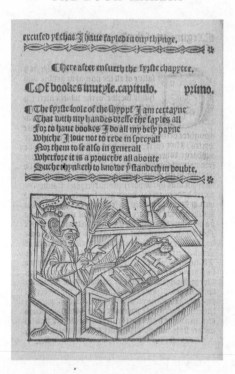

The Ship of Fools *(1517)*.

and published in Basel, and it spread across Europe like spilt ink through tissue paper, with fifteen editions in various languages before 1500, including Latin (in 1497 by Jacob Locher as *Stultifera Navis*), French, Flemish, and English. The popularity of these books mean the early copies that survive are often in a battered state: the 1517 copy in the Bodleian Library has the handwritten note, 'William . Crips . oeth [owneth] . this . booke . indede', and the photostat replacements from another copy for its missing signatures A1 and A8 suggest Crips was a little too vehement in turning the pages.

The book takes as its satirical target late-fifteenth-century folly: look at this ship of buffoons, Brant says, on its way to the fool's paradise of Narragonia, each figure ludicrous and pompous and wrong in their own particular way. Brant separates out these kinds and renders them vividly and memorably and with absurdity. Can

24

you see yourself among them? The drunkard. The gossip. The hypocrite. Are you an untrained doctor? A corrupt judge? An actor? A flatterer? Are you in denial about death? Do you ignore the holy days? Are you ungrateful? Impatient? Gullible? Judgemental? Slothful? Proud? Are you preoccupied with success? Do you eat immoderately? Do you lead the good astray? Do you – and here the categories of foolishness get a little more surprising – play musical instruments at night, or – stay with me – fail to complete pieces of architecture? Do you buy new books without reading them, 'oftentymes . . . pass[ing] the tyme in beholdyne the dyversytees of the coverynges' without finishing the text?

Are you – and this is Brant's best type of all – determined not to be a fool?

Eager to please Margaret, de Worde responded to her enthusiasm for Brant's book by having Henry Watson translate the French prose version into English. The book appeared in print in quarto (about the size and status of today's paperback) in July 1509, although Margaret had died a month before. De Worde's rival Richard Pynson was also at work on his own edition: a translation by Alexander Barclay appeared in December. De Worde worked fast, particularly when he sensed a race, and as he outstripped Pynson, his workmen left signs of haste in the finished book, like the occasionally poorly inked images.

Pynson's edition is in many ways a superior bibliographical object – the printing is better, the images sharper, the use of type defter with Roman letters for Latin juxtaposed with blackletter for English – but something of the quick and earthy humour of the satire is lost in Pynson's admirable but static folio, a work for the desk, but not the hand. The Bodleian has a copy of Pynson's edition once owned by the legal scholar John Selden (1584–1654) – the most learned man in the country, according to John Milton, himself not exactly bottom of the class. Selden's copy has the number 16 inked on the fore-edge, recalling a time when the book stood on Selden's shelf among his collection of 8,000 volumes, with the pages, rather than the spine, facing out.

25

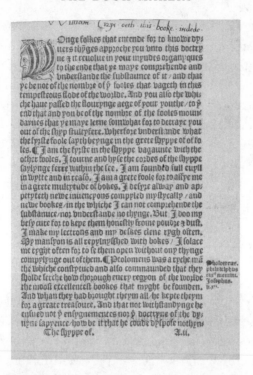

Historiated capitals from one copy of The Ship of
Fools *with an ownership note of an early reader.*

De Worde's edition is a different beast, and we can see his
emerging tactics all over his smaller quarto: the grimacing faces
in the capital letters; the slightly clumsy ornamental borders; and
the many woodcuts that litter the text.

Below is one of de Worde's representatively beguiling woodcuts
of a type of fool: a group of 'players of instrumentes', each of the
musicians manqué wearing their giveaway headpieces, complete
with pert ears – their song inducing not acclaim but only the emp-
tying of a chamber pot.

As we read de Worde's book, one curiosity that might strike
us, if we're paying attention, is that the same woodcuts reappear
at different points in the book: identical images for different varieties of fool. The illustration of 'folysshe physycyens' (Chapter
52) had already been used for 'Of the impacyence in sykenes'

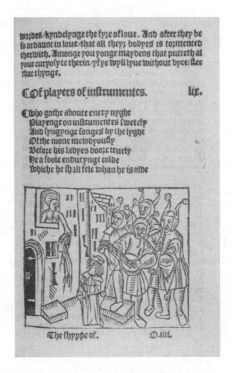

Musical fools in The Ship of Fools.

(Chapter 37) – and there are lots of other repeats, both within books and from one title to another. This was part of de Worde's thrifty economy: a woodcut block was an expensive piece of hardware, so better to reuse blocks already in-house than buy or commission new ones. De Worde repeated the manoeuvre across lots of publications. In *The Assembly of Gods* (1500), a series of reprints of Lydgate's shorter poems, de Worde used a woodblock intended to represent the assembled gods that had been previously used to illustrate the (very ungodlike) pilgrims in Chaucer's *Canterbury Tales*. And as the literary scholar Seth Lerer has shown, de Worde reused the same woodcut of a woman presenting a ring to a man across five different books of poetry, including Stephen Hawes's *Pastime of Pleasure* (1509 and 1517) and Chaucer's *Troilus and Criseyde* (1517). In his printing of Chaucer's narrative, de Worde filled in the 'banderoles' (the scrolls for text, from the Italian *bandiera*, 'banner', forerunners of the modern comic book's bubble of speech) with text – but he didn't in Hawes's.

Today we might see these visual repetitions as dubious short-cuts: failures of book production for which de Worde deserves reprimand. In fact, this kind of image recycling was common in print across the sixteenth and seventeenth centuries. We see it a lot also in broadsheet ballads – cheap, single-sheet verses to a named tune – where the same image can appear in incongruously different contexts, like the woodcut of a courting couple, embracing outside on the ground, which crops up in a number of ballads in the 1670s and '80s, including *The Beggar's Delight*, and *The Hampshire Miller, Short and Thick*. Readers would have expected these repetitions, and rather than feeling that something was amiss, may have drawn connections between the flashes of visual repetition. This was a culture deeply familiar with the re-presentation of biblical, and increasingly across the sixteenth century, classical, figures and narratives, and reiterated woodcuts no doubt prompted some readers to wonder – as de Worde's *Pastime of Pleasure* and *Troilus and Criseyde* overlap – how Hawes's allegorical journey through life connects with Chaucer's tragic poem of love set against the backdrop of the Trojan wars. One of de Worde's significances is that he (in Lerer's words) 'published virtually the entire canon of Middle English literature', and these visual connections were ways of building links between these literary texts, creating the effect of an imaginative field.

Part of de Worde's highly visual approach to the book was his reimagining of the nature and function of the title page. A title page probably seems to us today so evidently part of a book that it's hard to imagine a time when its form represented an innovation, but across the later fifteenth and early sixteenth centuries – let's call them the de Worde years – there was a movement from, in broad terms, medieval manuscripts with no title page, to 'incunables' (books printed in the infant years of print, before 1501, from the Latin *incunabula*, 'swaddling clothes' or 'cradle') with a brief label-title, to printed books with title pages we recognise today. Medieval manuscripts marked their beginning with an *incipit* (from the Latin, 'here begins' or 'it begins'), a short narrative statement opening the text, but not separate from it, a note of subject and maybe (but frequently not) author, often rubricated (decorated in red ink). A medieval text in manuscript often existed as one text in a larger group or anthology contained within a single physical codex, so the 'here begins' form made sense as a way of marking out the next text in a sequence. What would become the title is here the opening clause, and the invention of the modern printed title page meant in effect the uncoupling of this *incipit* and its movement to a place before, and outside of, the text: the creation of what Gérard Genette, in 1987, called paratext, the space outside the main text, a kind of surround, that conveys the writing to the world. Information about who actually made the manuscript usually came in the form of a colophon at the end or sometimes the start: colophons in manuscripts were sometimes tetchy, and often deeply humanized vignettes of labour expended, like the late-fourteenth-century manuscript now at Leiden whose Latin colophon translates as, 'This work is written, master, give me a drink; release the right hand of the scribe from the oppressiveness of pain.'

Printed texts, which tended to exist as distinct physical forms, rather than as items within a larger physical whole, began to feature simple, unadorned label-titles, applied to the otherwise blank leaf at the start of the text – a blank leaf that was there to serve as a protective covering during the book's transit. Printers began to see the potential in this new space for fuller titles, and by the early sixteenth century, the colophon shifted from the back of the book to the front and merged with the expanding label-title. Title pages were beginning to develop a logic we recognise today, listing some combination of title, author, printer-publisher, and location of production. They became spaces where the book could assert itself as legitimate, trustworthy – 'Imprinted at London by Simon Stafford for Cuthbert Burby: And are to be sold at his shop neere the Royall Exchange 1599' – even as it would advertise, sell, entice, persuade: 'A Pleasant Conceyted Comedie of George a Greene, the Pinner of Wakefield, As it was sundry times acted by the servants of the right Honourable the Earle of Sussex.'

De Worde's position as a pioneer of early print in a culture still steeped in manuscript traditions means his title pages exist at a kind of transitional point, exhibiting features both old and new. Let's take his edition of the sermon delivered at the funeral of Henry VII in 1509 by John Fisher, Bishop of Rochester. The title page contains the kind of arresting woodcut image that de Worde became famous for. I like the picture of a living Henry, flipped horizontal to denote death – when de Worde came to reuse the same woodcut for a later, 1521 sermon by Fisher against 'the pernicious doctrine of Martin Luther', he covered up the no-longer-relevant king with text. The 1509 book has an *incipit*-style beginning that recalls manuscript traditions and, fascinatingly for the status of early print, that positions the printed book as a medium for recalling and storing oral culture: a way of (my words, not de Worde's) freezing or preserving spoken words that would otherwise disappear into the air. De Worde's book, here, is commercially for sale for anyone with a few pence, but is at the same time framed as a royal commission ('enprynted at the specyall request of the ryght excellent pryncesse Margarete moder vnto the sayd noble prynce'). The account of the book's production, printed at the Sun in Fleet Street by de Worde, still comes at the very end of the book – the colophon not yet integrated into the title page. This, in 1509, both is and is not the book as we might recognise it today.

De Worde's styling of himself in the colophon as 'prynter unto the moost excellent pryncesse my lady the kynges graundame'

John Fisher, This sermon folowynge *(1509 or 1510).*

was part of a broader pattern of de Worde making books by, for, or about women: we might even say that de Worde created the idea of a market of women readers of print. We can see this in de Worde's prologues that address a female readership, and in his many vernacular translations of religious works that seek female buyers, or that were sent to women to read, like *The Image of Love* (1525), distributed to sixty nuns at Syon Abbey. We can also see de Worde's attention to women in two other important publications. The first is *A Shorte Treatyse of Contemplacyon,* printed in 1501, just after de Worde's move from Westminster to Fleet Street. The text is, the opening words tell us, 'taken out of the boke of Margerie kempe of lyñ': it's a shortened version of the manuscript we today call *The Book of Margery Kempe.* Kempe was a mystic who lived in fourteenth-century Norfolk, the mother of fourteen children, a pilgrim who travelled to Rome, Santiago, and the Holy

Land, and the author, in *The Book*, of what is often called the first autobiography in English. The latter claim is debatable, not least because Kempe's accounts of her spiritual visions, dictated by her to an amanuensis or scribe, are far stranger than that nineteenth-century term 'autobiography' suggests. But *The Book* is certainly a landmark in women's writing, and in the writing of the self.

De Worde's *A shorte treatyse* is an abridgement, produced by an unknown editor, a seven-page compact quarto that sits nicely in the hand, with a woodcut of the crucifixion recycled from an earlier Caxton book. It presents twenty-eight brief extracts drawn from the manuscript structured as a dialogue between a first-person female, who asks questions, and a first-person Christ who answers his 'daughter', with a narrator providing exposition – and the whole constitutes a guide to living piously. The most striking assertion is the need for this woman – let's call her Kempe, although her exemplarity, her lack of individuation, is the point – to turn away from the prospect of a martyr's death: the book opens shockingly with 'She desyred many tymes that her hede [head] might be smyten [struck] of[f] with an axe upon a blocke for the loue of our lorde Jhesu.' Rather than martyrdom, the woman is to think continually of Christ, to commune silently with him in prayer; compassionate weeping is a sign of her love for Christ, and patient suffering is the 'ryght way to heuen'. *A shorte treatyse* is a handbook for enduring with patience the scorn of the world that is, the text suggests, a uniquely female experience. It's complicated to claim this as a proto-feminist text because the version of patience it counsels seems to us today problematically passive and tolerant of adversity. But it is a text that centres female experience and suffering. While the conversion of *The Book* into this concise handbook sacrifices many of the riches of Kempe's manuscript, it has a spirit of practical application, of print's radical capacity to reach and shape and (de Worde would probably say) improve the lives of women readers.

The second example is briefer but more spectacular, and a reminder of two refrains running across the chapters to follow:

that printers printed not only books, but also sheets, broadsides, ephemera (we shouldn't be too literally bookish when we consider the history of the book); and that past cultures of print might be dramatically different from our own. The text is the only surviving example of an English printed birth girdle, a text designed to magically protect women against the dangers of childbirth: the printed paper strip would have been placed over the woman's womb during labour as a way of requesting divine aid while the prayers and incantations were spoken out loud. It was printed by de Worde near the end of his life, around 1533, and has been discussed recently by scholars Joseph J. Gwara and Mary Morse. The text survives as a single, damaged strip of paper, about 24 by 9 centimetres, printed on one side. At some point in the sixteenth or seventeenth century it was deemed worthless and was used as a binding support in a now unknown book. (Survival as waste is another refrain, as we saw at the start of this chapter.) At some point in the late-seventeenth century, the fragment was extracted from the binding by John Bagford (1650/1–1716), a shoemaker's son from Fetter Lane who became a key figure in the second-hand book market, and who collected vast quantities of fragments in pursuit of a history of printing he never got round to writing. The strip survives in one of Bagford's large albums of printed bits and pieces culled from books, now in the British Library. On such circuitous fables of textual descent – sheets passed from hand to hand, discarded, cut up, reused, lost, noticed, excised – our knowledge of early printing often depends.

A number of quite spectacular manuscript birth girdles survive: they were often given to aristocratic and royal women during labour, sometimes with coloured miniatures and prayers in Middle English, and served as something like relics. In this sense, the intimacy of manuscript seems appropriate. What de Worde produced is a printed version of this upscale manuscript tradition, cheap at one pence or less, and probably very popular – and in doing so, he made print a new kind of conduit for divine intercession. De Worde's printed text is in English and Latin, with prayers seeking the intercession of St Quiricus and St Julitta; appeals for Christ's support; a woodcut image of an empty cross with six nail holes; and cues for the reader to recite the Paternoster and Ave Maria. The story of Quiricus and Julitta is a horrific tale but it was well known in late-medieval Europe and was understood as a story of heroic martyrdom – ironically, just the kind of doomed story *A shorte treatyse* warns readers against. On Tarsus, the widow Julitta refused to recant her Christianity and was burnt and her body then later beheaded; her three-year-old son Quiricus was thrown down the stairs. The child's skull was broken, but before her own execution Julitta thanked God for the child's martyrdom. Quiricus and Julitta are invoked in de Worde's text as, presumably – but to us probably bafflingly – consoling emblems in a society with high rates of infant mortality. It's a highly personal text – a printed text to be pressed against a woman's body at a defining moment in her life – but it might have had a public function, too. The year 1533 was a time of widespread anxiety about the lack of a royal male heir for Henry VIII; Anne Boleyn was already pregnant on her marriage to Henry on 25 January 1533, and Gwara and Morse suggest this birth girdle might have been used to direct prayers to the new queen. 'The most enigmatic product' of Wynkyn's considerable output, they call it, but it's also representative in the way it combines de Worde's quick-on-the-scene sense of a manuscript tradition that he might divert, his devotional publishing, and his awareness of the importance of women as readers, patrons, and subjects.

Alongside his hits for a lucrative non-aristocratic market, and his deft responses to royal commissions, de Worde was working out how to satisfy another audience by printing learned foreign languages. The visit of Erasmus to England in 1499, and his reception by scholars like Thomas More and John Cole – the Dean of St

Paul's would go on to found St Paul's School – is expressive of an emerging humanist culture in which scholars sought to rediscover, study and translate texts from the past. But here de Worde hit a problem. He had inherited at least four or five complete founts of type from Caxton – along with a set of twenty-one large woodcut initials, many sets of woodcuts, and Caxton's signature printer's device – and he added further type from France or the Low Countries, buying either founts or matrices (a matrix being the mould used to cast a letter or 'sort') to cast his own. But he didn't have the necessary type for some of these foreign scripts. In 1528 de Worde printed a book by Robert Wakefield, Professor of Hebrew at Cambridge University. Wakefield produced an extraordinarily learned treatise on the virtues of Arabic, Aramaic, and Hebrew, based on his inaugural lecture, and had it printed as *Oratio de laudibus & utilitate trium linguarum: Arabicae, Chaldaicae & Hebraicae*. Typographically, this was a remarkable effort by de Worde: the first use of italic in England, one of the very first books to print Hebrew, and the first ever in England with Arabic characters. But how to print Arabic if you don't own any Arabic movable metal type – if your ambitions were in advance of the available hardware? De Worde could have left spaces at the appropriate points and added Arabic letters in by hand to every copy – a painstaking process, but one we can see playing out in copies of Richard Brett's book on languages, printed in Oxford by Joseph Barnes in 1597, which left gaps for Syriac, Arabic, and Ethiopian to be added in with a pen. Or he could have used Hebrew characters, which were available, although in short supply. But de Worde's solution was appealingly elementary: he cut Arabic words out of wood, and inserted these amid the metal letters as he set the pages. And although, in the punishing words of one scholar, they are 'misshapen', 'crude', and 'lack cursiveness', they also indicate a printerly scope, and an interest in other languages. The next book in England with Arabic type after de Worde didn't appear until 1592. De Worde had also printed the first Greek letters in an English book in 1517, likewise cut from wood. In experimenting with new

scripts, de Worde was partly reflecting emerging humanist investments in studying the languages of the Bible. But de Worde's
linguistic range was expressive, too, of the fundamentally cosmo-
politan nature of English printing, circa 1500.

So: de Worde, the quick-witted businessman, alert to what would
sell, appealing to precedent even as he created new markets.
De Worde the printer-publisher of apparently ceaseless energy,
committed entirely to this new world of printed books: while
Caxton had been a merchant first and a printer later, de Worde
had only known print. Someone comfortable toggling between
social worlds, a spirit both democratic and elite, the foreigner at
the heart of England's Fleet Street, and perhaps, given his many
devotional publications, someone of strong religious convictions.
De Worde – we can speculate a bit, but this seems right – the
agreeable presence, the friend, a man who others liked. Unlike
Richard Pynson, whose name flits fairly regularly through legal
records, de Worde left no records of crimes or arrests, although he
was briefly reprimanded for his part in printing *The Image of Love*
(1525), a book judged to be heretical, and sending sixty copies to
the nuns at Syon Abbey. He was, it's clear, a natural collaborator:
as when, in 1507, he worked with Pynson and John Rastell to produce a huge three-volume edition of Sir Anthony Fitzherbert's *La
Graunde Abridgement de le ley*, an influential legal guide. We can sense
something appealing, too, a kind of generosity, a looking outwards, in the work he devolved down onto less established printers, often his former assistants: former Wordeans such as John
Butler, John Gough, and John Byddell, for example. These good
relations clustered with particular closeness on the thoroughfares
around Fleet Street, but we know de Worde had national links,
too, in an age when such links were challenging to sustain. He
gave a set of his type to the York printer, Hugo Goes. He had

connections in Bristol and Oxford. In this sense of networked Englishness, de Worde was distinct from Caxton who had European links but no real close ties with English stationers. He worked fast and decisively – he didn't linger, and didn't much doubt, and he may have surprised himself (repressing the voice of Caxton that came into his head) at how willing he was to sacrifice tidy perfectionism for getting the books out there. De Worde's books were objects in the world, not ideals, and often carried errors – like the prayer in *A ryght profytable treatyse . . . of many dyuers wrytynges of holy men* (1500), a book designed 'to dyspose men to be vertuously occupied in theyr myndes [and] prayers', where the 'n' of 'clene' was printed, with humanising effect, upside down: 'Lerne to kepe your bokes cleue.'

We can draw a bit closer still by looking at de Worde's will, signed on 5 June 1534, six months before his death. The original will doesn't survive, but there are several copies from the time. Wills are in some ways impersonal documents, organised around set rhetorical conventions that work to flatten a sense of an individual – and de Worde's opens with the cadences of many others: 'I Wynkyn de worde citizen and stacionner of london Being hole of mynde and body . . .' But after de Worde requests that he 'be buried w[ith]in the body of the churche of sainte Bride in ffletestrete of London before sainte katherines aulter', and that his debts be settled, these standard formulations of piety give way to something more expressive. In dispensing his money and possessions, de Worde describes a local community teeming with figures who are there for a moment, and then gone. 'I beque[th] to Agnes Tidder widow three poundes sterling,' he begins, and 'to Jo[hn] Ly[n]en three pound[s] sterling,' and 'to Alice my maid seru[a]nte the value of three pounds sterling in printed Book[es].' Three pounds of books to Alice the maid. The books were probably left as items of value to be sold on, like pieces of furniture; less generously, perhaps de Worde was in effect clearing the remaining clutter through these bequests. But maybe Alice was a reader: a servant who paused to look over the piles of inky sheets stacked beside the press before they were sent to the binders to fold, sew and cover. His other servants get books, too: Robert Darby, John Barbanson, John Wishon, 'Hectour' and 'Simon'. The sudden specificity of these names makes them statements of both possession and of loss, markers of an historical presence now gone: like the 20 shillings of books left 'to hercules Diricke powchmaker soone' – that is, to Hercules Diricke, son of a pouchmaker. (Diricke is a Low Countries name, and the leather trade had many foreign workers.)

De Worde's community was close and it mattered to him. Seven of the named beneficiaries were his neighbours in Fleet Street. He clearly had important and numerous national professional connections – he forgave a £4 debt owed by Robert Woodward, the only stationer in Bristol between 1532 and 1552, who perhaps bought a press or type from him, or retailed de Worde's books – but in the will his professional connections are generally hyperlocal, a matter of yards away: to 'Nowe[ll] the bokebinder in shoo lane', round the corner, 20 shillings in books. The young men he taught and mentored into the world of printing also mattered: to 'euery of [my] apprentice[s] three poundes sterling a peec[e] in printed book[es]'. De Worde requests that his name be remembered in St Bride's after his death. He asks that the churchwardens Robert Water (a saddler) and James Pegge (a brewer), busy figures in the community, arrange for the purchase of lands and tenements to yield 'at the leste' 20 shillings each year to pay the priest for the performance of de Worde's 'obit' – an annual commemoration, his name and life recalled – and a Requiem Mass in St Bride's to 'my soule my frends soules and all christe[n] soules'. This was a turbulent time to hope for annual prayers for the soul of the departed: the beginnings of England's shift to Protestantism meant such practices were under threat, and it may be that de Worde's wishes were not enacted. Any money left over was to be divided equally between the churchwardens and their successors, and 'the poore people of the parrishe of sainte Bride' – 'for so longe tyme as the residew of my goodes shall endure'.

A stationer's will normally includes bequests for wives and children and an extended family. When the printer John Rastell died a year or two after de Worde in 1536, he bequeathed 'my house in St. Martyns, with my presse, notes and lettres comprised in the same' to his wife, Elizabeth, the sister of Thomas More. The presence of widows in many stationers' wills suggests women played major roles in early printing culture in ways that historians have until recently overlooked: not only after their husband's death, when they might inherit the printing business, but also and more commonly as active partners during their husband's life. In the 1630s Anne Griffin established what one recent scholar calls 'a loose network of widows who printed and published together', involving printers Mary Dawson and Elizabeth Purslowe, and booksellers Joyce Norton and Joan Man, among others.

But de Worde's will records no family. His wife, Elizabeth, had died in 1498 when they were still living in Westminster: the churchwarden's account for St Margaret's, Westminster, records payment of sixpence for 'the knell of Elizabeth de Worde with the grete belle'. Church records also list that in 1500 'Juliane de Worde' died and was buried in the church. We know Wynkyn remarried because he rented a pew for his new wife soon after Elizabeth's death ('Item of Wynkyns Wife for hir parte of a pew' at eightpence). 'Juliane', or Juliana, is perhaps that second wife, or maybe a daughter who died young. Plague was bad in London in 1500 and may have been the cause of death. We don't know. But we can say that de Worde's professional community became a kind of family: the apprentices like sons, the fellow stationers his brothers and uncles, the binders and pressmen and servants and printers always close by and in and out of the shop like a busy and expanding family. The witnesses to de Worde's will were prosperous figures, carefully selected by him in advance: John Studde, a wealthy St Bride's parishioner, and John Tourner, a successful stationer, plus the curate of St Bride's, Humphrey Towne, and a fourth name that is only a name, Thomas Cooke, who emerges briefly from the past only to return to its inky blackness again.

It's no accident that many surviving copies of de Worde's books are covered with annotations from early readers. De Worde was the man of the handbook, the guide, the compact volume one could carry and read. Annotations left by readers on books are another way in which books carry their own history as they move through time. The marks are often extremely vivid, even as they conceal their full story. Here are two brief examples. *The Fruytfull Saynges of Dauyd the Kynge & Prophete* is a collection of sermons on the seven penitential psalms, compiled by John Fisher, Bishop of Rochester, and printed by de Worde '[i]n the yere of oure lorde .MCCCCC.viii, ye .xvi. day of ye month of Juyn' (16 June 1508 – he couldn't resist a punctual colophon). Some copies were evidently marked out with a particular kind of material care: one now in the British Library is printed on vellum, not paper, with the fore-edges of the pages coloured gold. This copy has a partially legible handwritten annotation at the start: 'This book belongeth vnto syster [. . .]'. The name that follows has been crossed out with an intensity that suggests a desire to expunge, but it looks as though this book was owned and read by a nun living in Syon Abbey, a dual monastery of men and women, founded by Henry V on the northern bank of the Thames in Isleworth. Syon was famed for its library until the Abbey was destroyed at the order of Henry VIII. This book was commissioned by Margaret Beaufort – it is, the title page declares, printed 'at the exortacion and sterynge of the moost excelle[n]t princesse Margarete cou[n]tesse of Rychemou[n]t [and] Derby, [and] moder [mother] to our souerayne lorde kynge Henry the. Vij' – and de Worde, through Beaufort's mediation, had established links with Syon, and published several books with this particular institution in mind. This is the context that lies behind that moment when a sister whose name we don't know opened this book and added carefully her mark of ownership.

The Protestant violence that would destroy Syon, and that is perhaps registered in the deletion of this nun's name, is seen also in the marks added to a copy of *The Descrypcyon of Englonde* from 1502. This book is a history of Britain with material originally derived from Geoffrey of Monmouth in the twelfth century, mixed with geographical descriptions from the *Polychronicon* of the Benedictine monk Ranulf Higden (d.1364). It's a big folio for a nation to tell a story of its own past, a sustained attempt to invent a tradition and, through repetition, to make that tradition stick. The chronicle runs from Adam and Eve down to its moment of compilation under Edward IV (d.1483), but its central ideological claim is that Brutus of Troy, great-grandson of Aeneas, landed on an island called Albion around 1115 BCE, became its first king, and renamed the place 'Britain', after his own name. (It's nice to note that having sailed all the way from Troy, Brutus's first port of call was, rather implausibly, Totnes.)

The copy now in the library of the Society of Antiquaries in London is a particular register of the sixteenth-century life of this book. Page after page is covered with blocks of black ink, added by a reader with care and consistency. It looks like a redacted legal document.

What is happening here? The blocks of black ink obliterate, or nearly obliterate, every appearance of the word 'Pope', from Peter I on. These deletions are meticulous and they read like controlled rage: a careful and unswerving attempt to erase a memory. They are a response to the early years of the Protestant Reformation, when on 9 June 1535, Henry VIII issued a statute requiring his subjects to strike out all references to the Pope in their prayer books. This was book damage not as transgression but as legal requirement. 'All manner [of] . . . books used in the churches,' the statute prescribes, mixing legalism and violence in a very Henrician way, 'wherein the said Bishop of Rome is named of his

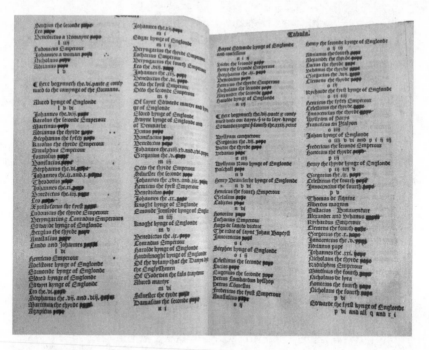

A redacted copy of The Descrypcyon of Englonde *(1502).*

presumptions and proud pomp and authority preferred, utterly
to be abolished, eradicated, and erased out, and his name and
memory to be nevermore (except contumely and in reproach)
remembered, but perpetually suppressed and obscured.' The
effects of this official policy of erasure are everywhere to be seen
in archives and rare book rooms: surviving copies of printed
books of hours show, in the words of historian Eamon Duffy,
'that most Tudor devotees dutifully blotted, scraped or sliced the
Pope . . . out of their devotions'. What's fascinating is how imperfect these efforts at deletion usually are: we can easily still read
'pope' through the ink in our Society of Antiquaries copy, and
the effect of these blots is – with lovely irony – to draw attention
to, rather than erase, the sustained presence of the Pope in British
history. The redactions become their opposite, a form of marking
out, and the book – 'Enprynted in flete strete in ye sygne of the

sone By me Wynkyn de Worde' – becomes a site not of forgetting but of remembering.

In his will, de Worde asked that his body be buried in St Bride's Church, opposite his home and office, before St Katherine's altar. St Katherine was a popular saint in England at this point, but she may have held particular significance for de Worde as the patron saint of the Dutch fraternity at the nearby church of Austin Friars. De Worde had certainly printed several books about St Katherine, including, at the very start of his career, *The Lyf of Saint Katherin of Senis the Blessid Virgin* (1492). On 29 December 1940, a German bomb struck and largely destroyed St Bride's, reducing the church to a smoking shell. During the excavations that followed, human remains were found close to the position of the altar: a part of a skull, some bones, and lead from a coffin. It's not by any means certain that these are the remains of Wynkyn de Worde – but they might be.

2. BINDING

William Wildgoose (*fl.* 1617–26)

On the morning of 23 January 1905, a very assured twenty-one-year-old graduate named Gladwyn Maurice Revell Turbutt knocks at the office door of Falconer Madan. Madan is the sub-librarian of the Bodleian Library in Oxford. The young man has a large folio leather-bound book under his arm. The man, and the book, have an aura of significance. Turbutt has a question about restoring the binding: he wants some advice. He is not used to waiting. He pushes open the door and strides in.

In order to understand Turbutt's 1905 visit to the Bodleian, we need to travel back almost three centuries, to the year 1623, and to a man named William Wildgoose. Wildgoose was a book-binder working in early-seventeenth-century Oxford, and his story is a kind of haunting. We know he was there because his name appears fleetingly in certain obscure administrative documents held by the Bodleian Library, and through these records we are able to reconstruct something of his working life, and the books we know he worked on; but his personal history remains largely a blank. In this, Wildgoose is representative of the historical fate of the overwhelming majority of members of his bookbinding profession before the eighteenth century. In other ways, though, Wildgoose is exceptional, since his name becomes linked, through his binding work, with perhaps the most famous book of all. This combination of absence and presence – Wildgoose's spectral mixing of obscurity and influence – is what this chapter sets out to explore. Wildgoose's story is the paradox of the trace: for something to be felt as absent, something needs to be left behind. History has closed to a dot on Wildgoose the man, but we still have some of the books that passed through his hands.

Wildgoose's name appears in the second day book of the Bodleian Library: a handwritten list of titles, in the form of unbound sheets, sent from the library to a small number of local binders between 1621 and 1625, with the binders' signatures. Across these day books, we have a brief roll call of Oxford binders in the early 1620s, and since history has not shone brightly on these figures, we should take the chance to name them in full, as a kind of payback for the work they did:

> Edward Miles, John Adams, John Allam, Dominique Pinart, Roger Barnes, Elias Peerse, John Westall, Henry Bluett, Francis Peerse, Robert Way, Richard Billingsley, William Johnson, William Davis, William Spire, William Webb, William Wildgoose, Christopher Crouch.

The entry for 17 February 1623 records ten titles under the heading, 'Deliured to William Wildgoose / These books following to be bound'. The list is written in the hand of Jean Verneuil (1583–1647), a Frenchman who worked as the library's underkeeper, sometimes referred to in records, perhaps a little sarcastically, as 'Monsieur'. At the bottom of the page, indicating receipt, is Wildgoose's signature: slanting, jagged, and written in thick ink.

We know from administrative records that Wildgoose was admitted *bibliopola* on 10 June 1617 – which means the university permitted him to work as a 'bookseller', although that term was looser than it is today, meaning bookseller, or bookbinder, or both – and we know he was reprimanded some time before this for dealing in books without being registered. In the day book, William Spire, Richard Billingsley, Henry Bluett, and John Allam recur more

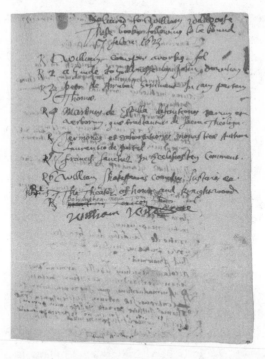

'*Deliured to William Wildgoose These books following to be bound 17 Febre. 1623*'. Bodleian Library Day Book.

frequently, so it looks as though Wildgoose was employed by the Bodleian when these men were busy. So he wasn't first on the Bodleian's list, but something like a reliable second-tier worker: a binder of good if not exceptional repute.

In the Bodleian account book there are two records of payments to Wildgoose, sums that indicate Wildgoose must have depended mainly on work elsewhere: 'payd to William Wildgoose for bookes bound for the Library 15s 6d' for 1621–2, and 'paid to Mr Wildgoose for binding £2 7s 4d' for 1625–6. These are just two notes in the louder chatter of regular library expenses – 'to the glacier for mending glasse in the Library and Gallery 21s 6d'; 'for chayninge of books 6s 9d' – and they locate Wildgoose within a community of manual workers working to keep the library going, of names shuffling briefly onstage, to fix a shelf or install a case, and then off again. Local parish records are briefly suggestive, too. We might think it's unlikely that there were dozens of individuals named William Wildgoose honking around Oxford, but in fact records suggest an extended family in the Oxfordshire area in the seventeenth century. There is a William Wildgoose, husbandman or farmer, of Great Milton, who died in 1614 (so not our man), with a will naming Ambrose, James, and Alice as children. There is a Thomas Wildgoose, also a husbandman of Great Milton, who died in 1633, with a son James and a brother Paul, and a will witnessed by a Nicholas Wildgoose. There is a Henry Wildgoose, yeoman, of Denton, Cuddesdon, who dies in 1617, who refers in his will to brothers James, William, Francis, Samuel, and Richard. And a probate document for a William Wildgoose, who died in 1633 – perhaps the binder? – is in the Oxford Consistory Court but it tells us only that his wife was Sarah. There is also buried in the archives of All Souls' College a brief record for 11 March in the first year of the reign of Charles I, of a 'Sale by Thos. and William Wildgoose of their lease of a tenement and 100 acres of land in Whateley [or Wheatley], Oxon, belonging to All Souls' College, to Richard Powell, of Forrest Hill, Oxon'. If this is William, this probably indicates not a home but a lease on a farm that he was selling in 1625 to generate income. It's certainly the case that William wouldn't have lived in Wheatley and worked in Oxford: that kind of commute (two hours' walk east from the Bodleian) is a twentieth-century construct.

So lots of smoke, but no smoking gun. But we can say something of the world in which Wildgoose moved. Early book culture in Oxford, like the London of Wynkyn de Worde, was largely the creation of foreigners, particularly north European immigrants, and sometimes there are enough archival scraps to sketch a life. The first printer in Oxford whose identity is known, Theodoric Rood, was from Cologne: Rood's name appears on a copy of Aristotle's work on the soul, *De Anima*, printed in Oxford in 1481. It's worth mentioning Balthazar Churchyard simply for the splendour of his name, but we can also say that he was a Dutchman working as a binder in Oxford in the 1520s (but not much more than this). Flemish binder Garbrand Harks appears relatively frequently in college accounts in the 1530s onwards as a supplier of books. Harks, like many binders needing to seek extra cash, also doubled as a wine dealer, and in general seems to have enjoyed a long but spiky career. Bust-ups were his thing. Harks got into legal trouble in 1577 over the return of a pawned bed (the details are opaque); in 1550, when he accused Elizabeth Clare, widow, of defaming his wife (Clare denied the phrase 'hereticke hore' but admitted 'butter mowthed flemmyng'); and in 1539 with the mayor of Oxford for 'having eaten this Lent with his family 20 legs of mutton, 5 rounds of beef, and 6 capons'. This does sound rather a lot, but Harks was still, presumably plumply, binding books for Magdalen College in 1542, and long after that. During the reign of Catholic Mary I (1553–8), Harks used his cellar at Buckley Hall for illegal gatherings of fellow Protestants. One more example of the early internationalism of Oxford book-makers: John Thorne, born Johannes (Hans) Dorne at Altstadt in Germany in 1483. Thorne began working as a printer in Brunswick around 1507 before moving to Oxford shortly before 1520 where he set up a small shop on the High Street, selling and binding. (He's described as Dutch but in this period Dutch could mean from the Low Countries or German, especially a speaker of Low German, also known as Low Dutch.) Thorne's shop, open daily except Sundays, was in the area of Oxford where bookbinders tended to congregate from the thirteenth century (before print, when binders were working with manuscripts) to the eighteenth: clustered around the university church of St Mary the Virgin, on the High Street that runs from Magdalen Bridge to Carfax – the equivalent of the area around St Paul's Cathedral in London, bustling with binders and bookmen. By the mid-sixteenth century, almost all the known binders have shifted 50 metres or so south of the High Street, around Oriel College between Grove Lane and what is now King Edward Street, a narrow compass teeming with innkeepers, physicians, apothecaries, tailors, and shoemakers. This is where Thorne's shop is located: a compressed space for living and working.

Everyone knows everyone. Gossip flourishes, and animosity, and lust. In 1529, Thorne's wife Joan is sued for slander – she said the father of Alice Hunt's daughter Barbara was Magister Bithe, not Alice's husband John the barber. Among the witnesses is Thorne's next-door neighbour Anne Bartram, wife of Richard the shoemaker. Joan loses the case and is fined 19s 6d, and has to make a public apology to Alice.

Miraculously, Thorne's thirty-two-page ledger or day book for most of 1520 survives – it's bound in an old vellum cover, about 18 by 13 centimetres, and is preserved in Corpus Christi College archives – and the 1,851 transactions give us a flavour of Thorne's bookselling life. We can't quite hear the shop doorbell ring on each entrance and exit, but Thorne's clumsy handwriting and sometimes approximate numeracy (his nineteenth-century editor, Falconer Madan, the Bodleian sub-librarian we briefly met above, notes that 'he shows a disregard of half-pence which is sadly unbusinesslike') records a daily list of books sold, similar to much of Wynkyn de Worde's output: lots of Latin grammar guides by bestselling authors John Stanbridge and Robert Whittington; works of theology; service books; sermons; books full of Luther's criticisms of the Pope; some 270 copies of titles by Erasmus, including his *Adages* and *Colloquies*; mountains of ballads; ABCs; books about cookery and Christmas carols and masses of almanacs. Thorne also sold lots of books that capture the rising interest in humanism in the 1520s, with its commitment to a return to classical texts as a source of eloquent speaking and writing: customers left Thorne's shop clutching Cicero's letters and his *On Duties*; Pliny's *Natural History*; Virgil's *Eclogues*; and works by the Roman grammarian Aulus Gellius. It's a mingling of the high and the low: proto-Protestant polemic alongside romances about Robin Hood. Cheap thrills and Ciceronian epistles – bound in limp vellum, parchment or leather, or sold in sheets. Some were new, some second-hand. There are expensive books, but nearly half sold for 6d or less, many for only 1d or 2d, books with the lowest survival rates today, probably flimsily bound and often stab-stitched (a needle with thread passing quickly through the text block and the wrapper). Most of the books were in Latin and only a few in English, and lots of the classics were printed abroad: Thorne probably picked them up during his regular European travels. In this sense, from the small 1520s bookshop tucked in a narrow district of Oxford, tendrils extended out across Europe. And while there were efforts by government to restrict foreign workers – as we saw in Chapter 1, a 1534 law made it illegal to import ready-bound books, and banned foreigners from working as retail booksellers – significant numbers of skilled bookmen continued to arrive from abroad, particularly in periods of crisis: hence the arrival of Huguenot binders in England during the French wars of religion in the 1560s. Falconer Madan catches Thorne nicely, although he perhaps misses the tendrils:

> We see him obscurely, seated in his shop, ready for every class of customer, with ballad and almanacks for those of light heart and light purse, portiforiums [portable breviaries, or books of prayers] and missals for the monks, and ponderous commentaries . . . for such as could carry them away.

The pile of books that reaches Wildgoose's bindery on that day in February 1623 expresses just this kind of internationalism, and also emphasises the relative marginality of English as a literary language. Since eight of the ten books are still in the Bodleian, it's possible to revisit the actual volumes that Wildgoose was working with. Four of the books were printed in London, three in Spain, and one each in Strasbourg, Paris, and Lisbon; six were in Latin, and four in English. The list also shows just how often, before the mechanisation of book production in the early nine-teenth century, the place of binding and the place of printing were often countries apart: before these books were books, they were sheets of paper, and they flew about Europe in a pre-modern swirl before being bound in England.

Wildgoose's list of titles probably seems to us, today, dauntingly learned and culturally distant, including the collected devotional writings of William Cowper, late Bishop of Galloway; John Downame's *A guide to godlynesse or a Treatise of a Christian life*; and two Latin works on Aristotelian philosophy. The idea of 'beach reading' was yet to emerge. But there is one book on this list that looms out from an unfamiliar setting, like a friend's face in a crowd: the book that Jean Verneuil describes as 'William Shakespeares comedies histories &c.' – or, to give it its full title, *Mr. William Shakespeares Comedies, Histories, & Tragedies*, published in 1623, containing thirty-six of his plays, the book we now refer to as Shakespeare's First Folio. But the lovely thing about Wildgoose's list is precisely this lack of emphasis: here is Shakespeare, one book among ten, a work of imaginative literature, not yet the icon it would become, levelled alongside biblical commentaries (drawing on Hebrew and Latin), sermons printed in Lisbon, and a work on aristocratic genealogies. So we should read the list in full before we begin to impose our own priorities:

William Cowper, *The workes of Mr William Cowper late Bishop of Galloway* (London, 1623)

John Downame, *A guide to godlynesse or a Treatise of a Christian life* (London, 1622)

Aimé Meigret, *Questiones Fratris Amadei Meigret Lugdunensis Ordinis Predicatorum in libros De generatione et corruptione Aristotelis* (Paris, 1519)

Francisco de Araujo, *Commentariorum in universam Aristotelis Metaphysicam* (Burgos and Salamanca, 1617)

Martinus de Espilla, *Diffinitiones rerum et verborum, quae tractantur de sacra theologia, & de rebus moralibus* (Burgos, 1612)

Francisco Sánchez de Las Brozas, *In Ecclesiasten commentarium, cum concordia Vulgatae editionis, et Hebraici textus* (Barcelona, 1619)

Laurent de Portel, *Sermones et exhortationes monasticae: religiosis personis necessariae, & saecularibus proficuae* (Lisbon, 1617)

William Shakespeare, *Mr. William Shakespeares comedies, histories, & tragedies* (London, 1623)

André Favyn, *The theater of honour and knight-hood* (London, 1623)

Janus Gruterus, *Florilegii Magni, seu Polyantheae tomus secundus Jani Gruteri* (Strasbourg, 1624)

Would Wildgoose have read these books? Almost certainly not: not just because his Latin wouldn't have been up to it, and not just because he had little time to waste in the face of the Bodleian's exacting deadlines and his continual hustling for other orders across Oxford. He wouldn't have read them because his relationship to these books was physical, a matter of converting flimsy sheets into sturdy bound codices. Wildgoose would have assessed them – held them hundreds of times, weighed them up, peered closely at points of physical weakness – but this was a kind of comprehension that conceived of books not as things of words but as taut combinations of packthread and stitches, of beaten pages and burnished leather. Wildgoose's head would have hummed with a set of attitudes like those expressed by the antiquarian Sir Robert Cotton (1571- 1631) in his instructions for the binding of his manuscripts: 'bind this book as strong as you can. Cut it smoothe. Beat it and press it well . . . Sew it with twisted and waxed threde.' When Wildgoose bound books, he wasn't attempting to represent in physical form the intellectual or literary content of the titles, or to visualise theme or narrative. The nature of the flowers or foliage pressed into the leather or even (for these Bodleian books) the elegantly simple quartet of lines that ran around the edges of the covers spoke not to the insides of the books but looked outwards, to wider design conventions within bookbinding in Oxford, London, and (with a lag in time) across Europe, and also to related crafts such as furniture design, metalwork, and architecture.

Deciding to be a bookbinder is perhaps never the savviest of career moves, but Wildgoose had picked a relatively good time and place. While London was indisputably the nation's centre of book culture, Oxford and Cambridge had vibrant bibliographical networks. In fact, by the seventeenth century there were also binders active in many cathedral cities and market towns, including Ipswich, Norwich, Hereford, Durham, York, and Worcester, and in Scotland in Edinburgh, Glasgow, Aberdeen, and St Andrews. The opening of the Bodleian Library in 1602 created new demand for the kinds of skills Wildgoose had developed serving as an apprentice, but even he would have had to admit that bookbinding was not a prestigious profession: money was short, and a career was precarious. We get a sense of this precarity from a petition, written in the name of the Chancellor of Oxford University in 1574, seeking to aid the binder Christopher Cavey who had served as an apprentice to Garbrand Harks:

> Christopher Cavie, bokbynder . . . is now by age, sycknes and otherwyse lacke of necessarie worke, by reason of the multitude of other bokebynders, brought behynd hande and in debte, not havinge of himselffe to mainetayne him, his wiffe and familie . . . I praye you . . . to lycence fullye and privilege this poore man to sell old bookes; and therew[i]thall to make a special provision that no other bookbynder in the universitie do intermedle in the same.

Even prominent figures might struggle. Roger Barnes was a binder of high standing in Oxford from around 1590 to 1631 who overlapped with Wildgoose: his name also appears in the Bodleian day books, and the two would certainly have met, talked, compared work. Barnes was better connected than most – his brother Joseph was the university's first official printer, and Roger had begun his career working as his binder – but on his death Roger's goods totalled only £11 14s 8d (about £1,400 today), including his binding equipment and tools. His brother Joseph, the university printer, left a relatively staggering £1,128 2s 9d. As historian

David Pearson notes, 'the way to succeed, in bookbinding, was to get out of it', and into a related but more lucrative bibliographical stream. So it's often the case that binders also worked as booksellers (dealing in both new and second-hand books), printers, and purveyors of stationery, to the point at which, in archival records, 'bookbinder', 'bookseller', and 'stationer' are sometimes used as synonyms. There was a lot of dabbling in other businesses, too, like innkeeping, or like Garbrand Harks's work in the wine trade, although one suspects, given the bust-ups and legal cases, that Harks was also fond of imbibing the stuff. In a survey of professional careers published in 1679, Richard Head describes this tendency of the bookbinder, after sufficient success, to move away into other work, leaving behind his binding tools like toys abandoned in a nursery:

His sewing-Press lies mouldy in the Garret, his Plow neglected lies, and his Knives rust; the skrews of his standing and his cutting-Presses have forgot their wonted duty, and stubbornly won't stir an inch for any; his Marble-moody-beating stone weeps incessantly to see the weighty Hammer lie rusting in a corner unregarded: In short, if he work it is for his pleasure, and what pains he takes now and then in binding of a book is his Pastime. The Sonne after his Fathers Decease scornes the mean Title of a Bookbinder, and therefore employs others, and is henceforward stil'd a Bookseller; and the rest of his Brethren, who are able, follow his example. Thus, as Binding formerly was the Rise of a lazy Bookseller.

The archival disappearing act performed by Wildgoose is typical of most early book-binders: as a class of skilled workers whose influence we can weigh in our hands, they have all but vanished from the historical record. Graham Pollard's hauntingly titled article from 1970, 'The names of some English fifteenth-century binders', conveys the mood of a battleground surveyed the day after, beginning as it does by noting the nicknames derived from binders' tools that previous scholars were compelled to use in the face of this anonymity: 'the demon, the dragon, and the monster binders; the greyhound and the huntsman; the half-stamp and the fishtail; the bat and the unicorn binders'. This culture of a kind of invisibility extended forward as far as the Restoration. Samuel Pepys's 1660s diary hums with excitement about the world of Restoration books: browsing the bookstalls in St Paul's Churchyard; acquiring the latest literary gossip in coffee houses; collecting more than 1,700 of the latest ballads; gawping at literary celebrities like Margaret Cavendish; buying and then concealing sexually explicit texts like *L'École des Filles* ('not amiss for a sober man once to read over to inform himself in the villainy of the world'). And Pepys spent a number of afternoons that stretched happily into evenings watching bookbinders at work:

> Friday 31 January 1668
> . . . and so back and took up my wife and set her at Mrs. Turner's, and I to my bookbinder's, and there, till late at night, binding up my second part of my Tangier accounts, and I all the while observing his working, and his manner of gilding of books with great pleasure, and so home, and there busy late, and then to bed.

Binders worked on account books and other handwritten texts, as well as printed books, either following conventions for binding printed books or producing so-called 'stationery bindings', and here Pepys brings along the notes he kept while serving on the Tangier Committee from 1662. (Tangier, along with Bombay, was part of the dowry of Catherine of Braganza, Charles II's Portuguese queen.) But despite the long hours and the pleasure, Pepys doesn't give his binder a name, and even his encounters with the most famous practitioners (Pepys was a delighted observer of technical skill, and of versions of celebrity) present us with little more than skeleton presences – names, but not quite individuals, like this account, from Friday 12 March 1669:

I took him in my coach with W. Hewer and myself towards West-minster; and there he carried me to Nott's, the famous bookbinder, that bound for my Lord Chancellor's library; and here I did take occasion for curiosity to bespeak a book to be bound, only that I might have one of his binding.

Bookbuyers at this time might purchase a book ready bound, but many books, and probably the majority, were sold as folded sheets, or in a temporary soft cover, and it was the customer's task, or pleasure, to take the unbound book – or more often a little stack of them – to the binder's. This is what Pepys frequently did, and so we might think of binding as a first or early act of reception, rather than the final act of production. The 'famous bookbinder' may be William Nott, tentatively known to binding historians as 'Queens' binder A' after books bound for Catherine of Braganza and Mary of Modena; but the real truth is that we can't even be sure of this.

What did Wildgoose's workshop look like? What was it like as a space to work in? Most binderies were independent businesses, run by a freeman who had acquired his skills as an apprentice, and who now employed several wage-earning journeymen, plus an apprentice or two. We can see a consistency of binding tech-niques across Wildgoose's books to suggest he was working alone; if he had others working for him, he was directing the bind-ing work with control. Wildgoose's ghostly presence means we can't know for sure, but we can get some idea of his world by going back to Roger Barnes, whose will, dated 15 October 1630, describes the distribution of goods to a community of family and colleagues. In so doing, the will sketches a network: to 'my sonne Robert Barnes the somme of ffive Shillings . . . To Grissell

Barnes my graundchild' 20 shillings; to 'Anne Barnes alias Lech-
field a little girle in my howse' 40 shillings; and to his eldest son
John, upon condition that he 'do keepe [and] mainteine' Anne
for five years, and then place her in service, the rest of his goods.
The overseers of the will – named in the document as Nicholas
Barton, a cordwainer (or shoemaker), and Henrie Carter, an
innholder – were to be given 'xij^d [12 pence] apiece to buy them
a paire of gloves'.

Upon Barnes's death, the contents of his bindery were inven-
toried and valued and so we have, in its moment of passing, a
glimpse into the kind of workplace that would have resembled
Wildgoose's, too:

> Inprimis a greate pressing presse, two cutting presses, one plowe
> to cut books, three oviles [ovals], a paire of Rolles, three phillets,
> foure small flowers, on[e] beating stone, two beating hammers,
> some plaining boords, backing boords and cording boords of all
> sorts, some finishing tools, five tubs to make pastbords.

We will come back to these tools in a moment. Also listed are 'three
olde books', 'two old sowing presses', and 'a trough to make past-
boords'. These items were a binder's resources – valued at a modest
£1 15s 0d, or about £215 in today's money – and we can imagine how Wildgoose used his. Work with a book would have fallen
into two stages: 'forwarding' (the binding of the book), and 'finishing' (the decorating). It was incremental work, a single book passing (historians estimate) about eighty times through the binder's
hands; work that could not be rushed; a blend of delicate precision,
patience, and toil; manual labour that allowed space for flourishes
of art. *The Bookbinders Case Unfolded* – a single printed sheet, of which
Pepys's is the only copy to survive – lists, in a spirit of celebration,
sixty-six discrete actions a bookbinder like Wildgoose would undertake in binding a single book, from 'Folding' to 'Lastly Pressing the
Book'. After folding, the first ten actions on the list are 'Quiring',

'Beating', 'Pressing', 'Collating', 'Putting Paper thereto', 'Sowing, with Appendices', 'Glewing', 'Drying', 'Opening the Packthred', and 'Scraping the Packthred'. Fifty-five more follow.

What arrives at Wildgoose's bindery – 'Deliured', as the Bodleian's day book has it – is not a pile of ten books but sheets fresh with print, perhaps stacked flat, or rolled. The slow process Wildgoose performs would have been pretty much the same for any bookbinder from the fifteenth century to the eighteenth. Wildgoose's first task is to check if any sheets are missing or faulty: crucial to prevent later charges of poor work, which flew about frequently. In fact, Verneuil has written 'Imperf.' next to the record for the seventh book on Wildgoose's list, André Favyn's *The Theater of Honour and Knight-hood*. Wildgoose's copy is no longer in the library – the Bodleian probably sold it when, in 1659, a donation of the same title came from the great legal scholar John Selden – so we can't be sure of the nature of the imperfection, but it probably suggests missing sheets, rather than faulty binding work. Having scanned for absences, Wildgoose checks to see if any pages need cancelling (or striking out) and replacing – such sheets marked with a slit – and if there are prints or maps to be inserted. Wildgoose folds the sheets into quires, or sections, taking notice of the catchwords (the first word of a page printed at the foot of the previous page) to ensure the sequence, and arranging these piles side by side in the correct order. The book, at this stage, isn't a physical whole – isn't in any real sense a book at all – but is a distributed series of sections, spread out on a desk, the parts not yet drawn into singularity. Wildgoose beats these sections with a heavy, 10-pound hammer, to flatten and regularise the paper: perhaps using, as Barnes did, 'two beating hammers' and 'on[e] beating stone'. At this point, Wildgoose's relationship to the book is about as physical and loud as it can be: illustrations of bookbinding from the period show a second worker delivering the blows in a separate room, due to the noise. These beaten sections are placed together in what Barnes's inventory calls, with endearing tautology, 'a greate pressing presse', to squeeze the

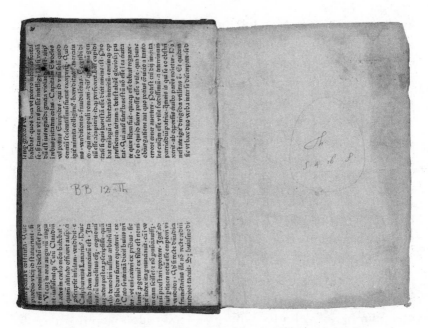

Printed Latin waste used as a pastedown in Wildgoose's binding.

book – or the thing that at some point soon (but not quite yet) will become the book – into regularity. The folded, hammered, pressed sections are then collated, and plates and maps inserted. Wildgoose then adds endleaves, inserted in the front and back to provide protection for the text when it presses against the boards. It's a feature of Oxford binders that they use fragments of old, unwanted printed books – the kind of fragment of Wynkyn de Worde's which we saw at the start of Chapter 1 – and sometimes manuscripts scattered after the dissolution of the monasteries and texts now fallen out of fashion, to line the insides of the front (or upper) and back (or lower) boards. (Hence, to astonished modern eyes, a medieval manuscript commentary on Aristotle, torn up and used to pad out a 1631 printed book on the Gospels.) Wildgoose has an old Latin book from the 1480s to hand that he bought for almost nothing to use as waste. He tears out pages and will, when the time comes, glue them on the inside of the front and back boards. (Marbled endpapers didn't begin to catch on in England for another decade or so, when they began to be imported mainly from France – and even then they were only ever used for more upmarket work; the kinds of bindings commissioned by the Bodleian would never have had them, even in 1680.)

The text block (that is, the brick of sequential sections) is sewn together, using a sewing frame: a thread joins the gatherings together and then onto between four and six raised leather sewing supports spaced along the spine which will soon be attached to the boards. This sewing, in the finished book, will be invisible, hidden behind the spine like wires inside a plug. Wildgoose rubs hot animal glue across the back of the sections to make things stronger still. While he's waiting for the glue to dry – fanning it every now and then – he starts work on another book on the list. It is his tendency, like many bookbinders, to work simultaneously on a number of volumes. The glue dry, Wildgoose proceeds with 'rounding' and then 'backing' the book: rounding means pulling and lightly hammering the flat spine of the text block into a rounded shape – something like a third of a circle – to ensure it can meet the strain of opening, and doesn't revert under pressure to its natural concave shape; backing means placing the text block in a press and then hammering the spine edges so that those sections splay out over onto the boards, placed on either side of the book. This twin process of rounding and backing gives a more organic shape to the spine, converting a square-edge block into a rounded back, meaning the strongest parts of the binding take the strain of a reader opening and closing the book: crucial for the longevity of the spine. Throughout all this, Wildgoose's relationship with the book, or the book-to-be, is something like the imposition of discipline on otherwise unruly materials: folding, ordering, flattening, beating, pulling, tightening, sewing. Wildgoose is working against entropy, battling the tendency of materials to revert or scatter.

Next are the pasteboards: not the wooden boards widely used in the sixteenth century, but boards about 8 millimetres thick, made

Ploughing the board edges, with (left) *a book in a standing press, and* (rear) *pages being sewn on a sewing frame, in a late-sixteenth century German bindery. From* Hans Sachs, Eygentliche Beschreibung aller Stände auff Erden *(1568).*

from layers of pulped paper and board scraps, glued together – the technique comes from centuries of practice in the Middle East – to form the front and back covers. Wildgoose would have had something like Barnes's 'five tubs to make pastbords', and would have produced them himself. Wildgoose beats the boards with a hammer to make them as dense, rigid and tough as possible; the boards are cut to size, and then with cords are attached to the text block. The form in Wildgoose's hands now resembles what readers expect: we can probably start talking about a book. Wildgoose puts the book into a standing press for several hours – perhaps overnight – to flatten and regularise the whole. Then he trims the edges of the boards – what binders called 'cutting the book', or ploughing. Barnes's inventory lists 'two cutting presses' to hold the book in place with covers closed, and 'one plowe to cut books', and Wildgoose would have had something similar. Wildgoose then sprinkles red ink across the edges of the closed pages, perhaps by knocking a brush against a hammer to scatter the ink, or perhaps by using his finger to let (in the words of one binding historian) 'a shower of small droplets fall on the tightly closed edges'. As he does it, Wildgoose perhaps thinks about the different tastes of his Oxford binding contemporaries: Edward Miles (*c.*1569–1638), who prefers a fine blue edge; Francis Peerse, who died a little over a year ago, in 1622, who liked olive green. This sprinkling, delicate after the noise of hammer blows, is both aesthetic (an artistic choice) and practical (concealing dirt). It also functions as a kind of indexing system in multi-volume works: as part of the Bodleian commission, Wildgoose binds two works on Aristotle in one book – what bibliographers call a Sammelband, from the German, meaning multiple texts in one book form, a common structure in the seventeenth century – and uses different fore-edge colours (red, then yellow) to denote each text. He slipped up on another Sammelband, sprinkling the page edges of Francisco Sánchez de Las Brozas's biblical commentary and Laurent de Portel's sermons in one colour, and so missing the chance for a demarcation. Other works demand different treatments: Wildgoose would sometimes paint the fore-edges black (using antimony or graphite) for funeral sermons and service books; he may even have had a pile of black-edged paper ready to go for the bereaved in a hurry. There were more elaborate possibilities, too: gilded edges using gold leaf, and gauffered edges – the latter meaning the use of heated rolls or finishing tools to indent into the edges small, intricate, repeating patterns. Later in the century, edge-marbling became fashionable. But these books for the Bodleain are simpler affairs. Wildgoose sews the headbands – bands of pink and blue thread sewn around a strip of leather and attached to the text block at the top and bottom – providing once again the binder's particular blend of strength and decoration; he cuts the inner corners of the boards at an angle; and then covers the book in brown, tanned calf leather, stretching it tight and pasting it down. Tanned calf leather is the most common binding leather at this time, plentiful as a resource in England, made from the hides of young cows; the flesh removed and the skins (in that unlovely term) 'dehaired', and the hides then soaked in tannic acid made from oak bark and water. The skins are dried and curried (that is, split with knives) then oiled, dyed, and polished before being delivered to Wildgoose. Calf leather is a material that takes well to the pressures from a binder's tools, and is the variety the Bodleian wants for its larger books that will be chained in the library. Wildgoose will have bound with other materials, too: after calf leather, parchment was most common in Oxford binderies at this time, often used for limp bindings. Wildgoose would have experience too with sheepskin (for less prestigious bindings, prone to wear and damage) and goatskin (for higher-end work, a strong leather imported mainly from Turkey and later, in the eighteenth century, from Morocco), but both were infrequently used in Oxford in this period. Wildgoose is not indulging in what we'd call fine binding, the kind of thing produced for a rich patron or (a little later in history) a collecting connoisseur: bindings that have traditionally attracted the majority of scholarship, but which, as David Pearson has made clear, vastly misrepresent the form of most early modern books. Wildgoose is working to make books that can sit on library shelves: silks and satin wouldn't go down well.

Wildgoose then sandwiches the book between two boards and wraps a cord around the whole to ensure that the glue takes successfully. As he stretches the leather over the cover of these books, Wildgoose is dealing with matter that was once animate:

in his hands is the skin of a calf, or what once has been a calf. Henry Vaughan's ghostly poem 'The Book' (1655) catches brilliantly that sense of a book as a recollection of these previous forms, as a glancing back to earlier lives. Addressing God, Vaughan imagines the prehistory of the physical components of a book – paper, once clothes worn by people with their own lives and thoughts, and leather covers, once a creature in a field eating grass:

> Thou knew'st this paper when it was
> Mere seed, and after that but grass;
> Before 'twas dressed or spun, and when
> Made linen, who did wear it then:
> What were their lives, their thoughts, and deeds,
> Whether good corn or fruitless weeds.
> . . .
> Thou knew'st this harmless beast when he
> Did live and feed by Thy decree
> On each green thing; then slept (well fed)
> Clothed with this skin which now lies spread
> A covering o'er this aged book;
> Which makes me wisely weep, and look
> On my own dust; mere dust it is . . .

Wildgoose is unlikely to have reflected too much on the animal origins of the book in his hands: he has an anxious eye on the credit and debit columns of his financial accounts. But Vaughan's imagination tells us something true about the Orpheus-like capacity of the book to gaze back on those earlier lives, and his poem lets us conceive of the book for a moment as one arrangement of materials which have a much longer, pre-codex history.

Wildgoose's decorating is restrained, and consistent. Before nineteenth-century industrial book production led to the possibility of the mass production of uniform books, binding was always the work of individuals working with their hands, the product of innumerable small choices.

Wildgoose has something like a style, and we can see it recurring across the books he binds for the Bodleian, but it's not quite a bibliographical signature. We might think of this as a withholding except Wildgoose never intends to be the centre of attention, or even to be legible as a presence behind his work. Bookbinding is not conceived – really, until the world of nineteenth-century fine bindings – as a medium of individual expression. Occasionally a single personality forces its way into visibility through a kind of excessive or even violent liveliness: the eccentric Oxford binder Richard Billingsley (c.1564–1606) produced 'infelicitous designs' (the adjective is the Bodleian assistant librarian Strickland Gibson's in 1914) which he signed and dated. But this is an aberrant instance, and it's not until the late eighteenth century that binders begin to insert small printed labels inside the front board with names and addresses. Before then, it's more helpful to think of style as something communal – 'an Oxford early-seventeenth-century binding', for example – a shared set of aesthetic and practical commitments that mark out a time and a city or even a nation.

Wildgoose has a set of probably brass tools for marking books: oval centrepieces to stamp the middle of the cover with a design of intertwining leaves; wheel-shaped tools or 'rolls' with patterns engraved around the rim to create continuous bands of decoration; fillets for pressing lines in the leather; and ornaments with floral designs. Wildgoose may have acquired his tools early in his career from metalworkers in Oxford, or potentially from another binder who arrived from abroad. In their design we see the evidence of a global flow of influence: oval or lozenge-shaped English centrepieces from about the 1550s, for instance, often featured interlocking foliage or abstract designs of geometrical symmetry, a so-called 'arabesque' (or 'moresque') design which found its origins in Islamic bookbinding from the fourteenth century. That Islamic aesthetic spread across Europe from the fifteenth century via the Italian trading ports, flowing along the routes carved out by money and the movement of goods, before reaching the shores of England, as so often belatedly, around the time of Elizabeth I – finding expression first in high-end workshops in London (the centre of the book trade), and then quickly filtering out more widely to Oxford and Cambridge, and beyond. The gold leaf used to produce gilded tooling followed a similar trajectory: from the Arab world in the early thirteenth century, if not before, through Europe and then to England in the sixteenth century.

Wildgoose takes a fillet – a revolving wheel, like a broad modern-day pizza cutter, with four lines engraved around the rim – and, pressing hard, runs it around each of the sides of the leather cover, front and back, to create a frame made of four parallel lines. The leather takes the impression well. This is a blind-tooled frame: blind in the sense that it is not coloured or gilded with gold leaf applied via heated tools. Wildgoose presses a fillet horizontally across the spine several times to create a series of panels. Then he adds little flourishes that serve to locate these books in Oxford at this particular time: to the narrow edges of the boards nearest the spine, he cuts a series of slanted lines, in two directions ('edge hatching') and on the spine, he cuts hatching lines into the top and bottom panels ('spine hatching'). Many of the books bound in Oxford in the early seventeenth century, particularly for the Bodleian, have a similar design: an outer frame of blind-tooled fillets, and spine and edge hatching.

Wildgoose laces two coloured ties (a mix of pink, yellow, green, blue, and white threads – a quietly excitable alternative to the normal green cloth) through holes drilled through the boards, to keep the book shut. The fashion for engraved brass clasps has fallen away a generation before, living on only in luxury bindings, devotional works and small, portable books like almanacs that need to remain closed. And then, perhaps with a sense of a final flourish, a satisfying little piece of theatre – if Wildgoose is given to such gestures – he beats egg whites into a froth, a drop of vinegar added to prevent this 'glaire' turning putrid, and paints three times over the leather, before polishing.

Wildgoose delivers the books himself the next day.

Jean Verneuil checks the volumes on arrival at the Bodleian and adds an 'R' to indicate receipt against each marked-off title in the day book. At this moment in the library, books are shelved according to format (folio, quarto, or octavo) and subject (Theology, Law, Medicine, or Arts). We can follow the life of Shakespeare's First Folio – let's call it Wildgoose's First Folio – as it enters the library and experiences, as we will see, an interesting mix of movement and stasis.

The First Folio is placed at the Arts End of Duke Humfrey's Library, with the shelfmark S 2.17 Art; a clasp is riveted to the front board and the volume – as was the case with all folios, until the 1760s – is chained to the library. Because of the chain, the book is placed on the shelf with the coloured edges facing outwards. (The shelving of books with spines outwards, and, subsequently, with tooled titles on spines, gradually became more common across the course of the seventeenth century.) The chain anticipates the reader as thief – and is an augmentation that will leave, when removed years later, two holes through the front board that look like cleanly efficient bullet wounds.

Part prisoner, part king, Wildgoose's First Folio sits shackled to this shelf through the mid-seventeenth century. It's there during the Civil War, when Charles I flees London and in 1644–5 sets up parliament in Christ Church Hall, about a ten-minute walk away. We can get a sense of how readers interacted with the book by examining the marks they left behind; not, unfortunately, the beguiling scribblings of notes in the margins which we see in many early modern volumes, and in many of Wynkyn de Worde's

Enthusiastic elbow damage in Wildgoose's First Folio,
opposite the balcony scene in Romeo and Juliet.

books, but more elementally the wear and tear of repeated use –
despite the oath that readers had to swear on entry to the Bodleian, to avoid 'changing, razing, defacing, tearing, cutting, noting,
interlining, or by voluntarie corrupting, blotting, slurring or any
other manner of mangling or misusing, any one or more of the
said books, either wholly or in part'. There are so many ways to
be a bad reader! Despite the good quality Crown paper, Wildgoose's book takes a battering in its first forty years, but that battering is unevenly distributed: the pages of *Romeo and Juliet* are
the most worn away by what one Shakespeare scholar describes,
with erotic intensity, as 'the friction of their hands and elbows'.
This is book damage as an index of readerly interest. The balcony scene is particularly marked: parts of the facing page are
almost worn through. *Julius Caesar* is also a clear favourite, perhaps

chiming – as a play about an assassinated ruler – with the regi-
cide times of 1649. After those come *The Tempest*, *Henry IV part I*,
Macbeth and *Cymbeline*. The tragedies are in general popular, but
many of the histories are little touched – particularly (some things
don't change) *King John*.

But despite the chains, Wildgoose's First Folio is soon on the
move. The Bodleian doesn't appear to have acquired a copy of
the Second Folio in 1632 – it's not clear why – but when the Third
Folio (1663/4) arrives, Wildgoose's First is promptly deemed
unnecessary. Bodleian librarian Thomas Lockey probably sells
it to the Oxford bookseller Richard Davis in 1664 for £24 in
what the Bodleian accounts from that year describe, with stylish
understatement, as 'Superfluous Library Bookes'. Lockey tends
to get heaps of criticism for the cheap sale of what later would
become (but certainly was not then) the world's most treasured
book: the loud clang of his decision sounds a bit like Poet Laure-
ate Robert Southey writing to Charlotte Brontë in 1837 ('Literature cannot be the business of a woman's life: & it ought not to
be'), or Dick Rowe in 1962 ('The Man Who Turned Down The
Beatles'). And it's true that the contemporary Oxford antiquarian Anthony Wood described Lockey as 'not altogether fit for that
office'. But Wood was a nasty gossip, and Lockey's sale was in fact
consistent with the Bodleian's attitude to old editions, as things to
be replaced by new editions, an attitude that persisted right up
until the mid-twentieth century. Others in the seventeenth century thought similarly. Pepys bought a copy of the Third Folio
on 7 July 1664, on his way back home from the New Exchange
on the Strand, along with a legal book and a Greek–Latin dictionary. He'd been in a not uncharacteristically hypochondriacal
mood that morning ('it happening to be a cool day I was afraid
of taking cold, which troubles me, and is the greatest pain I have
in the world to think of my bad temper of my health'), so perhaps he bought the books in a spirit of consolation. But when the
Fourth Folio was published in 1685, Pepys – like Lockey – seems
to have kept this and sold the earlier. The Fourth Folio is still in

the Pepys Library at Magdalene College, Cambridge: a room of shelves and books and furniture maintained, like a magical slice of the past, exactly as Pepys knew it.

More important than the scandalous sale of the First Folio is the counter-narrative: the Bodleian's early institutionalisation of Shakespeare as an author worthy of study. One way to respond to the list of books bound by Wildgoose is to note how Shakespeare, the provincial playwright who never went to university and who wrote imaginative literature in English at a time when that was only just about an acceptable thing to do, sits alongside folio works of learned devotion and Aristotelian philosophy written in Latin. It's important to emphasise what a major cultural shift this represents. If writing stage plays in English was seen as a pursuit of questionable legitimacy, then printing those plays carried even less prestige. Ben Jonson was ferociously mocked for his printed *Workes* of 1616: 'Pray tell me Ben, where doth the mistery lurke,' carped one contemporary epigrammist, 'What others call a play you call a worke.' And in January 1612, Sir Thomas Bodley, founder of the Bodleian ten years before, wrote to Thomas James, First Keeper of the Library, expressing why he thought it right to ban plays, and other related books, from the library:

> I can see no good reason to alter my opinion, for excluding suche books, as almanackes, plaies [plays], & an infinit number, that are daily printed, of very unworthy maters & handling . . . Happely some plaies may be worthy the keeping: but hardly one in fortie . . . Were it so againe, that some litle profit might be reaped (which God knows is very little) out of some of our playbookes, the benefit therof will nothing neere counteruaile, the harme that the scandal will bring vnto the Librarie, when it shalbe giuen out, that we stuffe it full of baggage bookes.

A library stuffed with baggage books (literally, movable books, but meaning here rubbish or trash) certainly doesn't sound good, and it's striking, given what happens to Wildgoose's First Folio, that the reputational damage Bodley fears is not from letting books go, but rather from letting them in. Did he really think only one in forty plays was worth keeping?

But attitudes were changing: Bodley's prescription came at a time when the status of literary writing in English was shifting – and Bodley's spiky exclusion didn't last long. By 1613, shortly after his death, the first playbooks – 'riff-raffe' books, according to Bodley's previous descriptions – entered the library. The arrival of Wildgoose's First Folio at the Bodleian is thus an important moment in the emerging canonicity of Shakespeare, and an important step towards an institutional recognition of the power and import of imaginative writing in English: what we today call 'literature'. Understood in this way, the Wildgoose First Folio's arrival is an occasion to be placed alongside the great theatrical revivals of Shakespeare's plays after the reopening of the theatres, closed between 1642 and 1660; the appearance of editions of Shakespeare's works in the eighteenth century, beginning with Nicholas Rowe in 1709 and Lewis Theobald in 1733; and later cultural celebrations such as actor David Garrick's 1769 Stratford Shakespeare Jubilee which, despite torrential rain on day two (the grand pageant called off), to a considerable degree invented the idea of Shakespeare as a tourist commodity, and of Stratford as a destination for the Bard-struck.

In the poem Ben Jonson wrote for inclusion in the First Folio, 'To the Memory of My Beloved the Author, Mr. William Shakespeare', Jonson anticipated these cultural investments by praising Shakespeare in terms which still ring out today: 'Sweet Swan of Avon!' and 'He was not of an age but for all time!' In Jonson's verse, Shakespeare outshines his peers Lyly, Kyd, and Marlowe, and, miraculously, 'though thou hadst small Latin and less Greek,' even matches 'thund'ring Aeschylus, / Euripides and Sophocles' and the best 'Of all that insolent Greece or haughty Rome / Sent forth, or since did from their ashes come.' And Jonson offers three lines that, had he opened the book he was binding, Wildgoose would have liked:

Thou art a monument without a tomb,
And art alive still while thy book doth live
And we have wits to read and praise to give.

Jonson's praise of his friend and rival ('I loved the man,' Jonson wrote, 'this side [of] idolatry') has a kind of conditional undertow, a flicker across the face amidst the smile, and here the logic of celebration is complicated. Dear Shakespeare, Jonson says, you will endure as long as your book endures, and as long as there are readers to read your book – but (implicitly) not beyond that. In setting Shakespeare free for all time, Jonson also chains him to his book. Shakespeare may not need a tomb (buried in Holy Trinity Church, Stratford-upon-Avon, Shakespeare didn't get a statue in Westminster Abbey until 1741), but he does need a First Folio. And he does need a William Wildgoose.

We vault forward three centuries. It's the morning of 23 January 1905. Twenty-one-year-old Gladwyn Maurice Revell Turbutt, a folio volume under his arm, has just knocked at the door of the Bodleian's sub-librarian, Falconer Madan. Turbutt is a bibliophile fresh from Magdalen College, and before that, Harrow School, and is possessed, in the words of one contemporary account, of 'a love of all that was ancient and beautiful'. He isn't short of confidence. Turbutt is at this moment beginning to study architecture in London, travelling often to France to understand the origins of Norman buildings. But this gilded moment will soon pass. Five years later, Turbutt becomes a lieutenant and – we feel the end looming into view even before we read it – is killed on 21 October 1914, aged thirty-one, along with many colleagues from the second battalion of the Oxfordshire and Buckinghamshire Light Infantry during the early stages of the Battle of Ypres, in Belgium.

But in January 1905 – his upright gait framed in Madan's office doorway – Turbutt is a long way from Ypres. The book under his arm is a copy of Shakespeare's First Folio, taken from the private library of Ogston Hall in Alfreton, Derbyshire, where it has been for 200 years. Ogston Hall has been his family's home since the early eighteenth century: the Turbutt country pile, a building of Victorian character layered over early Tudor origins, a place where words like courtyard and gatehouse and stable-range ring out down long halls. Aspiring architect that he is, Turbutt is preoccupied by recent additions: the five-storey castellated clock tower; the stained-glass windows describing the Turbutts' heraldry; the landscaped parks and formal gardens and the parterres and terraces.

Madan calls in the assistant librarian Strickland Gibson. Gibson opens the book, turns it over in his hands, peers closely at the spine. His eyes flick up to the young man, then back to the book. Turbutt waits, declines a chair, at ease with people busying themselves around him. Gibson notes the rip in the board where a clip has at some point in the past been torn away: the sort of clip that chained books to Bodleian shelves in the seventeenth century. Gibson is interested.

Gibson notices that the insides of the boards are covered with printed waste. Gibson sees that the waste used in Turbutt's copy of the First Folio is from a Latin edition of Cicero. Late-fifteenth-century. Now strongly suspecting that this was once Bodleian property, Gibson fetches the day book with which this chapter began to identify the volumes bound at the same time as the First Folio that the Bodleian once possessed. He reads Jean Verneuil's record: 'Deliured to William Wildgoose These books following to be bound.' He orders up the titles. And there is the clinching evidence: pages from the same copy of Cicero used as paste-downs in three other volumes on Wildgoose's list. By conjuring up the moment in February 1623 when Wildgoose tears out sheets from a copy of Cicero, printed in Deventer around 1485 but now no longer wanted, pasting sequential pages in as waste as Wildgoose works across Francisco Sánchez de Las Brozas's *In Ecclesiasten commentarium cum concordia Vulgatæ editionis, et Hebraici textus* (1619), then William Cowper's *Workes* (1623), then John Downame's *Guide to Godlynesse* (1622), and then Shakespeare's *Comedies, histories, & tragedies* (1623), Gibson proves that Turbutt's First Folio was once the Bodleian's, and once, a long time ago, passed through the hands of William Wildgoose.

One of the happy consequences of this First Folio's long static life in the Turbutts' Derbyshire library is that the book retained its original physical form. Most copies were lavishly rebound, as an act of honour, between about 1775 and 1950; of the 232 extant copies of Shakespeare's First Folio, only two others contain similar printed waste. But what we might call the lost Ogston Hall years bequeathed a wonderful lack of intervention, and the book that now sits in the Bodleian is close to the book that left Wildgoose's bindery 400 years ago, albeit a little darker, given the passing of time, and with some discreet conservation work from 2013. It's back in the Bodleian because the library, led by the dynamic, reforming head librarian, Edward Nicholson (1847–1912), organised a fundraising campaign to buy it back from the Turbutts in 1906 – the Turbutts who, faced with declining land values and rising taxation, lacked the riches that their parterres implied. In excess of 800 donors, the majority of them former students or members of the public offering a guinea or less, pooled resources to raise £3,000, about three times the market price. The library had never spent more than £200 on a single book before, but through a collaboration framed in patriotic terms, Nicholson and Madan managed to hold at bay the phenomenon that had begun to spread a particular kind of panic through Edwardian libraries: the rich American collector.

What we don't have, of course, and what we can't buy back, is a sense of Wildgoose as an individual: the man behind the careful fillets and the sewing and the hatching and the glued-in Ciceronian waste. Was Wildgoose calculating, or sentimental?

Parsimonious and a bit sour, or rashly generous and possessed of a booming laugh? Maddened daily by an incompetence he saw spreading all around him? Or a loner, standing apart?

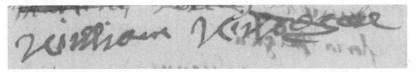

Wildgoose's signature, from the Bodleian Library Day Book.

3. CUT AND PASTE
Mary (1603–80) and Anna Collett (1605–39)

William Wildgoose took meticulous care in turning printed sheets into bound, coherent objects that could endure through time, giving sturdy physical presence to words and thoughts. This next chapter is about a competing impulse: another kind of book-making, from around the same moment in the seventeenth century. It concerns two women who cut up printed Bibles with knives and scissors so that they could scramble, reorder, and augment the text, releasing to the world a new form of biblical narrative that they called a 'Harmony'. This is book-making as a kind of collaging: the sound of a blade slicing through the page, a response to print that looks at first destructive, but that in fact produced some of the most magnificent volumes in the history of the book. We can begin the story with a visit by the King.

In March 1642, five months before the outbreak of the Civil War that led to his public beheading, King Charles I, accompanied by his son the Prince of Wales and a gaggle of very well-dressed courtiers, paused on a journey from Huntingdon to York to visit a small chapel and manor house. The residence was Little Gidding: a secluded religious community, and also a centre of book-making, 30 miles from Cambridge, set in acres of empty fields.

'Let's ride up to the house,' said the King, to an immediate chatter of agreement. A handwritten document now in the Museum of London with the rather unlovely name of 'MS Tangye 46. 78/675' describes this visit. It's one item from the collection of Cromwelliana amassed by the industrialist and Nonconformist Sir Richard Tangye (1833–1906), a huge pile of relics including Cromwell's button, coffin plate, death mask, and watch – the latter, according to the 1905 catalogue, 'in going order, except for the cat-gut, which has perished'. The handwritten account catches the sense of a sunny day, 400 years ago, and of an eerie calm: the wistful King touring the house and chapel while national conflict was drawing closer, like thunder on the horizon.

King Charles led his troupe of courtiers over the bridge to the chapel, a small building that could seat thirty. Dust was suspended in the air. The King 'took in his hands the Service Book and Bible, covered with Blue Velvet, which stood upon the Communion Table, and opened them, looking what Translation the Great Bible was of, and finding it the New, said it was well.' Then he read out loud: slowly and carefully, his voice echoing around the little chapel's wood-panelled walls and black and white marble tiles.

When he finished, he started to ask questions. 'How often is there prayers in this Church?'

'Three times a day.'

'That's very well done,' he said. 'How often is there Sermons in it?'

'Every Sunday and most Holy Days.'

'I like that well,' said the King. 'And is there no Catechising also?'

'There was, every Sunday.'

'But how often is the Sacrament administered?'

'Every first Sunday of each month in the Year.'

'A very good order,' said the King. 'And upon Sundays do all the servants come to Church, forenoons and afternoons?'

'They do all.'

The King: 'What strange reports are in the world.'

The Duke: 'Envy was quick-sighted.'

The Prince: 'Nay, can see what is not.'

The King closed the Bible. He kept his hands resting on the cover. He looked round the chapel. 'I knew what we should find here practised, no other but agreeable to the doctrine and discipline of the Church of England.' And then he added, explaining his interrogative mood: 'Whatever is reported, you now see and hear how things are.'

The King and his courtiers went into the manor house, to the Great Parlour, a large room with edifying but also rather exhausting sentences decorating the walls, like 'Love no sleep, lest thou come to poverty'. The King was shown a 'Great Book, as much as a man could well carry, laid upon the Table'. The King looked at the purple velvet cover and the binding, turning leaf after leaf, 'saying it was a rare, great and laborious work, as well as pleasant and profitable'.

'At first all cut out with Scissors and knives in small pieces,' John Ferrar explained, 'and there again brought into form, and conjoined together into a Body.'

The book was very big – about 75 centimetres tall and 50 wide – and heavy, too, at 23.5 kilos. The courtiers said that 'they never saw such a Book in Paper before of that largeness and size'. Titled *The Whole Law of God* (see plate section), the book described how the principles set out in the first five books of the Old Testament might apply to a later Christian society: it was a study of the relationship between the Old Testament and the New, a working out of which Old Testament laws to retain (like not worshipping false gods) and which to revise or discard (like special clothing for priests).

Biblical scholars would call this a work of typology, which means a reading of the Old Testament that understood narratives and figures like Adam, Noah, or Abraham as forerunners of later times. *The Whole Law of God* was a Royal Pentateuch – pentateuch from the Greek for 'five books' – but the text from Genesis, Exodus, Leviticus, Numbers, and Deuteronomy had been cut up with scissors and knives, and rearranged. More than a thousand printed images had been added, cut from prints or other books, trimmed, and neatly glued in.

'Very excellent,' said one of the courtiers, examining the collaged images, 'and of the best workmanship, graven by the best Artists beyond Sea.' (The prints derive from Dutch and Flemish

Genesis, chapter 1, from The Whole Law of God.

painters, influenced by Italian artists.) Looking closer: 'Many I know, but many I know not.' And: 'Here is several nations' workmanship.'

This was a handmade book – a unique object – but it was composed of print. As the King turned the pages, he felt a stillness he'd not experienced since before the death of his father. He looked closely at one glued-in image: a fleet of cloaked mourners walking behind a coffin. He turned a page: maps of Egypt and the Holy Land. Another: the heading 'Oblivion' and neatly cut up images of a mask, a mirror, and a chest of treasure. His mind an hour before had been burdened with the route to York and the prospect of rallying supporters for a conflict that now seemed inevitable. The continual sense of loneliness, and the dawning realisation that he was terrified. But here was a strange and beautiful book, a handmade thing, that rested outside of time. The minute care of it slowed everything down.

'My Lords,' the King said, 'you see the imployments, what they are, in this House. All is done in this House, yea the binding of it, yea all that belongs to it, and that most by the hands of Gentlewomen.'

He stood up, and closed the book. He fixed a smile for a little longer than seemed natural, as was his wont, so that the gesture became uncertain. Everyone waited, as was his wont.

'The garden,' he said. 'A little tour, please.'

At the back of the crowd that followed him outside was Mary Collett: she was worried that the King didn't realise the book wasn't quite finished. It had taken them two years to make and there was still more to do.

Seventeen years before, in 1625, Nicholas Ferrar (1592–1637) turned his back on spectacular academic success, a prominent parliamentary career, life at the Stuart court, and the business world of the Virginia Company, and bought a dilapidated manor house in the isolated parish of Little Gidding. Beside the manor stood a broken-down church, St John's, which had served, in recent years, as a pigsty and a farm building. There was nothing else within sight, except fields, and grazing sheep, and a single narrow lane.

The parish was Little Gidding, and from these unpromising beginnings, Ferrar created a tightly knit religious community that became famous, attracting praise and criticism in equal measure: part domestic university; part publishing house; part site of pilgrimage; part quasi-monastery, a century after monastic life had been violently obliterated from England by Henry VIII. Nicholas Ferrar was a youngest child but his charisma – 'the Mouth of them all', according to a visitor in 1634 – persuaded his family to join him in this permanent retreat: his mother, Mary (*c*.1554–1634), 'a tall, straite, cleere Complexioned, graue matron of ffourescore yeares of age'; his brother, John (1588–1657), 'his apparrell and haire soe fashioned as made him shewe Preiste like', and his wife, Bathsheba; and his elder sister, Susanna, her husband, John Collett, and eleven of their children, including their eldest daughters, Mary and Anna. 'Like a little college,' wrote Isaak Walton in 1670, 'and about thirty in number'.

The manor and grounds were restored, with 'sweete walkes . . . and gardenes on both sides' (the words come from a 1634 letter by a curious visitor), and so too was the chapel: 'all Covered with Tapestryes . . . with a Rich Carpet . . . and some plate as a Chalice and Candlesticke with wax Candles'. Amid this revived landscape, Ferrar established a life of communal devotion, based around vigorous moral debates, prayers, songs, reading, sewing, and – most famously – book-making. Ferrar devised a daunting daily service of devotion, beginning with a bell at 4 a.m. (5 a.m. for those indulgent winter lie-ins), and centring around three church services (6.30 a.m. morning prayer; 10 a.m. litany; 4 p.m. evening prayer), topped up with hourly services in the manor house. A major part of this programme was memorising the Bible: Nicholas supervised the recitation from memory of the Psalms and biblical passages between 4 and 7 a.m., and the cut-and-paste handmade books were originally designed to accompany the hourly services as a kind of hands-on memory aid. This sense of the purpose of what they referred to as Harmonies being mnemonic was what the poet George Herbert – a friend of Nicholas Ferrar, and a recipient of a now-lost Harmony made at Little Gidding – recognised when he 'encouraged' the continued application of 'women's scissors' as a means 'to keep that book always, without book, in their hearts as well as . . . their heads, memories, and tongues.'

The community was largely amicable, although cracks started to show through time: Nicholas's sister, Susanna, frequently resisted him, and his sister-in-law, Bathsheba, grew vociferously resentful at the regime, as (in her husband word's) 'greate passion and Violent words burst out'.

Word spread of Ferrar's little world of piety, education, and creativity, and visitors appeared with increasing frequency. While the elderly mother, Mary, grew irritated at yet more curious Cambridge undergraduates trudging across the fields, and pinned a warning sign above the fire, others were more welcome: among them, the poets George Herbert and Richard Crashaw, both of whose poetry was to be profoundly influenced by Little Gidding, and also King Charles I, who repeated his 1642 visit in 1646, after defeat at the Battle of Naseby, at night, and alone: the 'broken king' of T. S. Eliot's poem 'Little Gidding'. John Ferrar hid the King at a house close by in Coppingford, but Parliamentary soldiers closed in.

But the story of Little Gidding is not the story of Nicholas Ferrar – or at least, it is not only the story of Nicholas Ferrar, despite what most historians would have you believe. Little Gidding's fame rested on what look to us today like radical interventions in what is now called the history of the book, and the primary makers of these books were young women, particularly (but not only) two sisters, Mary and Anna Collett, usually unheard amid the very loud and domineering presence of their uncle, Nicholas. So let's shift focus, and imagine the scene in the Concordance Room of Little Gidding. It is 1634. The summer. Who is there? What is happening? What kind of book-making is going on?

The books Mary and Anna and their relatives made were Biblical Harmonies: thirteen complete Harmonies survive today, scattered across the British Library; university libraries in Oxford, Cambridge, Princeton, and Harvard; Windsor Castle; Ickworth House in Suffolk; Hatfield House in Hertfordshire; Lord Normanton's Somerley Estate in the New Forest, Hampshire; and in what is maddeningly known as 'private hands'. These were lavish folio books produced by scissors and glue, and the construction process went something like this. Mary and Anna obtained printed texts of the four Gospels – usually delivered by carriers from bookstall-browsing relatives in Cambridge or London – and, using scissors and knives, cut up these texts, often on a word-by-word level. What had been printed books were sliced and separated into sentences, clauses, phrases, single words. A door left open by a careless younger brother, and a gust of wind, and the word of God was fluttering through the air. Mary and Anna reorganised the text, distributing and glueing the pieces of the gospel into 150 chapters which told the chronological story of Christ's life. To this cut-up text, they glued in images: pictures removed from prints or sometimes other books, many of them imported from abroad (English Bibles rarely included illustrations), trimmed and reworked and sometimes conflated to produce something that would later be called collage.

What was this blend of care and violence all about? This was pious cutting, a strange kind of biblical scholarship which looks to us today more like a very neat version of a ransom note, or a Sex Pistols album cover. What they were after was harmony: harmony between the four different accounts of Christ's life in the four Gospels, achieved through this process of cutting, reordering, and glueing. Mary and Anna were building a book – and 'build' is probably the right verb: this isn't quite writing – that revealed but then reconciled 'agreements & differences' (as one title page put it) between Gospel accounts, and offered a coherent narrative, 'Digested into order'.

You can see what this meant overleaf: a page from the Little Gidding Harmony they were making in 1634, that in 1635 would be delivered to King Charles I, seven years before his horse-backed visit. It is now in the British Library, and it's an imposing volume, definitely as much as a man could well carry: more garden furniture than devotional handbook. The image shows a page that Mary and Anna worked on: the thirteenth of the

Gospel Harmony (1635).

Harmony's 150 chapters, titled 'JOHNS Baptisme, Preaching, Foode, & Rayment', the cut-up and rescrambled text presenting a description of John the Baptist's preaching; his arguments with the Pharisees; and the moment when he predicts (according to Luke) that 'one mightier than I commeth, the latchet of whose shoes I am not worthy to unloose'.

To produce this chapter, Mary and Anna selected the Gospel texts that narrate this moment: Matthew 3.1–12; Mark 1.1–8; and Luke 3.1–18. Taking their scissors and knives, they cut up these three accounts and on this page arranged the text in two different formats. In 'The Comparison', on the left, the three columns of text are aligned to produce a parallel edition of Matthew, Mark, and Luke – so the reader can scan across between them, seeing the differences and similarities. In 'The Composition', all the words from the three different Gospel accounts of this description of

Gospel Harmony (1635), close-up.

John the Baptist have been interlaced to create a single piece of continuous prose: this was three accounts harmonised into one. The image which I have reproduced above is a zoomed-in image of 'The Composition', and you can see here the level of detail involved in the production of this conflated account: the cutting up is sometimes at the level of the individual word. This is about fiddly scraps of paper that are hard to pick up, glue hardening on fingertips, the irritated search for a paper word that has flipped over – but it is also about the life of Christ.

You can probably just about make out the superscript 'Mr.' right at the start of the text beside the first 'THE'. This indicates that the ensuing text comes from Mark's gospel; the 'L.' at the start of the second, main, paragraph a few lines on, recalls Luke—although there is just one word, 'Now,' from Luke, before the text switches to Matthew ('M.'), for 'In those dayes', before flipping back to Luke for 'in the fifteenth yeare of the reigne of Tiberius Cesar'. What this means is that 'The Composition' combines both the texts into one, but leaves little editorial markers to signal the separate origins of parts of the whole. This is a new order that remembers the old order.

Mary Collett (1603–80) and Anna (1605–39) were the eldest daughters of the sixteen children born to Susanna and John Collett. They lived and worked at Little Gidding all their lives, both pledging a vow of chastity. In 1632, when the elderly matriarch, Mary, became too frail to lead much of the religious discussion and educational activities, her granddaughter Mary, dressed often in a 'friar's grey gown', became 'mother' to the community. Visitors to Little Gidding were struck by Mary's quiet charisma, particularly as it flourished after Nicholas's death in 1637. The poet Richard Crashaw, studying at Cambridge in the 1630s, was a frequent visitor – he liked to join in the all-night meditations – and was, it seems, a platonic admirer of Mary. In the 1620s, Nicholas arranged for her, and possibly Anna too, to be taught by a Cambridge bookbinder's daughter, and the binding of the 1642 Harmony that Charles I perused in purple velvet with elaborate good tooling is evidence of Mary's skills. A British Library copy of *Eikon Basilike* (1649) – the book justifying the reign of Charles I immediately after his execution – has long been claimed as the binding work of Mary, too.

We have to listen more carefully to hear Anna's voice, but it is audible. The Ferrar Papers is an archive that sits in Magdalene College, Cambridge – the same college that houses the Pepys Library – and it contains 2,280 manuscripts, plus around 600 loose prints, relating to the history of the Ferrar family between about 1590 and 1790. Largely unused in the nineteenth century, the archive was catalogued in stages over more than fifty years in the twentieth century. The majority of those manuscripts are letters, particularly of Nicholas Ferrar (1592–1637) and of the Virginia Company of London, but there are also letters in there to and from Anna Collett.

For the most part, these letters are written to her uncle, Nicholas. He calls her 'My dearest Nan'; she addresses him 'My Deare and ever Honoured Father Unckle' – 'for that Name [Father] you haue deserued and I accounte it a greate addiscion'. Anna's letters are full of a language of duty, thanks, of being bound to daily express gratitude, and of self-abasement ('But I dare not trust my owne iudgment in this waity matter'). Anna tends to slot tidily into the kind of hierarchy Nicholas clearly expected:

> Give mee leave I beseech you to tender unto you these Rude [i.e. ignorant, untutored] Lines as Parte to expresse the humble thankefullnesse wch daly I acknowledge my selfe Bounde to owe unto you For ye greate love wch you have bine pleased to bestowe on mee yt am altogether unworthy of ye leaste of your Favours wch So plentifully you have Showred upon mee.

This is from a letter dated 13 November 1626. On 9 November 1629, Anna signs off 'Your most obleiged Daughter to command Anna Collett', and it's hard not to feel the psychological walls closing in.

We might expect Anna to flicker and disappear in the face of this dominant charisma, but she didn't, and there's something nicely paradoxical about her repeated and articulate declarations of passivity ('my Honered father . . . y^r wisdom and Conciense shall by gods grace be my Ruler and guid'). At the end of Shakespeare's *The Taming of the Shrew*, written we think in the early 1590s, Katherine offers a long speech of duty to her husband-to-be Petruchio that renounces her earlier voluble and witty independence and instead preaches a kind of dumb loyalty ('Thy husband is thy lord, thy life, thy keeper, / Thy head, thy sovereign'). But Katherine's commitment to quietness and modesty is spread over forty-four lines, and as she holds centre stage to pledge a life of marginality, she offers a rousing speech to weakness. The ironies begin to crackle. Anna isn't ironic in her letters, but she does find a way for a kind of embedded self-expression: playing by the rules, but finding a voice.

We see a sense of a strong personality mediated through gendered conventions of pious modesty and spiritual devotion when, in 1631, Nicholas's nephew Arthur Wodenoth sought Anna's hand in marriage. Anna's response is a clear no, dressed in the language of stasis and compliance.

> Touching my Condission of lyfe such Contente doe I now fynde I humbly praise God y^t I neither wish or desyer any Change of it But humbly beg of God y^f he soe please to see it good and wth my Parence leave to give me grace and strength that I may spend ye remainder of my dayes w^{t}hout greater incoumbrances of this world wch doe of Nescessaty accompany a married Estate.

In their book-making, Mary and Anna would occasionally seize on a chapter topic to evoke something of their experiences at Little Gidding: they were not thinking in terms of autobiography, but they were drawn to a kind of rhyming of similar experiences through time. In Chapter 148 of their 1635 Harmony for Charles I, next to the biblical text, 'But there are written, that yee might beleeveth that Jesus is the Christ the Sonne of God', Anna and Mary cut out and glued in an image of a writing desk, book, and scroll; in Chapter 125, on 'The Ten Virgins', they included prints of women sewing and writing, with a book collaged in the centre of the page; and in Chapter 42 they included prints of women weaving, sewing, and praying. It's too clumsy to think of these scenes as representations of Mary and Anna: they were not interested in self-expression as we understand that term, as the voicing of individual desires. But Mary and Anna were using the conventions at their disposal to suggest a long history of the kind of gendered work that occupied their time, too. For Mary and Anna, a sense of self seems to have developed from conformity to, rather than (as we tend to imagine today) departure from, prior patterns of behaviour and personhood.

Nicholas's brother, John, wrote a very reverential but unfinished biography of him – a crucial early history that, in celebrating Nicholas, marginalised just about everyone else, including John himself, providing a pattern of Little Gidding history that has been largely repeated. But what's helpful in his biography is John's description of the mechanics of the cutting and pasting that Mary and Anna performed. The Harmonies were assembled in the Concordance Room at Little Gidding on large tables, the room hung with passages from Scripture pinned up on the walls:

> with their scissors they . . . cut out [of] each Evangelist such and such verses and thus and thus lay them together to make and perfect such and such a head or chapter. Which when they had first roughly done, then with their knives and scissors they neatly fitted each verse so cut out to be pasted down on sheets of paper. And so artificially they performed this new-found-out-way, as it were a new kind of printing, for all that saw the books when they were done took them to be printed the ordinary way.

John's quote catches a sense of both the novelty and the technical sophistication of the process of Harmony production: what he calls 'this new-found-out-way'. But there's also a hint of unease in here: a register of an anxiety felt by first readers, a sense of being disorientated by these books: 'All that saw the books . . . took them to be printed the ordinary way'. What, exactly, are these books?

Not everyone has been impressed with these hybrid works. Later (we might want to stress male) historians have been frequently

dismissive – and first prize here goes to the bookbinding historian Geoffrey Hobson, who, writing in 1929 of the 'pious tedium
of life at Little Gidding', described the cut-and-paste Harmonies
as 'dreadful monuments of misdirected labour', and, at best, 'an
admirable diversion for a rather backward child of eight'. Eight!
It's true that Hobson's son Anthony (eight at the time of Hobson's
writing) went on to become a distinguished auctioneer and bookbinding historian, as well as the author of six books and more
than two hundred articles on bibliography; but this still seems
a little harsh. Certainly, contemporaries came to very different
judgements. Charles I praised the Harmonies for their 'singular
composition' and 'exquisite workmanship . . . [not] paralleled . . .
by any man'. George Herbert prized the Little Gidding Harmony
he was sent 'most highly as a rich jewel worthy to be worn in the
heart of all Christians', and expressed delight 'to see women's
scissors brought to so rare a use as to serve at God's altar'.

We can get a sense of the production process by looking at the
leftover scraps that remain in archives today. The Ferrars sold Little
Gidding in 1760 and their library vanished, but bundles of papers
descended to Magdalene College, Cambridge, including thousands of letters and a collection of about 800 loose, unmounted
prints that lay for decades in an unopened box, unrecognised for
what they were. These prints, which vary in size from coin-sized
medallions to large double folios, are either images which the Ferrars expected to use in the construction of future Harmonies, but
never did, or the remnants of partially used sheets: the tatters left
behind by the scissor work of Mary and Anna. For a long time
they were assumed to be a rejected part of Samuel Pepys's print
collection, and so no one interested in Little Gidding took a look.
But once the lid on the box is lifted, they give a glimpse of the
book-making at Little Gidding, frozen in time.

The image shows one of the prints from Magdalene College: it's *The Last Judgement*, engraved after a painting by Marten
de Vos of Antwerp (1532–1603). Mary and Anna and the rest
of Little Gidding's Harmony-makers were fond of de Vos's

'The Last Judgement', after Marten de Vos of Antwerp, without sheep.

Mannerist work: it features regularly in the Harmonies, and a
surviving letter from 1635 has Nicholas, with characteristic hau-
teur, ordering his nephew to obtain prints by Adrian Collaert
and de Vos:

> send mee downe this weeke that sett [of prints] wch Bettys [Eliza-
> beth Collett's] Concordance is made upp wth being 51 in Number
> and of Adrian Collearts and M. de Vos ... Mr Tabor bought
> mee one of them at Sturbridge fayre [annual fair on Stourbridge
> Common, Cambridge] for seven shillings I suppose it is easy to
> be found.

It's not clear whether they really were 'easy to be found', but when
Mary and Anna came to Chapter 127 ('The Judgement') of the
1635 Harmony, they reached for de Vos's print. At other times,

they were interested in excising parts of prints for use in collages, and the missing sheep in the Magdalene College de Vos print suggest pieces removed for use elsewhere, leaving behind those rather haunting sheep-spaced gaps. If you visit Little Gidding today, not far from the main road at Sawtry, the tiny chapel that still stands is surrounded by fields of sheep, and the Ferrars had a particular weakness for animals: lots of Harmony pages feature animal collages – sheep, snakes, stalking foxes – illustrating text cut from, for example, Matthew Chapter 10 ('Behold, I send you foorth as sheepe in the middest of wolves'). 'Thees Pictures express the Cruelty of Wolves / And the Subtilty of Serpents', notes a characteristically literalist handwritten note.

These loose prints can help us conjure the process of Harmony manufacture in other ways, too. Leafing through the boxes of prints reveals parts destined for use in a Harmony, but stalled mid-production: a printed border of roses, for example, designed to frame a never-completed central scene. We get a sense of a vibrant, complex textual operation that has been packed up, suddenly, but which might resume at any point. On the reverse of a print from a design by Theodor Bernard of Amsterdam is a handwritten note: 'This parcell Contaynes a Hundred seuerall pictures they Cost 12 shillings.' The print, made of thick paper, has been folded twice to serve as a wallet for storing images as they were shipped into Little Gidding. Sometimes similar images were bound together with string, creating a little book; and where the string doesn't survive, the holes on individual prints can be matched up to evoke this improvised binding. It seems likely, but not certain, that there was a register, now lost, providing a central index – creating an archive to draw on for future, as yet unidentified, work.

Many of the Magdalene prints are augmented with handwritten notes, usually in the hand of Nicholas or John Ferrar. Reading these notes, we can listen in on the 1630s chatter of acquiring, cataloguing, and selecting prints. On the back of 'The adoration of the kings', from a design by Johannes Stradanus, is a passage of text in John Ferrar's hand. Ferrar requests that he be sent

> This Booke of Stradanus of the Stroy [Story] of the Gospell But espetially that if to be had a lim[b] of the Angell appeiring to Zakerias and if none of that of Stradens [Stradanus] to be had then you must Send me the Booke of that of Christ Acting in the tempell it is in Architecture manner black prints you Sent one of the Bookes which I returned having the same booke by me But coming now to peruse it I find wanting the First leafe of Story the Angell Coming to Zakerias and he Coming out to the Pepull [People] and could not Speake; if you Can not helpe me to that Singill Picture which is only that I want of the whole Booke then you must Send me the whole Booke Alsoe I shall have occasion to use more of that kind of Story and very picture if there be many other that have graven it after many other Formes the more variety the better in this and all other for my turne for they are of greate helpes when they are different kinds and formes both smaler and greter: This I pray observe in all Pictures you send me Variety in the same kind and Story the better.

The hum of purpose and activity and production and intent. Here is John's very specific desire for a particular scene: 'that *Singill Picture* which is only that I want of the *whole Booke*'. If he can't get this in isolation, 'then you must Send me the whole Booke'. John also wants other copies of similar prints: he is gathering resources, 'the more variety the better', particularly 'when they are different kinds and formes both smaler and greter'.

These incorporated images – often originally produced by sixteenth-century Antwerp printers and engravers – ensured that the Harmonies were not only beautiful objects, but also constituted apparently proto-Catholic, and therefore politically explosive, interventions in the heated political-religious debates of the 1630s. This was the decade when William Laud, Archbishop of

Canterbury, encouraged a heightened ceremonial form of worship that seemed to many to represent a Romanising agenda. And indeed, one of the important aspects of early modern life that Little Gidding reveals is the survival of forms of Catholic religious life within an officially Protestant England. One critic in 1641 described Little Gidding as 'The Arminian Nunnery'; in 1634, a young lawyer called Edward Lenton was dispatched by the local sergeant-at-law to find out if rumours of Catholic superstition were true; and George Herbert lamented the 'suspitions, slanders & scornes wch worldly persons would throw upon them'. Charles I's approving 1642 visit, with all those questions duly answered, took place in the context of these rumours. Nicholas Ferrar, in particular, endured heated speculation: he was, in the words of a contemporary, 'torn asunder as with mad horses, or crushed betwixt the upper and under millstone of contrary reports: that he was a papist, and that he was a puritan'. When, on his deathbed, Ferrar ordered his profane books ('comedies, tragedies, love hymns, heroical poems, and such like things') to be burnt, the bonfire that rose in the night in the grounds of Little Gidding seemed to confirm suspicions that he was a magician, his soul sold to the Devil like Christopher Marlowe's Dr Faustus, who declared, ''Tis magic, magic that hath ravish'd me.'

Little Gidding wasn't the crypto-Catholic cell that Puritans feared, or perhaps fantasised about. But it was a hub of activity, a buzzing textual factory, despite its seclusion amid the circling fields, with goods of all sorts (including but not limited to prints and book-making resources) flowing in and out, often conveyed by anonymous servants. ('Touching the Cake and Capons, I suppose it best to send them by Page.') In 1627, Ferrar wrote to his 'most Deare Mother', listing items due to be delivered 'by Saturday noon' – including 'An old Cloke[,] some glasses', 'Figgs, Almons,

Prunes' and, in 'a bundle sowed upp in Canvas', 'Lump sugar' and 'A seruice booke wth a couer of Blew Veluett'. Deliveries often included more bookish items: 'A Bottle of Red & a bottle of black Inke'; 'a lyttle Box [of] . . . seuerale letters or [printing] Characters [and] . . . Printers Inke wch must be layd ouer the letter by a ball of Leather'; and even, in July 1633, 'a Press' – perhaps a printing press, or possibly a standing press, of the sort William Wildgoose would have had, used to press pages after prints and pieces of text had been glued down onto paper. Surviving letters describe relatives required to search London bookstalls and Cambridge College libraries for Bibles and prints that could be used back at Little Gidding. In London, Nicholas's nephew Arthur Wodenoth, a goldsmith living at the Bunch of Grapes in Foster Lane, near Goldsmiths' Hall, served as something like Little Gidding's principal London agent: letter after letter describes his indefatigable attempts to secure specific materials for his uncle. 'I was yesterday att Printing Hows,' he wrote in a letter in 1632, 'when I understand that the Bible of the Romane letter is finished.' Ferrar's relative Robert Mapletoft, a Fellow of Pembroke, Cambridge, and chaplain to the anti-Puritan Bishop of Norwich and then Ely, Matthew Wren, was another regular searcher and his letters are full of the latest publishing news: '[T]he fayrest Latin Bible of the Vulgar edition and of you[r] size is that of Amsterdam by Johnson 1632.' Mapletoft was particularly good at scouring Cambridge College libraries for books that would help the workers at Little Gidding produce better Harmonies: in 1635 he reported back on the books he'd found while Mary and Anna worked on their Harmony of the four Gospels, including Perpinian's *Concordia Euangelica in quatuor Euangelistas* (1631), which 'goes by way of comparison, bringing the whole text of euery seuerall euangelist one after another and comments upon them'.

Those of us who think about the history of the book – like me, like you – are used to linking print with something like fixity, with the capacity to convert an in-flux medieval handwritten culture into uniform printed books. John Donne's 1590s and early 1600s poetry exists in a chaos of manuscript variants, partly because Donne was terrified of printed versions of his poetry reaching readers who didn't understand his complex and usually lascivious ironies, particularly after he became Dean of St Paul's and youthful get-thee-to-bed poetry looked awkward on a CV. As a result, copies of his verses circulated widely in manuscript, particularly among sniggering students at the Inns of Court, so that a poem like 'The Flea' is recorded today in forty-five early-modern handwritten versions (or, in the procedural language of textual studies, 'witnesses'), all of them different from one another in varying ways. How, then, faced with this multiplicity (a chaos, or a richness, depending on your inclinations) are we to talk about a single Donne poem called 'The Flea' – or even a single author named Donne? But one Latin Bible printed in Amsterdam by Johnson in 1632 looked like another, or at least it should do, or at least we expect it to, and from this sense of dependable repetition springs the (to us) entirely commonsensical but (for the history of written text) revolutionary notion of identical copies. Since every copy of Shakespeare's *Workes* should look the same (I'm stressing 'should': keep the equivocation in mind), we can all read the same text by the same author and respond to the same work of art. And from this unity springs a number of everyday but also quite profound concepts, including the very idea of the author, and of the literary work, and of the literary canon. But in their cut-and-paste Gospels, Mary and Anna Collett show a willingness to dismantle and reorder printed Bibles that drives a sheep through this particular royal procession. The Harmonies are a response to the culture and technology of the printing press by brilliantly skilled (but also amateur) book-makers, who converted printed books back into unique texts. Not for them the fixing potential of print, or the expectation that a grand folio religious work persists as an ossified thing, like text cut into stone. The teeming life that Mary and Anna's work displays is the very opposite, and to read these Harmonies today is to experience a kind of twin-pull: a sense of the intricacy and completeness of these volumes, but also an awareness of the cutting and pulling apart that lies behind the assembling. The Harmonies are poised awkwardly on the border of destruction and creation, and the creativity at work at Little Gidding rests on a prior act of cutting apart.

But that still doesn't quite answer the question of *why*. Why would members of an Anglican religious community choose to cut up copies of the Bible? From the vantage point of a twenty-first century in which the destruction of religious books, like the 2012 burning of a Koran by Terry Jones, Protestant minister in Gainesville, Florida, is a potent cultural taboo, how are we to make sense of this apparent act of destruction? In Thomas Hardy's *Jude the Obscure*, when Sue describes making a 'NEW New Testament' by 'cutting up all the Epistles and Gospels into separate *brochures* [from the French, literally 'a stitched work'], and rearranging them in chronological order as written' – 'I know that reading it afterwards made it twice as interesting as before, and twice as understandable' – Jude's response is the reaction we might expect from culture at large: ' "H'm!" said Jude, with a sense of sacrilege.' So what was going on at Little Gidding?

Part of the answer to that puzzle lies in the nature of seventeenth-century Protestantism, which encouraged believers to read the Bible for themselves, to wrestle with every word, turning the pages, finding their meanings, striking up an agonistic relationship with the text. As the book historian Juliet Fleming notes, print 'may . . . have represented a mode of materialising thought *more densely*'; and if Protestantism advocated interactions with not abstracted text but the embodied book in every reader's hands, and understood reading as a tussle, then accounts of devotional writing often presented hyper-sensual descriptions of religious writing that bordered on the erotic. Describing the murky textual history behind Bishop of Winchester Lancelot Andrewes's posthumous *Manual of Private Devotion* (1648), Richard Drake linked devotional writing not only to the handling of physical paper, but also and very strikingly with staining and marking. A proper religious interaction with text left a mess:

> Had you seen the Original Manuscript, happie in the glorious deformitie thereof, being slubber'd with His pious hands, and water'd with His penitential tears, you would have been forced to confess That Book belonged to no other than pure and Primitive Devotion.

'Being slubber'd with His pious hands' is a wonderful description of a religion of messy book handling, and of the paradoxical conviction that pure faith leaves its mark – and it is in this culture that Little Gidding's cutting and rearranging and glueing took place. 'To know the Bible in the age of print,' as the art historian Michael Gaudio nicely puts it, 'was to be adept at managing its pieces.'

But these cut-and-paste biblical Harmonies also tell us something important about the seventeenth-century book more generally. I noted earlier, rather nervously, the way print is often linked to an idea of fixing or stabilising text: and early works by those scholars who did much to invent the field of the history of the book, like Elizabeth Eisenstein's *The Printing Press as an Agent of Change* (1979), showed how the printing press could create a new kind of stable literary monument. There is much truth in that, but Mary and Anna Collett's spectacular cut-ups alert us to an important caveat: that is, their Harmonies show that for all the new permanence of printed books, the early modern was also a culture of a profound bibliographical inconstancy, at ease with (among other manifestations of bookish flux) taking scissors to its printed books. This cutting was often a very everyday version of reading: not scandalous or destructive, but a response to the ways books asked to be consumed. John White's *Briefe and Easie Almanack for this Yeare* (1650) – a kind of early-modern desk diary – requests that readers snip out 'the whole kalender' for 1650 for use elsewhere, 'which being cut out, is fit to be placed into any book of accompts [accounts], table book, or other'. In a 1710 copy of *Parker's Ephemeris* – a similar kind of almanac – a reader has sewn into the back of the book a paper wheel, made from cut-up printed pages, that can be rotated to reveal the astrological alignment of the present moment, and whether the 'Conjunction [is] good . . . indiferent good . . . very Good . . . very bad . . . most excellent . . . bad . . . [or] worst of All.' This is cutting up as an everyday mode of book modification. We know that from the earliest years of printing in the late-fifteenth century, readers snipped out printed woodcut roundels, initials, and images and glued them into devotional texts such as psalters and primers; and the manuscript of London alderman Robert Fabyan's *Great Chronicle of London* (*c*.1504) is covered with glued-in printed cut-outs: mixed-media, avant la lettre. Readers might cut to avoid laborious hand-copying; to cope, by excising and compressing, with that flood of print which Robert Burton in his *Anatomy of Melancholy* called 'the vast *Chaos* and confusion of bookes'; to expand or reformat texts; to create space for marginal commentaries; to remove censored material, particularly prayer book references to the Pope, Thomas Becket, indulgences and purgatory in response to legislation under Henry VIII and Edward VI; to correct or delete contentious, mistaken or knowingly false title-page claims (as was perhaps the case with at least two copies of *Aphorismes, or, Certaine Selected Points of the Doctrine of the Jesuits* (1609), both of which have the colophon's 'LONDON' removed); or to illustrate manuscripts with cut-out printed images. Seventeenth-century readers were at ease with the print-manuscript hybrid, and we have a spectacular example in the commonplace book of Royalist Sir John Gibson. Imprisoned in Durham Castle in the 1650s after being on the wrong side of the Civil War, and reflecting on the adversity he was enduring, Gibson assembled a manuscript full of quotations, many from the Bible and classical literature, that meditated on the suffering that the virtuous endure. He hoped

*John Gibson's multi-media commonplace book, featuring cut-out pages
from printed books that reflect on his unlucky fate.*

the compilation would serve as a justification of his life, and an
aid to his son as a 'companion some times to looke upon, in this
Vale of teares'. To these transcribed quotations, Gibson glued in
several pages cut from printed volumes, and added his own handwritten notes.

There is something breath-taking about these pages: Gibson is
using everything he can get his hands on to produce a text that
chimes with his particular blend of despair and defiance. But his
willingness to cut also reflects much more broadly the fact that
the coherent, bound, unannotated, 'complete' printed book, with
which modern book culture has been fixated – the perfect, 'clean
copy' that causes auctioneers to jig on the spot – was not yet the
dominant medium for conveying text. The establishment of the
book through iconic publications like Jonson's and Shakespeare's
Folios is of course one of the loudest and most important narratives of seventeenth-century literary culture – and we saw William
Wildgoose's role in that transformation. And I certainly don't
want to obliterate that shift with the all-or-nothing wrecking ball

of revisionism. But through much of the early modern period, the modern assumption that (in the words of Juliet Fleming) 'the work is coterminous with the book' – that one literary work equals one physical object – was not yet axiomatic. The book was not yet the exclusive or perhaps even dominant medium for carrying text (there were manuscripts, letters, single-sheet ballads, not to mention text-receptive walls and windows and plates and pieces of furniture), and the book was a material form that might easily be reworked. Books were usually sold unbound; several pamphlets might be bound together at a later date to create new composite wholes or Sammelbände, in which one physical whole contains numerous shorter texts that began life as separate publications; and readers might add blank pages to their printed texts to make space for their handwritten annotations. Some books were printed with extra-wide margins to enable just this sort of scribbling – a copy of Thomas Littleton's *Tenures* (1591) now in the Folger Shakespeare Library, for example, has huge margins that present the printed text as the starting point for a lengthy process of writing. *Annotate me!* this book declares.

Amid this culture, the printed book was a more tentative form than we might expect, a negotiable physical object, and cutting devotional pages was not necessarily the transgressive act later periods took it to be: 'it being the peculiar happiness of *Sacred Commodities*,' as that edition of Lancelot Andrewes noted, 'to be made *better by their using.*'

Many early modern readers expressed their investment in reading and knowledge and thought not by fetishising books, or putting them away in boxes or behind closed doors; to read was to mark, annotate, rebind, rearrange, reformat, cut. One way to think about Mary and Anna Collett is as quiet and dutiful nieces, barely visible beside their dominant uncle. Another is to recast them as radical book-makers, alert to the wonderful potential for inconstancy contained with the early modern printed book. We see this commitment to reimagining books in the following page: from the final chapter of the Gospel Harmony made for Charles I

St Matthew writing, with cut-up text, in the 1635
Harmony for Charles I (close-up on right).

in 1635 from cut-up editions of the English Bible and a wide range
of Antwerp devotional prints.

This is the Apostle Matthew writing his Gospel, turning to
face a beckoning angel, while, in the foreground, a desk bears the
props of writing: an hourglass, a book clasped shut, a quill in an
inkpot, and an open book bearing text which seems to be both on
the page, and floating above it, the text turned to be legible to the
reader, not as Matthew would write it: zoomed in on the right, we
can read 'And Loe / I am / with you al / way Euen unto / the End
of the World / Amen'. These are the closing lines of Matthew
Chapter 28: that moment when the risen Jesus tells the disciples to
'teach all nations', and disseminate the word. Matthew seems to
be both turning to face the angel for inspiration – suggesting he's
in the middle of writing – and presenting to us a finished narrative: a text complete.

This image of Matthew is built around a print designed by
Peter de Jode, engraved by Egbert van Panderen, and published
by Theodoor Galle. Early modern representations of Matthew
writing his Gospel were common, like Caravaggio's *Inspiration of
St Matthew* (1602), but Mary and Anna Collett have turned this

image into a celebration of book-making Little Gidding-style. Miraculously, what flow from Matthew's quill are printed words: words which have been cut up, rearranged, and glued down, oriented for us, the readers. The letters have a numinous quality as they float above the surface of the book: 'And Loe I am with you' hovers above the material world, even as these words are vividly made of cut paper and glue. The name Matthew derives etymologically from Latin *manus* and Greek *theos*, 'the hand of God', and so Mary and Anna Collett's final chapter reframes an iconic moment of writing as the work not of pen and ink but of knives and scissors.

On a Monday afternoon in 1936, T. S. Eliot left Cambridge, where he'd been conducting a PhD viva at the request of John Maynard Keynes, and made the thirty-mile journey by car out to Little Gidding. The weather forecast in *The Times* was poor – wind; rain;

cold – but it turned out, Eliot wrote in a phrase that it is hard to credit him writing, a 'really lovely day'.

Eliot was forty-seven and his status within English literary culture was, in the words of literary critic Frank Kermode, 'high and steady': *The Waste Land* was fourteen years behind him; the *Criterion* was a taste-defining journal that had published the leading writers of the early-twentieth century (Ezra Pound, Virginia Woolf, W. H. Auden, W. B. Yeats).

The car rattled out along narrowing blossom-covered lanes towards the small chapel with the dull facade. Accompanying Eliot was a coterie of Little Gidding enthusiasts, packed in like very learned Anglican sardines: among them, Hugh Fraser Stewart, Dean of Magdalene College and a scholar of the seventeenth-century French philosopher Blaise Pascal, and Bernard Blackstone, Fellow of Trinity College, who'd been trawling through Little Gidding's papers for years.

Eliot was visiting the house and the chapel in part because of his new-found Anglicanism: he had been baptised into the Church of England nine years before, and had become a British citizen in 1930. He was also a fervent royalist – a lifelong member of the Society of King Charles the Martyr – and was drawn to the stories of Charles I's visits. But perhaps strongest of all was Eliot's fascination with George Herbert – someone Eliot regarded as a great poet of spiritual insecurity and restlessness. Late in life, according to his second wife Valerie, 'Eliot sometimes thought of himself as a minor George Herbert.'

Six years after his visit, Eliot published the fourth of his *Four Quartets*, 'Little Gidding', transforming elements of his visit on that day in May into this time-warping poem. Preoccupied with Herbert, Nicholas Ferrar, and Charles I, Eliot seems to have known little or nothing about Mary and Anna Collett. But he was part of a long tradition of individual visitors to Little Gidding, a tradition stretching from Herbert and Richard Crashaw in the 1630s right through to those who visit today. The visitors' book by the chapel door today records a range of motives for these more recent journeys.

Part of the pilgrimage.
On the eve of my wonderful son's 34th birthday. I give thanks!
Interesting building.
Love it.
Remembering Howard King.
A return visit many years and poems later.
Married here 31.7.1971. 40 years ago.
I will come back.
My mother Frances Deller as a girl polished the brass Church Eagle.
Made the trip all worthwhile.
Really quaint place.
For the first time.
A farewell visit?

Eliot's lines from the beginning of his poem capture that sense, that Charles I presumably felt in 1642, of Little Gidding as a secluded end-point to any number of journeys.

If you came this way,
Taking the route you would be likely to take
From the place you would be likely to come from,
If you came this way in May time, you would find the hedges
White again, in May, with voluptuary sweetness.
It would be the same at the end of the journey,
If you came at night like a broken king,
If you came by day not knowing what you came for,
It would be the same, when you leave the rough road
And turn behind the pig-sty to the dull façade
And the tombstone.
And what you thought you came for
Is only a shell, a husk of meaning
From which the purpose breaks only when it is fulfilled
If at all.

4. TYPOGRAPHY

John Baskerville (1707–75) and Sarah Eaves (1708–88)

Have you noticed how picturesque the letter Y is and how innumerable its meanings are? The tree is a Y, the junction of two roads forms a Y, two converging rivers, a donkey's head and that of an ox, the glass and its stem, the lily on its stalk, and the beggar lifting his arms are a Y.

Carl Dair, *Design With Type* (1967)

From the scissors and glue and biblical collaging of Little Gidding in the 1630s, we travel forward a little over a hundred years to eighteenth-century Birmingham and a typographer and bookmaker of celebrated reputation, and his wife. We can get there via a trip to Cambridge.

If you make the happy decision to visit the Historical Printing Room at Cambridge University Library, a brisk twenty-five-minute walk from the train station, you can request to view seven brown wooden boxes containing, in their green felt-lined interiors, what appear at first to be rows and rows of bullets. But they are not bullets: they are John Baskerville's type punches, cut by his punch-cutter John Handy in the middle of the eighteenth century, working from drawings by Baskerville, each about 5 centimetres long with the shape of a mirror-image letter cut in relief into the top. The function of each punch is – or was, before they became historical artefacts to be consulted in a library – to be driven into bars of soft brass or copper, the hard tempered steel punch creating a matrix, about an inch and a half long, in the shape of a letter. This matrix, trimmed and locked into a mould by a type-caster, could hold molten type metal poured from a ladle, an alloy of tin, lead, and antimony. 'The type is cast in a mould that is held in one hand,' wrote a Swedish visitor to Baskerville's foundry in 1754, 'and can be opened and shut very quickly.' Hardening and expanding, the metal would form a left-right inverted letter, and then another, and then another, each of which, after a process of 'dressing' – the 'sorts' (pieces of type) rubbed smooth and square – had the capacity to mark paper with inked letters. An 'a', or a 't', and a 'p', or an 's'.

The expertise required to produce these punches was a closely guarded secret, whispered from master to apprentice. When Joseph Moxon came to write his great celebratory work on printing, disguised as an instructional manual, *Mechanick Exercises on the Whole Art of Printing* (1683-4), he could only confess his frustrated searches: 'Letter-Cutting is a Handy-Work hitherto kept so conceal'd among the Artificers of it, that I cannot learn anyone hath taught it any other . . . Therefore, I cannot (as in other Trades) describe the general practice of the Work-Man.' These type punches in the Historical Printing Room at Cambridge were hand-cut in Birmingham in the 1750s, a city at that time flush with skilled metalworkers and in particular locksmiths. The punches are heavy and cool to touch. Their mixture of weight and – as they narrow to a mirror-image letter – precision is a reminder that the earliest printers, in the fifteenth century, including Gutenberg in Mainz and Nicolas Jenson in Venice, were metalworkers by training, and that the beginning of printing was, like many technological advances, the migration of one set of skilled workers into a new, adjacent field.

The punches are not letters, but the source of letters: they are a very early stage of any printing, and they have, we can imagine, all books using this alphabet latent within them. 'You know B[askerville] imagines yt his Letter is every thing,' wrote the poet William Shenstone (1714–63), 'on wch ye merit of a book depends.'

Each box is labelled by hand: '40pt Italic 36pt Italic 28pt Rom. caps'; 'ITALICS English Pica Small pica Long primer Bourgeois

Brevier Nonpareil'; '60 & 48 pt Romans'. This is the language of typography, of italic and Roman letters in sizes ranging from very small to very large: 6-point nonpareil, from the French for 'having no equal'; 8-point brevier, named because this size was used to print guides to religious services in the Roman Catholic Church called breviaries (small, so you had to peer close); 9-point bourgeois, the term indicating a middling-size book, or a connection with the social middle classes, or maybe a link with Jean de Bourgeois, printer in Rouen around 1500; 10-point long primer, a size used early on to print prayer books or primers; 12-point pica, perhaps deriving from the Latin for ecclesiastical directory; and then up into the larger 28- (double English), 36- (double great primer), 48- (4-line pica) and even 60- (5-line pica) point types.

These punches have endured migrations. After Baskerville's death in 1775, his wife Sarah sold them to the French playwright Beaumarchais – the author of *Le Barbier de Séville* and *Le Mariage de Figaro* – for £3,700 (something like £325,000 today). Beaumarchais used them to print a celebrated 168-volume edition of Voltaire. The punches then moved around France, like a dusty, sunburnt hero in a picaresque novel. For many years they seem to have disappeared entirely. They passed to the Didot family of printers, punch-cutters and publishers, and then to the type foundry Deberny et Peignot, and then, in 1953, and to considerable fanfare – with ambassadors and vice chancellors shaking hands over drinks – director Charles Peignot donated them back to Cambridge University, where Baskerville had served a productive but financially unhappy spell (he used the term 'shackles') as University Printer, 1758–66. Admiring Peignot's Channel-crossing generosity, we can pass over the fact that some of the punches, and all of the matrices, appear to be missing.

These are the punches that once rested in Baskerville's hands, and which were the source of the letters which printed the books that went forth, as the historian Thomas Macaulay wrote, 'to astonish all the librarians of Europe'. The punches don't quite let us travel back to 1750, but they have journeyed forward across centuries to meet us today, and that journey through time seems to register in their cool and reassuring heaviness.

We can sketch the significance of Baskerville in clear terms. He came to printing late, publishing his first book aged around fifty, after an inventive but also meandering career – 'trained to no occupation', wrote his contemporary the Birmingham historian William Hutton, but a 'son of genius'. Baskerville worked first as a writing master, teaching handwriting, and then as one of the earliest experts in japanning in the Midlands – japanning being the lacquering or varnishing of metal goods and furniture to produce hard black or tortoiseshell surfaces for decoration, in imitation of the kinds of objects imported by the English East India Company that fascinated eighteenth-century consumers. 'Wherever he found merit he caressed it' (Hutton again), and Baskerville took this experience with letters and decorative metalwork and turned it in the direction of printing. These earlier printing-adjacent skills played out in the books he made.

Baskerville achieved an all-round bibliographical excellence. His black ink shone like no other because he mixed in the soot from the solderers' and glass-pinchers' lamps; it also dried quickly, enabling the reverse side of the sheet to be printed swiftly. His paper had a flat, shiny glaze due to 'hot pressing', a technique Baskerville guarded with secrecy, enjoying the mystery, but which probably developed directly from his japanning work. He improved the mechanics of the press itself. And central to his achievement was his typographical design – the shape of the letters which Baskerville conceived and cast, and the creation of a clean, spacious aesthetic that still shapes book production today.

His printed corpus of books was a classical, deeply canonical, and as Baskerville would have seen it, indispensable body of works – Virgil, Horace, Juvenal, Lucretius, Terence, Ariosto, the

Bible, the Book of Common Prayer, Sternhold and Hopkins's Book of Psalms – enriched with seventeenth- and eighteenth-century authors including Joseph Addison, William Congreve, Robert Dodsley, and Anthony Ashley-Cooper, 3rd Earl of Shaftesbury.

These were the volumes sent out into the world to convey Baskerville's design, and they were met with international acclaim. Benjamin Franklin (1706–90), the other great printer-autodidact of the eighteenth century who we'll meet in the next chapter, visited Baskerville in 1760 from Pennsylvania, bought his books fresh from the press, along with some of his japanned goods, and wrote letters enquiring about the particular qualities of his paper and his printing methods. Voltaire (1694–1778) corresponded and permitted Baskerville to set specimen pages of his writing in 1771. The French typographer Pierre-Simon Fournier (1712–1768) thought Baskerville's italic 'the best found in any type-foundry in Europe', and celebrated his letter forms in his *Manuel typographique* (1766). And when a youthful Giambattista Bodoni (1740–1813) left Rome in 1768, in the early stages of an influential career which saw him develop an unadorned, 'modern' typography, it was Baskerville's printing that pulled him towards England.

'Whatever passed through his fingers,' wrote William Hutton, 'bore the lively marks of John Baskerville.' Baskerville's first book was arguably his greatest. It took him three years to print: he was fifty-one when it appeared at a price of one guinea for a stack of unbound sheets. (We're still in an era when readers often bought sheets, and then took them to their own favoured binder to stitch and bind into a book.) This edition of the poetry of the Roman poet Virgil marked out Baskerville's terrain: a canonical learned Latin text, a thick quarto of almost 450 pages, printed in 18-point (or great primer), the letters recently cast to Baskerville's

Baskerville's Publii Virgilii Maronis Bucolica,
Georgica, et Æneis *(1757).*

specifications, and the whole designed and manufactured to produce an almost miraculous sense of calm.

There is on each page a balance and simplicity that creates a sense of space to breathe. No ornaments. No illustrations. This is in part about the placement of type in space – the French *mise-en-page* means 'putting-on-the-page' – but it is also the product of a 'kiss impression': a clean printing achieved by Baskerville's pressman Richard Martin applying the minimal pressure from the type. That delicate kiss is also the product of certain adjustments Baskerville introduced to the wooden press. He made the 'platen' or plate (which presses the paper against the type) and the 'stone' or bed (on which the locked-up type sits) out of 2-centimetre thick machined brass, and he used a 'tympan' (the frame on which the sheet of paper to be printed is placed, and which receives the pressure of the platen) of smooth vellum packed with fine cloth rather than soft packing to avoid creating too deep an impression.

Printed letters became cleaner, more consistent, and clearer: 'engaging, finished and equal to the occasion', in the words of the best writer on type, Beatrice Warde (1900–69). Perhaps the most famous definition of typography comes from Stanley Morison (1889–1967), who wrote in 1930 that it was: 'the craft of rightly disposing printing material in accordance with specific purpose; of so arranging the letters, distributing the space and controlling the type as to aid to the maximum the reader's comprehension of the text'. This seems a perfect description of Baskerville's work two centuries earlier. Just before his edition of Virgil appeared, Baskerville wrote to an unnamed friend, describing the labour and discipline behind this elegant book: 'I have pursued the Scheme of printing and Letter founding for Seven Years, with the most intense Application, to the great prejudice of My Eyes, by the daily use off Microscopes.'

I've seen many copies of Baskerville's books in many libraries, but I've seen none with sustained handwritten annotations by readers – the kinds of pointing hands or manicules, doodles, underlinings, strike-throughs or spiky one-word commentaries ('No!') added by readers to the books printed by, say, Wynkyn de Worde. Baskerville's books expect a different, more reverential form of reading. These books glide through the centuries rather as Baskerville himself moved through space, with his head held high. 'Although constructed with the light timbers of a frigate,' wrote Hutton of Baskerville's deportment, 'his movement was solemn as a ship of the line.'

The pages of copies of Baskerville's Virgil have gold fore-edges. The paper has a smoothness and a gloss like satin. The smoothness meant less force was required when printing to create an even impression, and less force produced a cleaner, sharper series of letters. The gloss was the consequence of each sheet being taken fast off the press – the ink still wet – and placed between hot copper plates, which meant the paper didn't absorb and dull the ink. The first half of the book is printed on smooth wove paper, with no watermark, manufactured from a mould covered with a fabric of very fine brass wires, rather than the parallel wires of 'laid' paper, producing an extremely smooth, 'woven' surface that was augmented by Baskerville's pressing technique. Baskerville didn't invent wove paper – that honour, at least in terms of Western book-making, should probably go to paper-maker James Whatman (1702–59) of Kent – but this 1757 Virgil is the earliest known use of it. A subscribers' list runs to eight pages and more than five hundred names, a roll call of the famous and the now unknown who responded to Baskerville's 1754 specimen sheet, from the Earl of Chesterfield to 'P. Crump Esq. of Newnham, Gloucestershire'. Benjamin Franklin, always nosing around for bibliographical excellence, bought six copies. The London publisher and bookseller Robert Dodsley bought twenty. Baskerville sent a copy to Voltaire.

This sense of radical clarity is sustained in Baskerville's edition of *Paradise Lost* and *Paradise Regained*, printed in 1758 in octavo (1,500 copies) and 1759 in quarto (700 copies). This is Baskerville's most successful book in terms of sales and reprints: the subscribers' list is sweepingly long ('His Gr. the Duke of Argyle'; 'Rev. Mr. Tho. Adderley, Schoolmaster, Nantwich'; 'Erasmus Darwin, M.D. Lichfield'; 'Miss Hubert, Woolston'). The book contains the only preface Baskerville wrote, a kind of autobiography through type, an entwining of life and letter-making that recounts the development of a passion for '*Paper, Letter, Ink*, and *Workmanship*'. 'Having been an early admirer of the beauty of Letters,' Baskerville writes, 'I became insensibly desirous of contributing to the perfection of them.' Baskerville's life is described as the pursuit of 'a *Sett* of *Types* according to what I conceived to be their true proportion'. As with his debut Virgil, Baskerville's ambition is to print important books that have already obtained canonicity:

> It is not my desire to print many books; but such only as are *books of Consequence*, of *intrinsic merit*, or *established Reputation*, and which the public may be pleased to see in an elegant dress, and to purchase at such a price as will repay the extraordinary care and expence that must necessarily be bestowed upon them.

Baskerville's books were not sent out to democratise print, as were, for instance, many of Wynkyn de Worde's. His books were costly items, slowly produced, and striving for physical excellence. The development of the skills to produce these books took time, and Baskerville describes a gradual process of technical refinement. Indeed in many ways, his career is a study in slowness, of patient accumulation: 'creeping slowly towards Perfection', he wrote of his press in 1752. His autobiographical vignette in *Paradise Lost* continues:

> After having spent many years, and not a little of my fortune, in my endeavours to advance this art; I must own it gives me great satisfaction to find that my edition of *Virgil* has been so favorably received. The improvement in the Manufacture of the *Paper*, the *Colour*, and *Firmness* of the *Ink* were not overlooked; nor did the accuracy of the workmanship in general, pass unregarded.

This struggle towards better and better books is Baskerville's personal project ('I formed to myself ideas of greater accuracy than had yet appeared'), but it is also conceived in terms of national pride, and a sense of an emerging English tradition of letter-cutting. Baskerville notes the contribution of the Caslon type foundry, established in London around 1720 by the gun-engraver William Caslon (1692–1766). For Baskerville, Caslon is an important but also flawed origin point for English letters ('he has left room for improvement'), and he signs off his preface with the hope to produce a folio Bible of 'the greatest Elegance and Correctness; a work which I hope might do some honor to the English Press'.

Baskerville did indeed produce a Bible in 1763 while working with considerable discontent as University Printer in Cambridge – overstretched, and under-rewarded. Baskerville's Bible was a huge, two-volumed folio, a grand, calm slab of printing that exhibited his by now recognisable style: the smooth paper, the lustrous black ink, the sense of space afforded to canonicity. The book cost subscribers 4 guineas (£4.20, or today about £400), with half paid upfront and half on delivery. A total of 1,250 were printed. One of these now sits in the Cadbury Research Centre at Birmingham University. Before finding this home, the book belonged to Dr. B. T. Davies of Birmingham University; before Davies, to the Ryland family (the bookplate of Samuel Ryland (1764–1843) is pasted on the marbled inside cover, with his motto, 'Not the last'); and before the Ryland family, in the later eighteenth century, the Bible belonged to Sarah Baskerville, John's wife. Her bookplate is glued in opposite the title page.

What was the style that Baskerville's letters possessed? To understand his letters we need to place them in contrast with what went before. Baskerville was a pragmatist who worked incrementally – refining and refining – rather than a revolutionary who started anew. Baskerville used as models for his type the letters of William Caslon and his brother Samuel, founts which were themselves based on the Dutch letter forms that had dominated English printing.

On the following page are some of Baskerville's letters from a specimen sheet from 1757: four sizes of roman types and two of italic. And on the subsequent page are some printed letters from Venice in 1476, made by the French engraver, printer, and type designer Nicolas Jenson (1420–80), often credited with producing the first roman type form. The text is a near miraculous hand-coloured printing of Pliny the Elder's *Natural History* from the first century.

Baskerville heightened the contrast between the thin and thick strokes of the letter – the thin strokes became narrower – and the centre or axis of his rounded letters was adjusted to a more vertical position. His letters grew slender and upright. Curved strokes became smoother and more circular, and so he opened

A

SPECIMEN

By *JOHN BASKERVILLE of Birmingham.*

I Am indebted to you for two Letters dated from Corcyra. You congratulate me in one of them on the Account you have Received, that I ſtill preſerve my former Authority in the Commonwealth: and wiſh me Joy in the other of my late Marriage. With reſpect to the Firſt, *if to mean well to the Intereſt of my Country and to approve that meaning to every Friend of its Liberties, may be conſider'd as maintaining my Authority; the Account you have heard is certainly true. But if it conſiſts in rendering thoſe Sentiments effectual to the Public Welfare or at leaſt in daring freely to Support and inforce them;*

I Am indebted to you for two Letters dated from Corcyra. You congratulate me in one of them on the Account you have Received, that I ſtill preſerve my former Authority in the Commonwealth: and wiſh me Joy in the other of my late Marriage. With reſpect to the firſt, if to mean well to the Intereſt of my Country and to approve that meaning to every Friend of its Liberties, may be conſider'd as maintaining my Authority; the Account you have heard is certainly true. But if it conſiſts in rendering thoſe Sentiments effectual to the Public Welfare or at leaſt in daring freely to Support and inforce them; my Friend I have not the leaſt ſha-

I Am indebted to you for two Letters dated from Corcyra. You congratulate me in one of the Account you have received, that I ſtill preſerve my former Authority in the Commonwealth: and wiſh me joy in the other of my late Marriage. With reſpect to the Firſt, if to mean well to the Intereſt of my Country and to approve that meaning to every Friend of its Liberties, may be conſider'd as maintaining *my Authority; the Account you have heard is certainly true. But if it conſiſts in rendering thoſe Sentiments effectual to the Public Welfare or at leaſt in daring freely to Support and inforce them; alas! my Friend I have not the leaſt ſhadow of Authority remaining. The Truth of it is, it will be ſufficient Honor if I can have ſo much Authority over myſelf as to bear with patience our preſent and impending Calamities; a frame of Mind not to be acquired without difficulty,*

Q. HORATII FLACCI   *EPISTOLARUM LIBER I.*

Specimens of Baskerville's type – four sizes of roman types, and two of italic.

up the eye of his 'e' in contrast to the narrower 's'. His letters became more regular. His serifs – the little projections that complete the stroke of a letter – grew more horizontal, sharper and tapered. His upper-case Q – a letter that became his typographical signature – has a tail that reaches out extravagantly beyond

Nicolas Jenson's printing of Historia naturale di Caio
Plinio Secondo *(Venice, 1476).*

the body of the letter, its thickness widening and narrowing as it
proceeds like an unfurling ribbon.

The lower-case 'g' is also remarkable, with its ear hanging to
the right, and its open lower bowl recalling the quick loop of a
pen in elegant hands.

Q. HORATII

The extravagant italic 'Q', from Baskerville's specimen sheet.

The Parisian type designer Pierre-Simon Fournier said Baskerville's letters were 'real masterpieces of sharpness', and we might want to draw a connection between his clear lettering and late-eighteenth-century Enlightenment cultures of rationalism and neo-classicism. Baskerville's letters produced clarity not obfuscation, and steadily conveyed important literary works out into posterity. We might also want to notice a paradox of type: at once beautiful, or admirable, or technically remarkable, printed letters also strive for a kind of invisibility as they articulate, and seek not to distract from, the meaning of the text. According to Beatrice Warde, writing in 1932, typography succeeds when we stop noticing it. Only 'ugly typography never effaces itself'. By these criteria, Baskerville's printed letters flicker between visibility and invisibility – they generate a sense of the artistry of their letter shapes, but they strive also for transparency in transmitting meaning, like (in Warde's famous analogy) a crystal-clear glass holding wine. Historians of typography often label Baskerville's letters 'Transitional' in the sense that they constitute a movement away from Caslon's heavier letters, and the earlier 'old-style', fifteenth- and sixteenth-century designs named after the poet (Pietro) Bembo and the French type designer (Claude) Garamond, towards the 'Modern' fineness associated with Giambattista Bodoni (1740–1813) and the letters cut in France by Firmin Didot (1764–1836). This may all seem rather a lot of pressure to place on a little letter, but even looking at the samples above, we probably sense immediately with Baskerville a sense of space, regularity, and confident calm.

A lower-case 'g' from Baskerville's specimen sheet.

These letter forms emerged from Baskerville's years working as a writing master, training young men, women, and children to write by hand. 'Once you have formed letters carefully with a pen,' wrote Warde, '– if you are sufficiently interested to ask why one thing looks right and another wrong – the shape of types will always be real and alive to you.' At twenty, Baskerville seems to have taught writing and bookkeeping at the Grammar School in Birmingham, and by 1737, according to Hutton, he had set up his own school in the Bull-ring. We have an early example of Baskerville's writing skills in the form of several scripts cut into a stone, 22 by 27 centimetres, like a more permanent version of an advertising hoarding, or a giant business card. The stone survives today in the Library of Birmingham.

From the top of this stone, Baskerville is showing us his letter forms in Fraktur (a variety of blackletter); then, in the second line, a lower-case roman with two upper-case initials; a 'By' in a flourished roundhand; his name in an Old English gothic; and the title *Writing Master* in a sloped italic capital. Choose carefully: some of these might spell out your name on a tomb for centuries to come. The stone resembles the pages of the printed copybooks Baskerville must have studied – guides which disseminated in print elegant handwritten letters to serve as models. As Ewan Clayton has recently demonstrated, Baskerville's carved letters, like the wonderfully flourished 'S' of his 'Stones', show a particular relationship with certain forms displayed in George Shelley's *The second part of Natural Writing . . . Several Delightful Fancies & Designs . . . Making a Complete Body of Penmanship* (1714).

Reproduction of Baskerville's slate made by the Library of Birmingham.

For all his international fame, Baskerville's printing success was the product of his local world. He was born into an eighteenth-century Birmingham that was experiencing a surge of entrepreneurial energy. This Midlands Enlightenment was driven by a group of extraordinarily talented men who, in the words of Birmingham's most recent historian, 'epitomized the atmosphere of optimism, uninhibited enquiry and material prosperity'. The ambitious industrialist Matthew Boulton (1728–1809) built mills, workshops, and accommodation for his hundreds of workers across the 13 acres of Soho on Handsworth Heath, and he did so with such Palladian élan that visitors thought the site resembled an aristocrat's country house, with landscaped gardens, an aviary, a menagerie, and tea rooms. It was at Boulton's Soho house that the

Lunar Society – named because the group met when the moon was full and so would light the night walk home – gathered for dinner and ranging discussion: a mix of rational philosophy and business networking, with lots of fortified wine, and a crucial catalyst for Birmingham's transition from provincial town to international powerhouse. The roll call of 'lunaticks' included scientists, industrialists, and intellectuals with names that still ring familiar today: physician, poet, and atheist Erasmus Darwin (1731–1802); chemist and theologian Joseph Priestly (1733–1804); inventor James Watt (1736–1819); potter and industrialist Josiah Wedgwood (1730–1795); and Samuel Galton Jr. (1753–1832), who combined with no sense of dissonance the vocations of Quakerism and gun-making. The society was in its origins an expression of friendship and a means for strengthening business connections, but it came soon to be seen as representing a particular culture: dissenting, urban, freethinking, scientific, profit-seeking, politically progressive, Francophile and sympathetic to aspects of the French Revolution (but not to the Terror), and committed to a rationalism which had the potential to slice through accepted beliefs and practices with a confidence that could be contemptuous. Baskerville's disdain for the irrational in all its forms – from received church ceremony, to a poorly managed business deal – made him a natural ally, and although he was not a central member, he circulated in this environment.

Within this broad spirit of entrepreneurial expansion, Birmingham had particularly skilled workers in metal, and saw a surge in the production of light metal goods. Writing in 1772, Matthew Boulton put down on paper an atmosphere of teeming productivity:

> Snuff Boxes, Instrument Cases, toothpick Cases – gilt, glass and steel Trinkets, Silver filigree Boxes, Needle Books etc etc – all manner of plated Goods, as Tea Kitchins, Tankards, Cups, Coffee potts, Cream Juggs, Candlesticks – sauce boats, Terrines etc etc – Bronz'd Tea Kitchins and Tea Kettles as well plated as Tin'd inside, Saucepans, Cheese Toasters etc etc etc.

Amid this buzz of 'etc etc etc.', printing and book production had recently emerged as one aspect of Birmingham's growth. The Licensing Act of 1662 had attempted to reinforce the Crown's authority after the trauma of the Civil War by limiting the number and location of printers. The Act stipulated that printing could only take place in London, by a fixed number of recognised presses; in Oxford and Cambridge, under the authority of the universities; and in York, under the control of the city's Archbishop. This was an attempt by the Crown to stifle and direct the energy of print. But the Act lapsed in 1695, and by about 1750, most provincial towns in the nation had their own printer. Birmingham's history of print seems to have begun in 1712 in the person of the city's first printer, Matthew Unwin.

Baskerville's pivot to printing occurred around 1750, just as it was establishing itself as a properly national trade. Baskerville's desire to print was shaped by his previous work as a writing master and his japanning business, and also the wider entrepreneurial culture of Birmingham; but his late blooming was also probably catalysed by more specific events.

The first was the appearance in the July 1750 issue of the *Universal Magazine* of an article on 'The Art of Cutting, Casting, and Preparing of Letter for Printing, with a neat Representation of a Letter-founder's Work-house'. The *Universal Magazine* was designed, its cover page declared, to be 'Instructive and Entertaining' for 'Gentry, Merchants, Farmers, and Tradesmen'. Much of what the article printed was a condensed version of what Joseph Moxon had written in his *Mechanick Exercises* (1677–83), but the *Universal Magazine* conveyed to a wide audience a how-to guide to the fundamentals of making type: drawing letters, cutting punches, striking and justifying matrices, making type metal, and casting type. Like many aspects of book production, the methods for manufacturing type did not change hugely between the mid-fifteenth and the mid-nineteenth centuries. Baskerville, reading fast and taking it all in with the hunger of the autodidact, would have learnt that the letter-cutter should use 'hammers and files of all sorts' of the kind 'watchmakers use'. He would have learnt the mastery of angles required for the design of letters; that the molten metal, poured into the mould, is lead hardened with iron stub nails, mixed with antimony, and the whole beaten and melted in an iron mortar in a furnace, and then ladled into an iron pot; that 'a workman will ordinarily cast about three thousand of these letters in a day'. He would have grown used to the bodily language of type: the 'face' of the letter which fronts the 'head' with a 'beard' or 'neck', and, beneath this, a 'back' and 'belly' and 'body'.

Baskerville would have studied the image of the interior of William Caslon's foundry (see plate section): the four type-casters standing on the left; the boys in the middle breaking off the 'jets' or 'breaks' of metal attached to letters as they came from the mould, and rubbing the letters smooth. Baskerville would have gazed upon the large devices to the left and right of the table: moulds, but enlarged by a factor of ten to proudly display their intricacies, and to hover like allegories of technical advancement.

About the time Baskerville was likely to have been reading this article, a second crucial event took place in the form of the arrival in his life of Sarah Eaves. Sarah was a vital catalyst in Baskerville's printing career: his book-making would not have flourished as it did without her. For a long time she looked an unlikely wife and business partner. Born Sarah Ruston, in Aston, near Birmingham, Sarah, aged just sixteen, married Richard Eaves of Yardley in 1724, and had three boys and two girls: Robert, John, Richard, Sarah, and Mary. The marriage soon began to crack, due largely to her husband's plotting and lies: Sarah had married a criminal. Richard Eaves forged his brother's will, falsely writing that Robert Eaves bequeathed all his estate to his 'loving brother'. Fearing the consequences of the discovery of this forgery, which could have resulted in his hanging, Richard abandoned Sarah in 1743 and fled to America, leaving her to grieve alone for their son Robert who had just died. Richard then falls out of the historical record for nineteen years – his presumably criminal activities in America unknown – until he reappears back in Birmingham in 1762, trying and failing to take control of family lands.

Between 1750 and 1764, Sarah and her four surviving children lived with Baskerville in his grand house and gardens named Easy Hill. Sarah was described as his 'housekeeper', but everyone seems to have understood her to be his wife in all but legal detail – they couldn't marry with her husband still alive somewhere in America. Sometimes the comments were nasty. William Shenstone circulated gossipy little verses at Baskerville's expense, but Sarah had been through enough not to be buffeted by a poet with a curling lip. Sarah was spoken of as Mrs Baskerville for several years before the two officially married in June 1764, aged fifty-six and fifty-seven, released by Richard's death the month before. John treated Sarah's children as his own; he called John 'his eldest son' and his 'intended successor', and John's death in 1763 was a bitter blow.

It was around 1750, when Sarah and her children moved in with Baskerville, that his experiments in printing began. Her presence, ambiguous or discordant to a judging outside world but clear and right to Sarah and John, enabled Baskerville to work with new enthusiasm. Sarah released his imagination: he always could speak his mind, but with her around, he could speak the thoughts behind his thoughts. In his preface to *Paradise Lost*, Baskerville wrote that 'amongst the several mechanic Arts that have engaged my attention, there is no one which I have pursued with so much steadiness and pleasure as that of *Letter Founding*'. Steadiness and pleasure can only take place within an environment that affords the same.

But Sarah did more than bring emotional stability. She also had a level of expertise in printing, cultivated during her years with Baskerville. After he died in 1775, Sarah published two new editions of works previously printed by her husband, partly in a spirit of homage, but also an expression of her own book-making agency: *An Introduction to the Knowledge of Medals* (1775) by David Jennings, an octavo finished with marbled fore-edges and sold by the famous radical London bookseller Joseph Johnson in St Paul's Churchyard, London; and a duodecimo in Latin of Horace's *Works* (1777). Both books display a level of printerly confidence and skill that mean Sarah must have spent a large amount of time working at the press with her husband while he was alive. Historians have often suggested widows might take over a husband's print shop on his death, obtaining a kind of belated agency, but clearly Sarah was actively involved in the book-making during her husband's lifetime. The unfortunate recent claim by an emiment design historian that 'Sarah Eaves's only claim to fame seems to be her role in Baskerville's scandalous domestic situation' is itself scandalously wide of the mark.

We can see Sarah's hands-on involvement even more directly in Baskerville's japanning success. We don't know how exactly Baskerville acquired his skills, but he was an early champion of an industry that became a crucial trade for Birmingham and Wolverhampton for about 200 years. In 1742, Baskerville applied for a patent to manufacture 'exactly true and level' metal goods, like tea trays and other household goods

> which I propose to Japan or Varnish . . . [to] produce a fine glowing Mahogany Colour, a Black no way inferior to that of the most perfect India Goods, or an Imitation of Tortoiseshell which greatly excels Nature itself both in Colour and Hardness, and each Colour admitting of the most perfect Polish, whose Beauty, without violence, will not be impaired in several Ages.

Baskerville's success was profitable enough to enable him to acquire Easy Hill, 8 acres of land to the north-east of Birmingham. He built a house with an elegant mahogany staircase leading to a gallery, from the windows of which visitors could gaze on the gardens and, glimpsed through trees, the workshops and warehouses. Easy Hill became Baskerville's home until his death. He bought a coach with japanned side panels (the 'pattern-card of Baskerville's trade', according to William Hutton), which was pulled around Birmingham by four cream-coloured horses. Baskerville, who even 'in the decline of life . . . retained the singular traces of a handsome man', sat in the back, and 'delighted to adorn [himself] with gold lace'. Part Wynkyn de Worde, part Liberace.

Visitors noted Sarah's centrality to the running of both the japanning and printing sides of Baskerville's business. When Lady Shelburne visited Easy Hill in 1766, while her husband Lord Shelburne and Baskerville chatted about books, Sarah gave her a tour of the japan workshops, 'which business', Lady Shelburne recorded in her diary, 'she has chiefly the management of'. The business expanded under Sarah's watch between 1754 and 1767, with the arrival of nine apprentices, more than any rival employed. The japanning was crucial because the profits funded Baskerville's enthusiastic but developmental early years in print in the 1750s, and also because the years spent perfecting the manipulation of metal and the mixing of lacquer informed Baskerville's work in type-casting and ink-making. As Yvonne Jones has recently noted, Baskerville's ingredients for japan varnish included lamp black, linseed oil and amber rosin—the same components which the printer T. C. Hansard claimed in 1825 to have identified as Baskerville's secret recipe for his ink.

In the early twentieth century, Baskerville's eighteenth-century type was brought back from relative obscurity into surging popularity by the Lanston Monotype Corporation of London. The Monotype Corporation was built around the Monotype machine, patented in 1885, which offered a new, machine-based way of casting type. It had a touch of the Heath Robinson about it. Via the use of a rather daunting typewriter-style keyboard, powered by compressed air, users could type out characters which produced a series of perforations on a spool of paper, and this spool of paper was in turn fed into and read by a casting machine, rather like a pianola roll, which caused individual hot metal pieces of type to be cast.

The related rival Linotype machine produced whole lines or slugs, but the single letters of Monotype meant errors could be more easily corrected. These machines strove for 'non-distribution': after traditional letterpress printing, individual letters must be laboriously placed back ('distributed', or 'dissed') in their original compartments, ready for reuse, but Monotype meant the letters could be simply dumped and re-melted before another round.

In order to promote this technology, Monotype's typographical advisor, Stanley Morison, produced a series of revived historical types, including Garamond, Bembo, Poliphilus, Bell, and Fournier. Baskerville was foremost amongst these. While Baskerville's punch-cutters cut his seventeen sizes of type with some degree of variation in the proportions, the Monotype re-cutting in 1923 was based on the 18-point great primer design used by Baskerville in his edition of Terence's *Comoediae* (1772), and also in his Bible. ('Calculated for people who begin to want Spectacles,' Baskerville wrote of his great primer, 'but are ashamed to use them at Church.') The result of the revised reissue – the new letters a little cleaner and finer and more modern than the originals – was that Baskerville quickly became widely used and once again influential: as Beatrice Warde wrote in 1927, Baskerville 'attains permanency only by being re-discovered'. The Monotype series was acquired by Cambridge University Press in 1924; one of the earliest books to use the Monotype Baskerville was the *Journals of T. J. Cobden-Sanderson* (1926) – of which, much more in chapter 9. In the words of Morison himself, 'the prophecy may be confidently made . . . that his [Baskerville's] design will retain its already established position as one of the half-dozen standard book and jobbing founts of the world'. Select 'Baskerville' next time you write a Word document – or look closely at the font you are reading now – and imagine a smile flickering across the spectral faces of John and Sarah.

Baskerville lives on, with a modern spin. And so too does Sarah. In 1996, Slovak-born American type designer Zuzana Licko (b.1961) created a font, digitally and not in metal, which she named 'Mrs Eaves' (Licko removed the full stop after 'Mrs' to enable her to claim copyright over the title). It was released by the type foundry Emigre, run by Licko (who doesn't ride a coach with japanned side panels) and her husband. Compared to Baskerville, Mrs Eaves is smaller, and heavier, with wider characters and thicker serifs, and the contrast in thick/thinness between the letter stems and hairlines (something Baskerville had been criticised for) has been reduced; but Mrs Eaves clearly recalls Baskerville, particularly in the lower-case 'g' and the famous capital 'Q'. 'Just enough tradition with an updated twist,' said Licko in an interview in 2002. 'Familiar enough to be friendly, yet different enough to be interesting.' In the words of the design historian Paul Shaw, Mrs Eaves 'has a quiet strength. It is very readable . . . and avoids fussiness.' The font's relatively wide proportions mean it is popular for displaying text in headings or blurbs on books: Mrs Eaves gives presence to text – a presence which has the effect of slowing down reading. It is currently used for WordPress, and for the titles of Penguin Classics books, along with a host of other products including Radiohead and Coldplay album covers and bottles of pinot noir.

Let's end this chapter by imagining a scene. It is 1821. George IV has just been crowned King. The first ever edition of the *Manchester Guardian* newspaper has just been published. We are in an ironmonger's on Cambridge Street, Birmingham. The sign above the door reads 'Messrs Gibson & Sons'. Mr Gibson himself – tall, stooping, courteous but clearly wily – ushers us through the main shop into a back room. The light is low. Candles flicker. Standing on a table in the centre of the room is a lead coffin. Gibson takes 6d from each of us, puts the coins in his coat pocket, and opens the lid. The swiftness of his movements suggests he has done this many times before. He whispers, 'Closer, closer.' We peer over, nervous at first, but soon with more confidence. Inside is a corpse, wrapped in a white linen shroud. Across the corpse's breast is a branch of laurel, well enough preserved that it looks as though it was placed there last week, although the body has been dead for forty-six years. The eyes are missing, but the skin, eyebrows, and teeth still bear some relation to a man's face. The smell is terrible: a sharp, putrefied stink. Gibson closes the coffin lid after fifteen seconds. 'Europe's greatest printer,' he says. 'Come back next week for another look.'

Baskerville's corpse, like his type, endured a posthumous life not of dignified stasis but of a kind of shunting travel: a series of lurches. In his 1773 will, Baskerville prescribed that his wife ensure his 'body should be buried in a conical building in my own premises, heretofore used as a mill', a demand that expressed what Baskerville described as his 'hearty contempt of all superstition', particularly 'the farce of consecrated ground'.

Baskerville believed it was rational morality that determined a good and godly life, and not 'certain absurd doctrines & mysteries about which . . . the ignorant & bigoted . . . have no more conception than a horse'. We see this in Baskerville's epitaph, which he, like Benjamin Franklin – coming up soon in the next chapter – wrote himself, and ordered to be inscribed on his conical tomb:

Stranger –
Beneath this Cone in Unconsecrated Ground
A Friend to the Liberties of mankind Directed his Body to be Inhum'd
May the Example Contribute to Emancipate thy Mind

From the Idle Fears of Superstition
And the Wicked arts of Priesthood.

At some point in the years following Baskerville's burial, after the estate was bought by John Ryland (1726–1814), the conical building seems to have been destroyed: perhaps during riots of 1791, when crowds targeting religious fanatics attacked and burnt what had been Baskerville's estate, and other properties associated with Francophile dissenters; perhaps in the subsequent construction of canals across the land. In 1820, workmen digging for gravel struck lead and discovered a coffin which was moved to Messrs Gibson & Sons ironmongery in 1821. But this wasn't Baskerville's final resting place. In 1829, the coffin was moved to a plumbing and glazing shop in Monmouth Street, where a nineteen-year-old Thomas Underwood visited and sketched a ghoulish visage. After this, the whereabouts of the corpse was unknown, until in 1893 churchwardens at Christ Church, noting an unmarked vault, removed a coffin and opened it up before a crowd of gathered dignitaries. The name 'Baskerville' was spelt out in metal printer's letters on the side. Four years later, in 1897, Christ Church was facing demolition, and Baskerville's corpse was moved again to a vault under the Church of England cemetery at Warstone Lane.

Baskerville, who had railed against ceremonial Church orthodoxies, had ended up in precisely the wrong place – although one suspects, knowing Baskerville's restlessness in life and in death, that this is not the end of the printer's migrations.

5. NON-BOOKS
Benjamin Franklin (1706–90)

Benjamin Franklin may be the paradigmatic example of a life full to bursting. We've just met him, in passing, as a visitor to and admirer of Birmingham's John Baskerville, but let's put a few, but not all, of his achievements in a single sentence. Franklin was, in his own words, 'the youngest Son of the youngest Son for 5 Generations back'; born to a Boston candlemaker who had emigrated from Ecton, Northamptonshire, Franklin became an American printer of national significance; the editor and publisher, at twenty-three, of what became his nation's most important newspaper, the *Pennsylvania Gazette*; an internationally lauded scientist of electricity who broke through the frosty anteroom of London's Royal Society – *a colonial autodidact!* – to become a celebrated Fellow; a prolific humourist who invented a tradition of wry, plain-speaking wit (among his pseudonyms: Silence Dogood, Margaret Aftercast, Ephraim Censorious) later sustained by Mark Twain, Will Rogers, Garrison Keillor, and others; the author of the only pre-nineteenth-century American bestseller still read today (his *Autobiography*); a Pennsylvanian politician and civic reformer of tireless energy (founder of the Junto, a self-improvement society; of the Library Company of Philadelphia, the first subscription library in North America; of the American Philosophical Society; of the Union Fire Company; of the University of Pennsylvania); the author of essays on phonetic alphabets, demography, paper currency; a leader of resistance to the Stamp Act (1765) which imposed taxes on colonial legal documents and printed materials and, ultimately, to British colonial rule of America; Grand Master of the Masons, Pennsylvania; the Deputy Postmaster General of North America; the Ambassador to France; a famous Londoner; a famous Parisian; a famous Pennsylvanian; a celebrity in a time when that concept was only emerging (guests at his 4th July celebration in Paris, 1778, stole cutlery as souvenirs); one of the five Founding Fathers who drafted and signed the Declaration of Independence (1776); and the inventor of the Franklin wood-burning stove, the lightning rod, bifocal glasses, a chair that converted into a stepladder, the glass armonica, a new kind of street lamp (a funnel dispersing the smoke), a rocking-chair-with-fan, a laundry mangle, swimming fins, a flexible urinary catheter, and a 'long arm' for removing objects from high shelves.

Do you feel small? Don't feel small. Franklin knew his faults as much as he cherished his fame: the absent husband away for his wife's death; the man prone to jettisoning friends who ceased to be useful (former friend John Collins, too often drunk, whisked off to Barbados to work as a tutor: 'I never heard of him after'); the public moraliser who refused to name the mother of his illegitimate son; the life punctuated by furious arguments and – in tense and no more admirable counter-balance – the obsession with public credit and reputation. And – in ways that are becoming increasingly apparent at the time of writing – an active complicity with the slave trade. President John Adams (1735–1826) hailed Franklin's benefaction 'to his country and mankind', but described also his personal hypocrisy and vanity: 'He has a Passion for Reputation and Fame, as strong as you can imagine, and his Time and Thoughts are chiefly employed to obtain it.' Immanuel Kant (1724–1804) called Franklin 'a Prometheus of the modern age'. In Greek myth, Prometheus stole fire from the gods and gave it to humankind in the form of civilisation. But he was also punished by Zeus: tied to a rock, Prometheus endured an eagle eating his liver and, when his liver grew back overnight, the punishment resumed. Prometheus is a figure of cunning, benefaction, significance, transgression, fame.

The medium Franklin moved in was ink: he waded in it, up to his neck. The printing trade was his start, the profession that made him. While Franklin grew up at a time when printing in colonial America was not yet established, the trade was coiled like a spring, and his timing was right; to a considerable extent, Franklin released it. The first printing press was not established until 1638, when locksmith Stephen Day sailed from Cambridge, England, to Massachusetts, carrying a press in pieces. In 1722, when Franklin was sixteen, serving as an apprentice with his printer brother, James, there were just four cities in North America with presses, and only eight printing shops in all: five in Boston, and one each in Philadelphia, New York, and New London. The first successful American newspaper, the *Boston News-Letter*, appeared in 1704; until 1719, it was the only one in the colonies. (By the time of the American Revolution in 1775, there were thirty-seven.) And while a paper mill had been set up in Germantown, Pennsylvania, as early as 1690, materials for printing, including lead type, were generally imported from England well into the eighteenth century.

But the 1720s and 1730s, when Franklin established himself as a printer, were also the decades when printing as a trade spread rapidly across the Colonies; newspapers were formed and grew influential; the economic and cultural status of the printer-publisher rose steadily, from menial worker to, in the figure of Franklin, something like a literary-intellectual entrepreneur who might shape the public sphere. While London was still the dominant locus of printing, by 1740 fifteen printing shops were working across nine cites in British North America, with presses as far south as Charleston, South Carolina. Boston and Philadelphia were major centres of print.

Franklin, as we will see, was a crucial agent in these transformations, and exercised a profound influence on the nature of print culture. In his *Autobiography*, he even imagined himself as a kind of book. But his achievements in print are not quite what we might expect. His output was dominated not by the great folio volumes that have traditionally organised the history of the book, but rather cheap, ephemeral texts. It was on this transient version of print that, paradoxically, Franklin built his cultural capital, and his future fame: his success requires that we take these slight publications seriously.

Printing brought Franklin sufficient riches and fame that he could, upon retiring from active printing in 1748 aged forty-two – eight years younger than the age at which Baskerville began – pursue a second life of politics and science. He left his Scottish business partner, David Hall, in charge of the presses. But even when Franklin had achieved international fame later in life, he still signed himself 'Ben Franklin, Printer'.

It starts early, in Boston, America's biggest metropolis, in 1717. Having alarmed his Puritan father with talk of a life on the seas, twelve-year-old Franklin is set up as a printing apprentice with his elder brother, James, who, after serving his apprenticeship in London, returned to Boston with a press and type to found and edit the *New-England Courant*, the fourth paper in the Colonies (and the third in Boston). Benjamin Franklin does the grunt work – 'I was employ'd to carry the Papers thro' the Streets to the Customers' – but he is ambitious, and resentful of being held in check by an elder brother. He writes pseudonymous letters under the name of Silence Dogood, a middle-aged widow who mocks aspects of colonial life. Franklin's letters are a hit; when it's known that Silence is widowed, men write in with proposals of marriage. No one realises it's Franklin; his brother's friends praise the writing and James publishes the series before finding out the author is his younger brother. Franklin, who left school at ten, has a powerfully 'Bookish Inclination'; he feeds off scraps in his father's 'little library' and then whatever volumes he can find. 'Often I sat up in my Room reading the greatest Part of the Night, when the Book was borrow'd in the Evening and to be return'd early in the Morning lest it should be miss'd or wanted.' His youthful language and conception of the world is forged by

John Bunyan's *Pilgrim's Progress* (1678), Daniel Defoe, and Cotton Mather, and Dryden's translation of Plutarch's *Lives* (1683): that work of twenty-four pairs of Greek and Roman biographies (like Alexander the Great and Julius Caesar), conveying, to the young Franklin, the potential scope of a life.

In 1723 Franklin, squirming under his brother's rule, flees the Boston print shop. He is illegally breaking the terms of his apprenticeship: he is on the run. Having arrived dishevelled and almost penniless in Philadelphia on 6 October, he is bewildered and alone but seized also by the symbolism of a new start in this new place, Pennsylvania Colony having been founded only forty years before by William Penn. 'I walk'd up the Street, gazing about, till near the Market House I met a Boy with Bread.' His future wife, Deborah, happens to see the down-at-heel seventeen-year-old and thinks he has 'a most awkward ridiculous Appearance'. Franklin – 'forgetting Boston as much as I could' – finds printing work with ex-Londoner Samuel Keimer (1689–1742), a patchy printer who'd spent time in the Fleet Prison for debt before himself trying to start again in Philadelphia. Keimer is a bad poet, too, with a habit of composing verse directly in type, without recourse to pen and paper. Franklin quickly decides that Keimer ('slovenly to extreme dirtiness', and an 'odd fish') knows 'nothing of Presswork' (that is, of working the press, in contrast to composing or ordering the metal type). Keimer's hardware consists, in Franklin's words, 'of an old shatter'd Press and one small worn-out Fount of English'. ('English' is a type size: the equivalent of 14 on your word processor, and, Franklin probably thought, unhelpfully large. 'Font' (or occasionally 'fount') from the French *fondre*, to melt or cast, means a complete set of type, and the design it represents.) Keimer asks Franklin to finish printing an elegy on a recently deceased young poet and printer's assistant. Franklin's prompt, good work ensures future employment. This is the first work that Franklin prints in Philadelphia: not a book, but a fragile single leaf on the death of a young man with the impossibly poetic name of Aquila Rose (*aquila* is Latin for 'eagle'). All known copies disappear by the early nineteenth century until, 200 years later, a book dealer finds a sheet in a scrapbook and sells it in 2017 to the University of Pennsylvania, where it now resides.

A pattern forms that will be repeated in Franklin's early career. He vaults past the lesser talents he sees around him – the two established Philadelphia printers 'wretched': Keimer 'a mere Compositor', Andrew Bradford 'very illiterate' – and catches the eyes of powerful men. Sir William Keith, Governor of Pennsylvania, sees a young man of promising parts and on his urging Franklin sails to London to gain a printer's education. He arrives in London on 24 December 1724 to find Keith has failed to send the letters of support. ('He wish'd to please everybody; and having little to give, he gave Expectations.')

Forced on by his ceaseless drive, and managing to hold at bay some if not all of his friend James Ralph's calls to the taverns, playhouses and brothels, Franklin secures work at two major London printers where he learns quickly. Once more, wayward friends set off his industry; senior men are impressed. At the print shop of Samuel Palmer (1692–1732) on Bartholomew Close, Little Britain, Franklin works as a compositor; he sets the type for the third edition of William Wollaston's *Religion of Nature Delineated* (1725), an early work of Deism that argues ethics can be implied from the natural world, and need not depend on revealed religion. It's the kind of work John Baskerville would have liked. But Franklin feels he could do better, and writes 'a little metaphysical Piece' titled *A Dissertation on Liberty and Necessity, Pleasure and Pain*, arguing for the incompatibility of an omnipotent God and human free will. The pamphlet carries no note of author or place of publication. It's bad: Palmer thinks it 'abominable'. Franklin quickly regrets it, burning the copies he can find. But Franklin's fierce industry (he works after hours to print the 100 copies) brings him to the attention of a powerful group of London intellectuals, including iconoclastic philosopher Bernard Mandeville, author of *The Fable of the Bees*, and collector Sir Hans Sloane. Franklin once more weeds out weak friends. Amid attempts to arrange a meeting with Isaac

Newton – 'of which I was extremely desirous' – his wayward friend James Ralph is cast off and ends up in a 'small Village in Berkshire, I think it was, where he taught reading and writing to 10 or a dozen Boys at 6 pence per Week'. Franklin ignores the sheets of epic poetry Ralph sends him; 'in the Loss of his Friendship I found myself reliev'd from a Burden'.

Franklin is being shaped by everything bookish. He borrows second-hand volumes about medicine and religion from 'one Wilcox a Bookseller, whose Shop was at the next Door', at the sign of the Green Dragon. He moves from Palmer's print shop to John Watts's: a more prestigious establishment in Wild Court, near Lincoln's Inn Fields, where he works first as a pressman, taking the physical strain of pulling the press, and then as a better-paid compositor. Watts prints big, literary works in lavish editions: the majority of Watts's work comes through partnership with the dominant publishing house of eighteenth-century London, run by the Tonsons, based in the Strand, who had established their reputation through the publication of literary works by Alexander Pope and John Gay, and of earlier authors including Spenser and Shakespeare. Unlike Palmer's, Watts's office doesn't share the printing of single works with other printers: this means, as book historian Hazel Wilkinson notes, that a voracious autodidact like Franklin can read whole works as he prints them, peering closely at the copy and setting type. Among the titles printed during Franklin's time at Watts's are Addison and Steele's *Spectator*; Latin comedies by Terence; contemporary drama by Thomas Southerne; satires by Edmund Young; a French edition of Plato's *Republic*; and several volumes of poetry. If Franklin was consuming material as he set type – and everything we know about him suggests he would have been – this is a rich and varied curriculum.

Franklin sets out to distinguish himself among the twenty-two apprentices trained by Watts in ways that sometimes misfire. Refusing to pay the traditional 5 shillings initiation fee, Franklin is considered by the other compositors 'an Excommunicate, and had so many little Pieces of private Mischief done me, by mixing my Sorts [pieces of type], transposing my Pages, breaking my Matter [columns of set type]'. In the beer-soaked world of the printing apprentice in eighteenth-century London, Franklin is the abstemious 'Water-American'.

My Companion at the Press drank every day a Pint before Breakfast, a Pint at Breakfast with his Bread and Cheese; a Pint between Breakfast and Dinner; a Pint at Dinner; a Pint in the Afternoon about Six o'clock, and another when he had done his Day's work.

Franklin thinks this a 'detestable Custom' and proposes what he calls 'some reasonable Alterations in their Chapel [printing house] Laws'. It's easy to imagine how these rational proposals sound to the ears of Franklin's fellow apprentices: he urges his peers to leave off their breakfast of 'Beer and Bread and Cheese' and to instead eat 'hot Water-gruel, sprinkled with Pepper'. *No, thank you!*

Franklin, now full of what London can offer, his head eternally generating new schemes, some of which never materialise (like the establishment, rather implausibly, of a swimming school), sails back to Philadelphia and in 1728 sets up his own print shop in partnership with Welshman Hugh Meredith (1697–*c.*1749) in a narrow brick house on Market Street.

Type arrives from London. Orders trickle, and then flow: William Sewel's *History of the Quakers* (1728), three-quarters of it printed by Keimer but Franklin printing the remaining 178 pages plus title page for each copy. 'It was a Folio, Pro Patria Size, in Pica with Long Primer Notes.' (Pro Patria is a Dutch paper size, derived through association with the Pro Patria watermark: about 33 centimetres by 20.)

Franklin, understanding he has to conspicuously surpass (to the point of humiliating) his rival, throws everything he has at the printing of his sheets of Sewel's *History*. Keimer has been inching his way through the printing of this book for five years. Franklin composes a sheet a day – which means four large pages – and Meredith works the press.

It was often 11 at Night and sometimes later, before I had finish'd my Distribution [placing letters after printing back in their cases] for the next day's Work: For the little Jobs sent in by our other Friends now and then put us back. But so determin'd was I to continue doing a Sheet a Day of the Folio, that one Night when having impos'd my Forms [bodies of type, secured in an iron frame or 'chase'], I thought my Day's Work over, one of them by accident was broken and two Pages reduc'd to Pie [a disordered pile of type], I immediately distributed and compos'd it again before I went to bed.

Franklin, realising that building 'character and credit' is crucial, not only works with irresistible force; he makes sure his neighbours see this industry. He wears plain clothes and pushes a wheelbarrow full of paper through the streets to convey the impression of honest labour. He wants to be a walking emblem of industry. 'I see him still at work when I go home from Club,' an eminent neighbour says, 'and he is at Work again before his Neighbours are out of bed.' Virtue is crucial, for Franklin; but so is the chatter about virtue.

The personalities who dominate the early years of Franklin's printing are soon pushed to the fringes and finally expelled. His partner Hugh Meredith – in Franklin's judgement, 'no Compositor, a poor Pressman, and seldom sober' – agrees to leave the business for a life as a farmer in North Carolina: Franklin pays him £30 and a new saddle.

Through drive, intelligence, determination, and a variety of low cunning, Franklin is established as the major printer in Philadelphia. It's 1730. Franklin is twenty-four. His ambitions can now unfold.

To understand Franklin – for all the scale of his personality – we need to think about the history of cheap print, because, in the startling words of one recent account, 'Franklin was only marginally a printer of books'. He floated high on a sea of what bibliographers call 'job printing', and the book that most effectively propelled Franklin towards the dominance he held, and still holds, in the American imagination, was a flimsy, transient form: the almanac.

The history of the book as a discipline has been preoccupied with what we might think of as landmark publications: it's a history typically organised around big volumes. Books like Johannes Gutenberg's 1450s Bible, the earliest full-scale work printed from movable metal type on Royal paper measuring 60 by 42 centimetres per leaf; or the *Biblia Polyglotta*, printed at Christopher Plantin's shop in Antwerp between 1568 and 1572, in eight folio volumes, with parallel texts in Hebrew, Greek, Syriac, and Aramaic, and translations and commentary in Latin, a wonder of *mise-en-page*; or the great seventeen-volume statement of Enlightenment thought, the *Encyclopédie* of Denis Diderot and Jean le Rond d'Alembert (published 1751–66); or the 435 hand-coloured, lifesize prints in John James Audubon's *Birds of America* (1827–38). We've met, already, Ben Jonson's *Workes* (1616), and *Mr. William Shakespeares Comedies, Histories, & Tragedies* – the book we shouldn't really call the First Folio (1623) – and we'll soon get to know *The Works of Geoffrey Chaucer* printed at William Morris's Kelmscott Press (1896), the product of four years of bibliographical labour, a wonder in off-white and (according to Edward Burne-Jones) 'a pocket cathedral'.

It's difficult to describe these books without using the word 'monumental', but these titles are deeply unrepresentative of the kinds of texts that typically emerged from binders' offices and printing chapels and that filled the stalls of booksellers and the pockets of readers. The flip-side to Shakespeare and Kelmscott and Diderot and d'Alembert is the world of jobbing printing: the production of cheap, everyday, usually ephemeral texts, the torrent of non-book print that has circulated in the world since the 1450s. And still does today. Look around you: the takeaway menu; the supermarket receipt. Packaging is very easily the largest consumer of print in 2024. Gutenberg changed the world with his Bible, but what kept the metaphorical tills chiming were the thousands and thousands of single-leaf indulgences he printed: a kind of pre-printed devotional receipt, printed on one side, with a blank space left for the name of the purchaser, who, showing the indulgence to a Church confessor, would have their sins forgiven. Indulgences like this were often printed as multiple settings of the same block of text, placed in one forme: the printed sheet would then be cut to produce two, four, or more copies. The Church ordered hundreds of thousands; printers were frantic; and institutions grew rich to the muttering sound of sins disappearing into the air. On 22 October 1454, Pope Nicholas V needed money to help defend Cyprus against Turkish invasion and issued indulgences to raise the funds. Forty-six copies survive today of this so-called thirty-one-line indulgence, issued at Erfurt, Germany.

Compared to Gutenberg's Bible, each one of these copies is a slight thing, printed oblong on vellum, a single side, with a blank for the date, name and home town to be added by hand. (In leaving those blanks, this indulgence did what lots of early cheap print often did: it welcomed, rather than excluded, handwritten augmentation.) It might have fluttered easily to the muddy Erfurt ground on a day in 1454; many of those forty-six extant copies survive only because they served as binding waste in later books. But today it's the earliest dated document we know printed by movable type, and it represents the kind of everyday, cheap, jobbing work that kept the print trade alive. The first surviving dated text we know that Caxton printed is an indulgence, too, with handwritten names (Henry Langley and his wife) and a date (13 December 1476) added in the gaps in the print. And alongside the indulgences, all manner of other kinds of jobbing work was produced by printers in the centuries after Gutenberg: pamphlets, certificates, blank chits, broadside ballads, business cards, the forms through which people were baptised, married, and buried. The huge numbers of copies printed meant that loss rates were high: literary historian Tessa Watt estimates that the survival rate for sixteenth-century English ballads is about one in 10,000 copies, and the survival rates for indulgences are almost certainly even lower. This has major consequences for how we relate to our printed heritage, and for how we imagine our history. The printed past that libraries gather and curate is necessarily out of synch with the daily encounters with print which men and women would have experienced in the first centuries of printing. As the historian Elizabeth Eisenstein has argued in her pioneering work, the printing revolution is not 'centrally about the history of books': it's broader than that – a sea of 'images and charts, advertisements and maps, official edicts and indulgences'.

Benjamin Franklin was sustained by just this kind of printing work. In this, he was like his colonial peers: since it was cheaper to import large books from London, American printing before about 1740 tended to concentrate on small books, pamphlets, government printing, sermons, and ephemera. Franklin had his moments with big volumes. Most notable was his 1744 publication of Cicero's *Cato Major*, a 44 BCE essay on ageing and death, translated by James Logan. Seventy-three copies survive today of a print run of 1,000, and it's often held up with admiration as the best example of colonial printing: printed in Caslon type in black and red on either American-milled or Genoese paper, depending on the copy. Logan's translation had been circulating in manuscript some years before, and Franklin actively pursued it – rightly perceiving the volume not as a source of financial profit (it wasn't), but a means to acquire cultural capital in powerful, learned circles. Two years earlier, in 1742, Franklin began printing *Pamela; or, Virtue Rewarded*, Samuel Richardson's epistolary novel about fifteen-year-old maidservant Pamela Andrews and her attempts to fend off the unwanted advances of her wealthy employer, the enigmatically titled 'Mr. B'. *Pamela* was a huge hit in London, but at seventeen sheets this was a large book, and it took Franklin more than two years to complete both volumes, working again in Caslon type on American paper. Franklin sold it unstitched – folded, in sheets – for 6 shillings, and as a result of being exposed to the world in this way, only one copy survives today. But by the time Franklin's edition was published, the market was awash with cheap imported copies, and Franklin still had thirty-six sets of *Pamela* when he sold the stock of his bookshop to his new partner, David Hall, in 1748. The lesson he learnt – and Franklin was all about lessons learnt – was to avoid heavy investment in a single title: big volumes did not seem a smart route.

Jobbing work meant printing many copies quickly, moving rapidly from order to order with no thought to posterity. (Most of these items lack an imprint and were only ascribed to Franklin, or Franklin and Hall, by the meticulous study of account books and ledgers by Franklin's pre-eminent bibliographer, C. William Miller.) Jobbing commissions were frequent and not labour-intensive: they were usually quickly dispatched by the printer after putting longer-term projects on temporary hold. In 1742, Franklin repeatedly suspended work on *Pamela* to print lottery tickets; licences for pedlars and public houses; sheriff's warrants; naval certificates; 1,000 hat bills; Irish Society tickets for Philip Syng; and thousands of advertisements, for, among others, sailor runaways, and for Samuel Lloyd's mare. These are printed works whose loud local voice is lost in the long hum of history. Soap wrappers for his brother John in Boston; bookplates for libraries; medical cures by Dr. Brewster. If we could walk down 2nd Street, Philadelphia, in the spring of 1757, past the former offices of Franklin's rival Andrew Bradford, we might see one of the play bills Franklin and Hall printed for the visiting London Theatre Company (of 4,300 copies, only two are known to survive today); or if in 1761 we turned up Market Street, past the former printing office of Samuel Keimer, before he disappeared on a boat to Barbados, we might notice pasted on a lamp post or passing between hands a copy of instructions for operating a watch Franklin and Hall printed for Owen Biddle. One of the features of print that is most often invoked is its capacity to endure, but this is a world of transient texts: of print read, then dropped, or lost, or used to light pipes, or to stop mustard pots, or to wrap pies, or, with modern

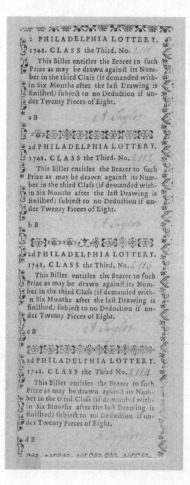

Franklin's printing of Philadelphia lottery papers (1748).

toilet paper still awaiting its great movement (it came in 1857), as what the seventeenth-century English poet Alexander Brome referred to as 'bum fodder'.

Franklin, focusing not on the grand volumes which have bewitched book historians, concentrated his attention in particular on three kinds of printed text whose import and profit far exceeded Cicero's *Cato Major*, or Richardson's *Pamela*.

The first was paper money. Franklin printed money for the governments of Pennsylvania (from 1729 to 1764), New Jersey (1728–46), and Delaware (1734–60), producing about 800,000 individual paper bills, of which just ten survive today in public collections. (But perhaps you have some squirrelled away at the back of a drawer.) Paper money was a polarising issue – farmers and tradesmen liked it; the rich did not – and Franklin contributed to the political controversy by advocating for it in *A Modest Inquiry into the Nature and Necessity of a Paper Currency*. Franklin also had some clever ideas about the printing process, and from 1739, the verso of his bills carried the impression of leaves to prevent counterfeits: Franklin placed a leaf on a piece of wet fabric and pressed this into smooth plaster, and used this negative impression as the mould for melted metal type. Franklin had a capacity to see what was not there, and then to find it, or invent it. He devises and builds a copper-plate press – 'the first that had been seen in the Country' – to produce these engravings. Among the anti-counterfeit devices on a twenty-first-century United States $100 bill, including a 3D security ribbon and colour-shifting ink, is Franklin's quietly judgemental face; he has been peering out from the back of the notes since 1914, along with Independence Hall in Philadelphia on the reverse. The bills are known as 'Bens', or 'Benjamins', or 'Franklins' – to be rich is to be 'rolling in the Benjamins'.

Franklin's second crucial kind of non-book printing was his newspaper, the *Pennsylvania Gazette*. Franklin's life in newspapers illustrates that double tendency of media companies to be both dynastic (you know who I mean), and ruthlessly competitive. Franklin exploits his capacities in both of these areas, learning voraciously, as was ever his mode, while a boy working for his brother's *New-England Courant*, and displaying a commercial cunning in out-manoeuvring his rivals. This meant plotting a way past Andrew Bradford's *American Weekly Mercury* – 'a paltry thing', in Franklin's words, 'wretchedly manag'd, and no way entertaining' – and appropriating Samuel Keimer's *Pennsylvania Gazette*. Keimer had set up the *Gazette* after Franklin's loose-tongued print-shop colleague George Webb – a former Oxford undergraduate, trying his luck as a poet in America – betrayed Franklin's plans to start a newspaper to Keimer. Franklin wrote articles for Bradford's *Mercury*, under the name of 'Busy Body', mocking Keimer's paper and chipping away at his authority. But in fact Keimer was a flabby rival, possessed of the editorial acuity of a blunderbuss, and reliable only in his unravellings. Keimer made the baffling decision to include in each edition a long excerpt from Ephraim Chambers's *Cyclopaedia; or, an Universal Dictionary of Arts and Sciences*, which meant that Keimer's paper, retitled the *Universal Instructor in all Arts and Sciences: and Pennsylvania Gazette*, carried incomplete and largely arbitrary essays, 'staggering along', as Miller nicely puts it, 'under the dull burden of encyclopaedia entries'. 'It will probably be fifty Years,' Franklin wrote, 'before the Whole can be gone thro.' And by the time he and Hugh Meredith bought the paper in October 1729 'for a Trifle', Keimer's *Gazette* was still inching its way through the article on 'Air'. (Keimer, like the eccentric minor character he could only ever be, moves to Barbados, 'and there lived some Years, in very poor Circumstances', where he edits, with some controversy, the *Barbados Gazette*. Exit Keimer.)

Published by Franklin and Meredith until 1731, by Franklin on his own to 1748, by Franklin and Hall until 1766, and after that by Hall and his successors until 1800, the *Gazette* became the most popular paper in the Colonies. The sum of 10 shillings bought you a year's subscription – that's about 2 pence for every weekly, four-page issue – and subscribers grew from a feeble ninety in the last days of Keimer's ham-fisted editorship to more than fifteen hundred in 1748.

What is a newspaper at this moment in history? And what qualities did Franklin's possess that marked it out for success? In 1729, there are seven newspapers in the English colonies: three in Boston, one in New York, one in Annapolis, and two in Philadelphia, including Franklin's *Gazette*. (Southern newspapers developed more slowly, not flourishing until the time of the American Revolution.) A typical edition of the *American Weekly Mercury*, edited by Franklin's Philadelphia rival Andrew Bradford, is a slender thing, dominated by brief summaries of foreign news that offer pockets of seemingly arbitrary information while leaving most of the globe untouched. The *Mercury* for 1–8 January 1722, for example, is largely devoted to brief reports of news from Paris, Venice, and London, mingling discussion of plans for the French coronation with vague notices of the movements of the Ottoman fleet, plus a certain amount of moralised sensation (the body of a newborn child found in Southwark with its bones broken, crammed into an earthen pot, the 'Authors of this Barbarity' unknown). American news is brief: a short note from Philadelphia (the Delaware River is 'open and free of Ice'; people are sailing to the islands of St. Vincent and St. Lucia 'on the Encouragement of 10 Acres of Land on those Isles given *gratis* to every white Person'), and there are advertisements for 'Jesuits Bark' (a cure for malaria from tree bark) lately imported from Peru, and several seeking to track down apprentices who have fled. This is primarily a scattered account of news from elsewhere. Newspapers like the *Mercury* show how partial and selective this sense of the global was: a *Mercury* reader's world is centred on London and Paris, orbited by Amsterdam, Astrakhan, Bologna, Dublin, Genoa, the Hague, Madrid, Milan, Moscow, Rome, Stockholm, Vienna, and Warsaw. What we call America means Philadelphia, New York, and sometimes Rhode Island. In *Imagined Communities*, historian Benedict Anderson argued for the importance of popular print culture in creating the idea of national belonging: newspapers enabled readers to imagine themselves as part of a shared culture of ideas, investments and events that spread beyond their local world, uniting readers who had never in fact met each other through a sense of commonality.

When Franklin assumes control of Keimer's *Gazette*, the quality of production and content is immediately and conspicuously better. Franklin's paper, like most other colonial newspapers, was printed on both sides of one small folio sheet, folded to produce four two-columned pages, about 30 by 20 centimetres per leaf; but it was also a better object. As Franklin himself wrote, 'Our first Papers made quite a different Appearance from any before in the Province, a better Type [a mix of English, pica, and long primer] and better printed.'

But it is the quality of Franklin's writing, too, that sets the *Gazette* apart – 'one of the first good Effects of my learning a little to scribble'. Franklin's *Gazette* still includes reports from foreign newspapers, but Franklin increases the local and colonial content, cuts the tiresome encyclopaedia recyclings and adds instead a series of essays, either reprinted from English journals (the *London Journal*, *Spectator*, *Tatler*), or written by Franklin's friends or Franklin himself (including his discussion in favour of paper currency that won admirers in high places). There are more advertisements. In a way that seems unimaginable amid the information overload of the twenty-first century, news was often thin on the ground – if the Delaware River froze over and ships didn't come in, the news was stuck in the ice too – and Franklin became adept at improvising content, often through the composition of original writing, including essays, anecdotes, or (greatest of all literary genres) fake reader letters.

The effect of all this was to produce a set of juxtapositions that at first might seem unstable: European and domestic news next to excerpts from Xenophon or *The Morals of Confucius*; bawdy anecdotes written by Franklin and inspired by Boccaccio's *Decameron*, next to letters from readers (many of them written by Franklin under various pseudonyms); the first important newspaper interview, with Andrew Hamilton, Speaker of Pennsylvania's House of Representatives, in 1733, alongside mock news that crashes through our modern sense of acceptable limits but which proved hugely popular in its time ('And sometime last Week, we are informed, that one Piles a Fidler, with his Wife, were overset in a Canoe near Newtown Creek. The good Man, 'tis said, prudently secur'd his Fiddle, and let his Wife go to the Bottom'); the first American political cartoon, advocating for the union of the thirteen Colonies with Great Britain to fight the French and Native Americans in 1754 as part of an editorial titled 'The Disunited State'; jokes ('Lost Last Saturday Night, in Market Street, about 40 or 50s. If the Finder will bring it to the Printer hereof, who will describe the Marks, he shall have 10s. Reward'); satirical sketches (on his rival publisher: 'When Mr. *Bradford* publishes after us, and has Occasion to take an Article or two out of the *Gazette*, which he is always welcome to do, he is desired not to date his Paper a Day before ours'); mocking accounts of the clergy; obituaries (Franklin's inclusions did much to establish and popularise the form); and essays written by Franklin motivated by a growing sense of outrage at the experience of English rule (the dire conditions of English prisons, and the suffering endured by the Irish as a result of 'their griping avaricious Landlords').

If this sounds thematically and tonally miscellaneous, it's because it was: in this sense, the newspaper was the perfect form for Franklin whose interests were so ranging. But Franklin also edited into the *Gazette* a coherence that took the form of a preoccupation with moral improvement: 'I considered my Newspaper also as another Means of communicating Instruction,' wrote Franklin in his *Autobiography*, and this commitment played out in essays that often originated in his autodidacts' club, the Junto, prescribing reason, good civic words, and moderation, like 'a Socratic Dialogue tending to prove, that, whatever might be his Parts and Abilities, a vicious Man could not properly be called a Man of Sense'. The *Gazette*'s contents tended to be secular and preoccupied with the virtues and opportunities of trade; and the *Gazette* was a newspaper, and Franklin an editor, increasingly convinced of the importance of the press as a means for what he called 'Zeal for the Publick Good'. This meant the cultivation of informed, civic-minded leaders and represented a commitment which ultimately found expression (although after Franklin's ties to printing had been in effect suspended) in Franklin's successful advocacy of American Independence.

But there is one topic among the *Gazette*'s noisy miscellaneity that is disturbing, if not unexpected, for a modern reader, and that clashes loudly with the expectations of virtue and the commitments to freedom that Franklin himself established. This is the presence of advertisements for slaves, and the role in these of Franklin as a kind of broker, and his print shop as a space for these transactions. Recent work by historian Jordan E. Taylor has done much to uncover the intimate links between eighteenth-century American newspapers and the transatlantic slave trade, articulated through both notices about runaway slaves, and – Taylor's particular focus – through thousands of advertisements for slaves for sale that 'empowered enslavers and strengthened the slave system'. In the thirty-seven years that Franklin published the *Gazette*, his newspaper printed at least 277 advertisements offering at least 308 slaves for sale (and these are conservative counts). In the 1740s in particular Franklin's *Gazette* was the crucial site for these advertisements.

Many of these instructed potential buyers to speak to 'B. Franklin, and know further'. Franklin's *Pennsylvania Gazette* on 17 February 1765 ran an advertisement for 'A Negro Man Twenty-two Years of Age, of uncommon Strength and Activity'. In the subjectivity-stripping register of capitalist commodification, 'Any Person that wants such a one may see him by enquiring of the Printer hereof.' (Advertisements typically denude slaves of anything as individuating as character, and use instead stark identity-categories such as wench, woman, lad, boy, fellow, man, girl, or child, with few details save age, health, sex, and skills.)

That last phrase instructing interested readers to contact the printer is crucial: it was the clause that typically signed off these advertisements, and it implicates absolutely the newspaper printer in this slave-trade economy. Franklin is here the middleman, linking buyers and sellers and oiling the wheels of a slave economy: the advertisements serving as informal proxies for the auction or merchant firm. The buyer power here in these acts of human trafficking is clear: in an 'enquire of the printer' advertisement in the *Gazette* for 1733, Franklin offered a 'very likely Negro Woman aged about Thirty Years' with a son 'aged about Six Years, who [. . .] will be sold with his Mother, or by himself, as the Buyer pleases'.

Franklin was certainly not alone in this practice. The first known newspaper advertisement for a slave was posted in the *Boston News-Letter*, the first long-running newspaper in British North America, published by John Campbell and printed by Bartholomew Green, in 1704: 'A Negro Woman about 16 Years Old, to be Sold by John Campbell Post-master, to be seen at his House next door to the Anchor Tavern.' The practice continued through much of the eighteenth century, declining in New England and Pennsylvania by the 1790s only when slavery was gradually barred (the legal Atlantic slave trade was closed in 1808). Franklin's brother, James, advertised slaves in his *New-England Courant*: immediately above a notice for wines, rum, and spirits in the edition of 5 November 1722, for example – while a young Benjamin was working for his brother – is the advertisement for 'A Likely Negro Woman to be sold. Inquire of the Printer of this Paper.' Learning from his brother's example, Franklin became the first printer outside Boston to broker slaves regularly through his newspaper, and his commercial success (but moral failure) catalysed similar advertisements in newspapers in New York City, Baltimore, and Providence. Franklin later in life was known as a vocal and influential abolitionist, but as Taylor notes, British North American newspapers like Franklin's which supported revolutionary politics, republican ideals, and a language of freedom might also at the same time – and in an enactment of what historian Edmund Morgan called the 'American paradox' – sustain this slave economy through advertisements. 'For most of the eighteenth century,' writes Jordan Taylor, 'to be a newspaper printer was to be a slave trader.'

In the early years, Franklin strove for a kind of total control over the *Gazette*: he set copy, printed the pages off on the press or directed others to do so, gathered news and advertisements, wrote original compositions, faked letters from outraged readers, dug at and mocked and undermined his rivals, and in general took the literary quality of journalism to new levels. Seeking to secure widespread distribution, Franklin landed the job of postmaster for Philadelphia in 1737, replacing Bradford who had prevented coach riders from delivering the *Gazette* outside Philadelphia. In time, as his network of printing partnerships expanded – James Parker in New York (1742); his nephew James Jr. in Newport (1747); Thomas Smith in Antigua (1748); Parker and Holt in New Haven (1754) – Franklin's engagement became less hands-on, and more managerial. But it's nonetheless true that Franklin created a newspaper that was, to a unique degree in the history of journalism, expressive of the personality of its editor, for good and bad, even as its inclusions wandered and ranged. Franklin's most thorough biographer, J. A. Leo Lemay, summed things up nicely: 'Perhaps no other newspaper had ever been as audacious, entertaining, literary, humorous, salacious, intellectual, political, financial, scientific, philosophical, or witty as Franklin's *Pennsylvania Gazette*.'

The third kind of publication that was at the heart of Franklin's success – again, in contrast to the big folios we might expect – was his *Poor Richard* series of almanacs. In publishing almanacs, Franklin was following the scent of the bestseller. Almanacs compressed the world into miniature form: like 'infinite riches in a little room', as Christopher Marlowe's Barabas said of his wealth, almanacs were cheap, small, eminently portable books which provided readers with monthly calendars; astrological and meteorological prognostications; details of fairs and journeys between towns; chronologies of history; medical advice; a 'zodiacal body' anatomising the influence of the planets on parts of the body; and more. They were the most popular kind of printed book in seventeenth-century England, selling in numbers so large they scarcely seem credible. In 1666, 43,000 copies of Vincent Wing's almanac alone were printed, and print runs for texts compiled by Rider, Saunders, Gallen, and Andrews were 18,000, 15,000, 12,000, and 10,000, respectively. The market was crowded, frantic, and profitable: Thomas Nashe in 1596 said selling almanacs was 'readier money than ale and cakes'. Precisely because of this everywhere-quality, almanacs were ephemeral: fixed to a particular year, their moment quickly passed, and in a period before the notion of collecting 'popular culture' was established, they were usually discarded. As book historian Eustace Bosanquet notes, 'The entire productions of many of the [English almanac] authors of this period have disappeared . . . we know of such authors as George Williams, Doctor Harycok . . . Barnabe Gaynsforth . . . [and] Thomas Stephens, Gent, . . . [only] by their names appearing among the licenses.'

The first edition of Franklin's *Poor Richard, 1733* was printed during 1732; it sells for 5d a copy – or 3s 6d for a dozen – and contains, as the title page declares, 'The Lunations, Eclipses, Judgment of the Weather, Spring Tides, Planets Motions & mutual Aspects, Sun and Moon's Rising and Setting, Length of Days, Time of High Water, Fairs Courts, and observable Days.' It was a huge commercial hit – 'vending annually near ten thousand', according to Franklin, in a colony with a 1730s population of less than 15,000, with 'scarce any neighborhood in the province being without it'. The almanac was a perfect form for Franklin, with an inclusive sweep of contents (everything from the stars tracking across the heavens to the crops growing under our feet), and a loosely Christian kind of practical virtue. Almanacs represented that particularly Franklinian combination of big sales with plain-talking humility: cash, and a homespun manner.

Here is the page for May 1737, crammed with information: days of the month and the week; planetary positions, weather, and Church days; the time of high tide at Philadelphia; the moon's positions; and the sun's rising and setting. Amongst this

III Mon.   May hath xxxi days.

Rich *Gripe* does all his Thoughts & Cunning bend
T'encreafe that Wealth he wants the Soul fpend :
Poor *Shifter* does his whole Contrivance fet,
To fpend that Wealth he wants the Senfe to get.
How happy would appear to each his Fate,
Had *Gripe* his Humour, or he *Gripe's* Eftate ?
Kind Fate and Fortune, blend 'em if you ca n,
And of two Wretches make one happy Man.

Poor Richard, 1737. An almanack for the year of Christ 1737 *(1736)*,
showing the crammed page of information for May, which includes (right)
italicised proverbial wisdom.

data, Franklin squeezes in proverbial sentences, filling the gaps in
the page with his ideology of thrift, trade, and profit – 'No better
relation than a prudent & faithful Friend.'

Franklin is using the cheapest of books to educate a vast reading public towards his idea of virtue. In the twenty-sixth and final
edition of *Poor Richard* for 1758, the text composed by Franklin
as he sailed towards England, he gathered about 100 of these

aphorisms and wove them into the speech of 'Father Abraham' ('a plain clean old man, with white locks'). 'The harangue of a wise old man,' as Franklin put it, 'to the people attending an auction.' This piece of writing, variously known as 'Father Abraham's Speech', 'The Way to Wealth', or 'La Science du Bonhomme Richard', is the most widely reprinted text by Franklin: before 1800, there were thirty-six reprintings of *The Way to Wealth* in America, twenty-eight editions in French, eleven in Italian, three in German, and in London the text appeared in numerous journals and as a chapter in Anne Fisher's hugely popular guide for children, *The Pleasing Instructor* (1795). Franklin himself was proudly aware of its influence; in the *Autobiography* he wrote:

> The piece, being universally approved, was copied in all the newspapers of the Continent; reprinted in Britain on a broad side, to be stuck up in houses; two translations were made of it in French, and great numbers bought by the clergy and gentry, to distribute gratis among their poor parishioners and tenants.

We get a sense of it, here, in the following extract: this is Franklin, reporting how he overheard one Father Abraham (written by Franklin) dispensing wisdom that he had gathered from reading *Poor Richard* almanacs (written by Franklin):

> Sloth, by bringing on diseases, absolutely shortens life. *Sloth, like rust, consumes faster than labor wears, while the used key is always bright*, as Poor Richard says. *But dost thou love life, then do not squander time, for that's the stuff life is made of*, as Poor Richard says. How much more than is necessary do we spend in sleep! forgetting that *the sleeping fox catches no poultry*, and that *there will be sleeping enough in the grave*, as Poor Richard says.

The collective wisdom was the unsurprising philosophy that hard work, thrift, and moderation produced both material comforts and spiritual salvation: it was a statement of Franklin's faith in reason and capitalism ('the people were the best judges of my merit; for they buy my works'). As a reading experience, it is saved – at least for us today – by Franklin's humour ('The people heard it, and approved the doctrine, and immediately practiced the contrary') and his self-awareness ('The frequent mention he made of me must have tired any one else, but my vanity was wonderfully delighted').

We can track Franklin's deep engagement with all aspects of the print trade not only through the titles he produced, but also, and more elementally, in his relationship with two of the materials that made up printed texts: type, and paper.

Setting up a print shop from something like scratch means ordering lots of type: and this means lots of weight. (In his *Autobiography*, Franklin boasts that while working in London as an apprentice at Watts's, 'I carried up and down Stairs a large Form of Types in each hand, when others carried but one in both Hands.') In 1727, with no domestic type makers available (American printers typically relied on Dutch imports, as the English had), Franklin draws on his London experience and orders his first quantity of types from the London foundry of Thomas and John James, in Bartholomew Close near Samuel Palmer's office, at that moment the most important foundry in England. (There were at least four significant foundries in the country at this time: the Andrews foundry in Oxford, and in London the foundries of Grover, Mitchell, and James.) Franklin had observed the process of type manufacture during his London years: the end of a narrow punch cut and filed to produce a letter or mark in relief; the punch pressed into softer copper to make a matrix (from the Latin, 'womb'); the matrix fixed in the hand-mould; molten type metal poured into a vertical cavity at the top of the mould to yield, when hardened, an individual letter or symbol called a sort (hence the unhappy condition of being 'out of sorts'). It was a process made to fascinate Franklin, and while working for Keimer he'd designed a mould and matrices, and cast the first types in North America. For his new print shop, from the James foundry Franklin imports about 300 pounds in weight each of long primer (10 point) – used in the *Poor Richard* almanacs – pica (12 point), and English (14 point), and about 100 pounds of double pica (22 point) for titles. Franklin adds in about 30 pounds of question marks (although he isn't really the doubtful type) along with a mix of ornaments (decorative, not illustrative, devices, such as might mark the end of a chapter), fleurons (from the Old French *floron*, 'flower': stylised leaves or flowers in type) and a small amount of planet sorts and (in 1734) blackletter long primer to mark out holy days in almanacs, and for German language advertisements in the *Gazette*.

Sorts are made from an alloy of lead (80 per cent), tin (7 per cent), and antimony (13 per cent), and because this relatively soft metal compound is grasped between fingers, dropped, pressed hard in a press over and over, sorts have a habit of developing idiosyncrasies, like a crack in the crossbar of a long primer 'A'. We get a lovely sense of the worn-through-workness of type in an inventory of Caslon type owned by Franklin and Hall in 1766, compiled by James Parker on the occasion of the ending of the Hall–Franklin partnership:

> 436 lbs. Long Primer, well worn
> 318 lbs. Small Pica, almost worn out
> 421 lbs. Pica, Old, and much batter'd
> 334 lbs. Old English, fit for little more than old metal
> 223 lbs. Great Primer, well worn
> 158 lbs. Double Pica, pretty good
> 91 lbs. Double English Do. [Ditto]

In these descriptions of exhausted type we can sense the industry which fired Franklin. These particular forms of brokenness, like micro-personalities, enable the sharpest bibliographers to track particular letters – not just letter types, but individual sorts – as they make impressions across texts. This has led to attributions of otherwise unsigned printing work to Franklin, more accurately establishing his canon; and it has also meant noticing how a set of type might move between different print shops. The pica and English type which Franklin originally acquired from the James Foundry in London passed to Sister Ann, Franklin's brother James's widow, in Newport, which she used well into the 1740s. (If you want to see how the seemingly prosaic act of listing a printer's works can produce riveting scholarship, spend an hour with C. William Miller's *Benjamin Franklin's Philadelphia Printing 1728–1766*: this is enumerative bibliography as a deep dive into the past.)

By 1737 Franklin needs to order new stock from London. Sensing the wind's direction before the sails filled, Franklin chooses the elegant type designed by contemporary engraver and toolmaker William Caslon, ordering Caslon's pica and small pica (11 point) in 1738, long primer and flowers in 1739, English and brevier (8 point) in 1740, and great primer (18 point) and paragon (20 point) in 1741. (Caslon's small pica had a shortage of 'p' and 'u' sorts which necessitated Franklin's compositors using inverted 'd's and 'n's, until 1739.) Through Franklin's patronage, Caslon's letters, influential in London printing circles by 1730, are introduced to the American Colonies and by about 1750 are dominant. Franklin buys the same Caslon type for the new partnerships he is forging into a network of print shops: this consistency of type enabled not only the cultivation of a Franklin house style, but also the sharing of print jobs between partners – as Franklin (in Philadelphia) and Parker (in New York) split the printing of particular almanac editions in the 1740s and 1750s. This practice of multiple printers sharing the production of a book, something Franklin had experienced at Palmer's in London, was regular practice. As book historian Peter Stallybrass has noted, the title page of 'The Fifteenth Edition' of Isaac Watts's *Hymns and Spiritual Songs* assigns the book's printing to Franklin in Philadelphia, in 1741, but in fact it had been split between Franklin in Philadelphia and James Parker in New York, and the sheets were then sent to Charles Harrison in Boston where they were bound into a book.

Even after his focus has shifted, after 1748, from printing to scientific experiments and politics, Franklin sustains a keen interest in typography: he is among the subscribers to Baskerville's edition of *Paradise Lost* (1758) and, as we've seen, visits Baskerville in Birmingham shortly after; later still, Franklin was delighted with the type produced by the Fournier family which he used at his small press in Passy, France, late in life.

We can see Franklin's contribution to the American history of paper-making, too.

We'll come to paper and its very global history in Chapter 6. For now we can note that Philadelphia was blessed with fast-flowing creeks and a population large enough to supply the necessary piles of rags for conversion into sheets. It's a process that never ceases to be a kind of magic: old rags cut, beaten, and soaked in water to produce pulp; a metal mesh and frame plunged into a tub of the mix by a vatman; the frame removed, shaken left to right, forward and back, for a few seconds, the water draining to leave a thin layer of woven fibres, knotted together, and dried by the coucher between woollen blankets or 'felts' – this whole process of dipping, removing, and tipping taking about twenty seconds, and a well-drilled partnership of vatman and coucher producing four reams, or 2,000 sheets, of paper each day.

But in the early years of Franklin's printing business (around 1728–33), domestic paper was regarded as cheap but not quite good enough – brown paper was fine for wrapping soap, and the rough blue could serve for a cover, but neither would do as a substrate for that government proclamation Franklin hoped would catch the right eyes. He purchased his paper from abroad, mostly Dutch-made, imported via British wholesalers, and sold by local merchants. From the 1730s, a vigorous local paper industry was emerging thanks in part to Franklin's influence as a purchaser (regularly from 1735), patron, and more broadly symbol of domestic commercial confidence. In 1734, Franklin advertised 'Ready Money for old Rags, may be had of the Printer hereof' in his *Pennsylvania Gazette*, and between 1742 and 1749 sold Anthony Newhouse 49,242 pounds of rags which Newhouse sold back as hundreds of reams of paper used by Franklin to print provincial paper money. The best paper-makers and mill-owners were immigrants who brought skills from Europe (Germany, Switzerland, the Low Countries) to the nascent American paper trade. The earliest American paper mill had been established by William Rittenhouse on Paper Mill Run, one of the tributaries of Wissahickon Creek, in 1690. Rittenhouse, born in a village in the Ruhr region of Germany, had learnt Dutch paper-making skills while serving an apprenticeship in Germany, before emigrating to Pennsylvania in 1688. Franklin's rival Andrew Bradford bought his entire output for himself, further forcing Franklin into purchasing expensive foreign paper.

From the 1740s, Franklin bought paper from Johann Conrad Schütz, originally from the Palatinate, Germany, whose mill produced paper carrying a fleur-de-lis watermark and, for Franklin, a countermark with the initials 'BF'. Swiss paper-maker Jacob Hagy took over Newhouse's mill on Trout Run in 1752, and his paper, with in its distinctive 'IH' watermark, was being used by Franklin and Hall from 1754.

The 1730s were, in the words of C. William Miller, 'the cradle age of the rising paper industry fostered by Franklin in Pennsylvania', and the 1740s represented the industry's youth. By the 1750s and 1760s the industry was full grown, and Philadelphia became the primary site of paper-making into the nineteenth century: Franklin's ledgers show the increasing use of American paper for his own printing, and Franklin himself boasted in 1788 to his French friend Brissot de Warville that he helped establish eighteen paper mills.

Franklin's immersion in book culture was so complete that he repeatedly imagined his life, and even his physical self, as a printed book. As a young man in 1728, Franklin, like his English counterpart John Baskerville, composed his own epitaph, which – eternal self-promoter that he was, even in the image of death – he was fond of copying out for friends.

> The Body of
> B. Franklin, Printer;
> Like the Cover of an old
> Book, Its Contents torn out,
> And stript of its Lettering and
> Gilding, Lies here, Food for Worms.
> But the Work shall not be wholly lost:
> For it will, as he believ'd, appear once more,
> In a new & more perfect Edition,
> Corrected and Amended
> By the Author.
> He was born on January 6, 1706.
> Died 17

The wit of the piece lies in part in its playing with the very impossibility of the self-composed epitaph: Franklin leaves a blank for the date of death because he cannot complete the text. (His actual gravestone reads simply 'BENJAMIN And DEBORAH FRANKLIN 1790'.) But its importance also lies in its relation to a longer tradition of figuring a person as a book. We see an early example of this in Giuseppe Arcimboldo's portrait, probably based on the humanist and historian Wolfgang Lazius (1514–65), in which the physical components of Lazius are made out of, or have turned into, books and bookish props: the effect is, unnervingly, of realistically rendered components cohering into a nightmarish body. (I find the hair from the fanning pages particularly uncanny.) Even if we don't interpret this as a bookish version of Frankenstein's monster, it does at the very least seem to be taking the idea of being well read to an extreme.

The effect of Arcimboldo's piece resides in part in its literalisation of the metaphor of the man or woman as book: a tradition

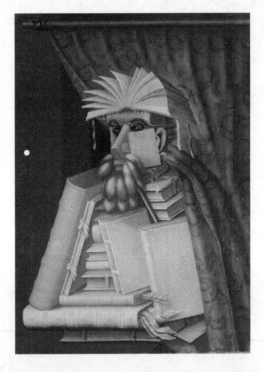

Giuseppe Arcimboldo, 'The Librarian' (1566?).

growing out of the medieval trope of Christ's crucified body as
a charter recording a written agreement by which all humanity
will receive eternal bliss in exchange for loving Christ. We see this
metaphor brilliantly developed, and secularised, across a number
of Elizabethan writers who, wrestling with the relatively new fact
of a dominant print culture, think hard, and imaginatively, about
what a book could mean. One of my favourites is Samuel Daniel's sonnet from *Delia* (1592) in which the narrator, bewailing his
fate in love, turns his own face into a tragic book:

> Read in my face a volume of despairs,
> The wailing Iliads of my tragic woe,
> Drawn with my blood and printed with my cares
> Wrought by her hand, that I have honor'd so.

John Donne pulled the conceit in different directions. In his seduction poem 'To His Mistress Going to Bed', Donne imagines undressing a woman by thinking about book covers and contents:

> Like pictures, or like books' gay coverings made
> For lay-men, are all women thus array'd;
> Themselves are mystic books, which only we
> (Whom their imputed grace will dignify)
> Must see reveal'd.

And in his prose Meditation 17 – 'No man is an island . . . ' – Donne figures death not as book destruction (a page ripped out) but, instead, a process of translation: 'All mankind is of one Author, and is one volume; when one man dies, one Chapter is not torn out of the book, but translated into a better language'. We see the trope sustained in Shakespeare's writing: a 'man's brow,' says Northumberland in *Henry IV Part 2*, is like 'a title-leaf', which 'Foretells the nature of a tragic volume'. Lady Macbeth chastises her husband for his lack of dissembling by declaring, 'Your face, my thane, is as a book, where men / May read strange matters.' Macbeth tells his followers, 'Kind gentlemen, your pains / Are register'd, where every day I turn / The leaf to read them.' Shakespeare seems to have been struck by the darkness in all this, by the potential for the person-as-book trope to signal a life gone radically wrong. The collapsing King John gives audiences a devastating bibliographical self-description as he fails to live up to the assumption that a king should be a grand printed folio: 'I am a scribbled form, drawn with a pen / Upon a parchment, and against this fire / Do I shrink up.'

Franklin's relation to this tradition was, as we might expect for a man of such prompt efficiency and optimistic energy, less agonised: the book provides for Franklin not a model of tormented selfhood, but a language for talking about his self in terms of improvement, correction, revision, audience, and influence, and his work as a printer (an experience Shakespeare, Donne, and Daniel did not share) enables him to bring some nicely specific bibliographical imagery to his epitaph (the gilding stripped away; the typical title page promise of 'Corrected and Amended').

In fact, Franklin's epitaph is part of a larger tendency within his writing to slide between person and book. We see this happening in the notebook technology Franklin develops in pursuit of what he hubristically calls 'moral Perfection'. Franklin uses the shape of the page to track and correct his vices:

> I made a little Book in which I allotted a Page for each of the Vir-
> tues. I rul'd each Page with red Ink, so as to have seven Columns,
> one for each Day of the Week, marking each Column with a Letter
> for the Day. I cross'd these Columns with thirteen red Lines, mark-
> ing the Beginning of each Line with the first Letter of one of the
> Virtues, on which Line and in its proper Column I might mark by
> a little black Spot every Fault I found upon Examination, to have
> been committed respecting that Virtue upon that Day.

Franklin's list of thirteen virtues includes temperance, silence, order, frugality, industry, cleanliness, and chastity. Against humil-ity he adds, with no apparent sense of irony, 'Imitate Jesus and Socrates.'

Opening his book; marking a column; aiming to live without inky blemish and so without vice: this was Franklin's way of striv-ing 'to live without committing any Fault at anytime'. He worked first in a paper notebook, but then used the ivory leaves of a mem-orandum book to facilitate erasure and rewriting:

> so I should have (I hoped) the encouraging Pleasure of seeing on
> my Pages the Progress I made in Virtue, by clearing successively
> my Lines of their Spots, till in the End by a Number of Courses,
> I should be happy in viewing a clean Book.

Is this noble? Petty? Pragmatic? Perhaps it's all of these: the image of Franklin marking his little notebook table with a small dot when he realises he is unclean is more than a little ridiculous, and we can feel for a moment what D. H. Lawrence felt, writing on the other side of Romanticism, when he recoiled from the notion of a clean book as a good man – or vice versa – as the worst form of Enlightenment moral control. Lawrence couldn't stand Franklin. 'This is Benjamin's barbed wire fence,' Lawrence wrote of Franklin's tables in 1924. 'He made himself a list of virtues, which he trotted inside like a grey nag inside a paddock.'

Just as his note-taking moral technology blends person and book, so Franklin's *Autobiography* is shot through with a printer's language. Reflecting on the fundamental content he feels for his life, Franklin writes that 'I should have no Objection to a Repetition of the same Life from its Beginning, only asking the Advantage Authors have in a second Edition to correct some Faults of the first.' Franklin repeatedly used the printer's term 'erratum', or its plural 'errata', to describe errors he made, and their subsequent correction – finding in his own life the equivalent of the kind of print-shop slips which he made. For 'lie' read 'live'. For 'included' read 'concluded'. Franklin thought a lot about errors. After blundering in an edition of the *Pennsylvania Gazette* in March 1730 – Franklin printed 'After which his Excellency . . . *died* elegantly at Pontack's', instead of *dined* – Franklin (writing under the pseudonym 'J.T.') recalled a series of historic, high-profile typos to provide a kind of genealogy for the compositor's slip:

> in a certain Edition of the Bible, the Printer had, where David says *I am fearfully and wonderfully made*, omitted the Letter (*e*) in the last Word, so that it was, *I am fearfully and wonderfully mad* . . . [A 1631 London Bible printed] *Thou shalt commit Adultery*, instead of *Thou shalt not* . . . and in a whole Impression of Common-Prayer-Books; in the Funeral Service, . . . [at] *We shall all be changed in a moment* . . . the Printer had omitted the (*c*) . . . and it read . . . *We shall all be hanged.*

Franklin took this language and used it to describe himself. His decision as an apprentice to take flight from his brother's print shop was cast as 'one of the first Errata of my life'. His typically shoddy treatment of his future wife, Deborah Read – 'another of the great Errata of my Life' – was later revised by their marriage in 1730: 'Thus I corrected that great *Erratum* as well as I could.'

Here is Franklin, aged seventeen, sailing from New York to Philadelphia in pursuit of work as a printer, not yet knowing (although he probably senses it) the scope of what he was going to achieve. Amid a dramatic storm that tears the sails to pieces and drives the ship towards Long Island,

> a drunken Dutchman, who was a Passenger too, fell over-board; when he was sinking I reach'd thro' the Water to his shock Pate [wild hair] and drew him up so that we got him in again. His Ducking sober'd him a little, and he went to sleep, taking first out of his Pocket a Book which he desir'd I would dry for him. It prov'd to be my old favourite Author Bunyan's Pilgrim's Progress in Dutch, finely printed on good Paper with copper Cuts [engravings], a Dress better than I had ever seen it wear in its own Language.

In his *Autobiography*, books as physical objects have a capacity to draw Franklin's attention away from anything else. What begins here squarely in a tradition of adventurous romance, with a large dose of Franklin's sense of his own heroism, quickly transitions – such are Franklin's priorities – into bibliographical description. It's as if we can hear the poor Dutchman gasping on all fours while Franklin closely examines the binding.

6. PAPER

Nicolas-Louis Robert (1761–1828)

The man with the best claim to revolutionising the paper industry died in something approaching poverty, in a village in northern France, on a hot day in August 1828. You won't know his name. He was sixty-six, and for many years had endured poor health working as a teacher in a primary school he had founded in Vernouillet. The pay was pitiful, but he passed quiet days with his wife and children. He wrote poems for his friends. He also spent – probably, surely – many hours reflecting on the arguments and the missteps: the ways he had been left behind. Nicolas-Louis Robert was 'frail and ingenious', as one historian has it, but also 'broken and discouraged'.

What Robert invented, but spectacularly failed to profit from, was the technology that produced (in the words of its 1799 patent) 'continuous paper': that took paper-making out of the hands of the vatmen, couchers, and layers, and placed it on the rotating belt of a machine. Under the name of Fourdrinier, that machine was soon humming across European and North American factories, making vast quantities of paper, not as sheets but as loops of 'indefinite length', at speeds unimaginable to even the most brilliantly skilful of artisans who had made paper in Europe since the twelfth century, in the Islamic world since the eighth, and in China since the second. Robert's machine presented a crucial new chapter in the (at that point) sixteen-century-long history of paper; it was, in the overheated but not untrue words of paper's towering historian, Dard Hunter, 'destined to revolutionize civilization', and facilitated, among its many other consequences, the rise of the newspaper in the nineteenth and twentieth centuries, and with it, a whole new relationship to information. But

Robert died a long way from acclaim or success or even recognition. Given the significance of his invention, the monument that stands in front of the church in Vernouillet, erected in 1912, seems to mark not memory but eclipse.

A similar kind of injustice – a sense of both unrewarded ingenuity, and a fading from the historical record – defined the closing years of several others associated with the paper-making machine. This was a technology that seemed to disown its origins. Saint-Léger Didot (1767–1829) supported Robert's early experiments but lost his paper mill and his business and died broke; John Gamble was a pivotal figure in exporting the technology to England, where it first flourished, but his effacement from history is such that it's not even clear when, exactly, he died. Even Henry Fourdrinier (1766–1854), with his brother, Sealy (1773–1847), the head of the Fourdrinier firm for whom history at least has some memory, became bankrupt despite the success of the machine with his name, and survived until the age of eighty-eight, 'in humble but cheerful retirement' in a Staffordshire village on handouts raised by a testimonial organised by *The Times*.

In part these bathetic ends to talented lives are a reflection of the Wild-West-like instability of patent law at this time: early inventors struggled to hold on to ideas, and copycat models sprang up. It's also a story of debtors who defaulted on promised payments, draining the inventor until they couldn't go on: like Emperor Alexander I of Russia, who you'd think might have the cash, but who handed over nothing of the ten annual payments of £700 promised to Fourdrinier after the 1814 installation of two machines at Peterhof. But there is also a larger truth about the ways in which a great invention necessarily exceeds, and therefore betrays, the life of any single originator.

Robert turned over this fact – probably, surely – as he took his daily early-evening walks round the sun-dappled square of Vernouillet.

There were writing surfaces before paper: baked clay tablets with wedge-shaped cuneiform marks from *c.*3000 BCE Uruk, in present-day Iraq; papyrus reeds gathered from the banks of the Nile, peeled and layered to produce sheets, combined into scrolls; wax tablets, pairs bound to produce a diptych, or several bound to produce a codex (the Latin for 'block of wood', or 'tree trunk', and meaning later a block split into leaves or tablets for writing); parchment and vellum, made from animal skins, de-greased, de-haired, stretched and scraped, but often with veins and hairs still visible. Chinese writings were found by the Yellow River in a flood in 1899: three thousand pieces in all, from about 1300 BCE, inscribed on tortoise shells and animal bones. The urge to write – to make a mark, to signal presence, to transmit and store information – is registered in this variety of substrates, a variety which suggests both technological innovation and the need to use whatever is to hand.

Paper – which means, in words unlovely but true, 'thin, felted material formed on flat, porous moulds from macerated vegetable fibre' – may have been developed in China in the year 105 CE. *Pass me that sheet of macerated vegetable fibre!* It was almost certainly not an invention that came from nowhere but a modification of what Lothar Müller calls the 'proto-paper' already in use. The inventor may well have been Ts'ai (or Cai) Lun (*c.*50-62–121 CE), a court official in charge of weapons for the Eastern Han dynasty. (Historians like to repeat the fact that he was a eunuch, although it's not clear why this is important.) The process Ts'ai Lun introduced went something like this. The inner bark of the mulberry tree was soaked in water with wood ash and then processed, or mashed up, until the fibres separated. The watery fibres were poured onto a screen – cotton or hemp fabric stretched on a wooden frame – resting in water, and were spread out by hand. The screen was lifted and left to dry with the fibres on it: when dried, a sheet of paper was pulled off. It was a slow process – a paper-maker might produce a few dozen sheets a day – but also, across centuries to come, a process that was remarkably constant.

From Asia, the technology spread to the Arab world, perhaps via a battle in 751 CE on the banks of the Tharaz River near Samarkand, in modern-day Uzbekistan, where Arab soldiers captured Chinese paper-makers and with them secured paper knowledge. The romance of the story suggests a tidy myth serving to scoop up a more gradual process of dispersal across a series of military conflicts, and along the trade route of the Silk Road. But it's certain that paper spread quickly across the Islamic world. It also developed as a technology, as Arab makers, needing to find resources abundant in their own lands, moved away from natural mulberry and began to use man-made linen and hempen rags – so linking paper production to cities, to areas of denser population, and to textile production. Paper mills of unprecedented scale and sophistication appeared in Baghdad in 793–4. Government bureaucrats began to use paper in place of papyrus and parchment and the Stationers' Market (*Suq al-Warraqin*) thronged with shops selling books and paper. The great writing culture of Islam between the seventh and thirteenth centuries, in which dazzlingly skilled calligraphers in Medina and elsewhere produced paper Korans, was fed by this later paper production. Paper mills followed in Damascus (soon famous for its delicate, light 'bird paper' – *waraq al-tayr*), Tripoli, Sicily, and through Tunisia and Egypt. In the tenth century, floating ship-mills, powered by the current, moored on the Tigris above Baghdad. By the eleventh century, mills were producing paper in Fez: the delayed take-up perhaps due to the sustained dominance of parchment in a herding society.

When knowledge of paper-making arrived in Spain in about the eleventh century via North Africa, paper was a medium, and paper-making a set of skills, definitively shaped by earlier Arab and, before it, Chinese, cultures. Perhaps because of this belatedness, European attitudes to paper-making were initially characterised by an arrogance built on deep foundations of ignorance. Europeans initially distrusted paper as a medium introduced by Jews and Arabs: in his *Against the Inveterate Obduracy of the Jews*,

Peter the Venerable, Abbot of Cluny (*c.*1092–1156) condemned rag paper – 'made from the scrapings of old cloths or perhaps even some more vile material' – through an explicit association with Judaism. By the time Europeans had understood paper's revolutionary potential, they set about systematically forgetting its Arabic, Chinese past, appropriating paper as their own, and refashioning its history into a story of European ingenuity. This was in part because of a booming early modern European paper-making industry that began to export to North Africa and West Asia: by the eighteenth century, when Europeans started to write paper's history, paper-making had diminished massively across the Islamic world. For hundreds of years, Europeans had no sense that paper-making began in China ten centuries – *ten centuries!* – before it reached Spain. When, in the seventeenth century, Europeans witnessed paper-making in Japan and China, they assumed the origin of this Asian craft was Europe; Diderot and d'Alembert's *Encyclopédie* (1751–66), that central text of the French Enlightenment that provided '*a Systematic Dictionary of the Sciences, Arts, and Crafts*', knew nothing of an Arabic past. If Europeans had really been interested in origins, they would have understood how the Chinese used a wide variety of grass and bark fibres, and so would surely have arrived at the idea of wood pulp as an alternative source to rags less belatedly than the 1840s.

By the thirteenth century, paper mills were booming in northern Italy: the mountainous town of Fabriano was the site of numerous paper-making innovations that drew on the town's rich tradition of weaving and of metalwork (a blacksmith is *il fabbro*). Water-powered rag stampers hammered the macerated rags with a new efficiency; animal glue (boiled-down hooves of deer and sheep: the stench was overwhelming) was used as 'sizing' – a substance to stop ink from seeping through the paper and so to enable writing; and stiffer moulds were made from fine wire rather than bamboo or reeds. Medieval Fabriano was also the site of the invention of the watermark: a piece of wire attached to the mould producing the makers' initials, or an image of a crown or a pot or a fool's cap, symbols that linger today in the language of paper size. Around this time Europeans began to wear more linen than wool: supplies for rag paper increased, therefore, and paper mills were established in Nuremberg (1390), Ravensburg (1393), and Strasbourg (1445). In England – which at this point was late to just about every party – William Caxton, who, as we've seen, learnt to print in Cologne, had to import paper from the Lowlands because England had no paper-maker until John Tate established the Sele Mill in Hertfordshire in the 1490s. The earliest extant paper from Tate's mill survives in the form of a single-sheet papal Bull from 1494. (We saw Wynkyn de Worde using Tate's paper in Chapter 1, with pages showing Tate's elegant eight-pointed star watermark.) Throughout much of the sixteenth and seventeenth century, British mills produced only a small amount of white paper, and mostly made coarse, brown papers for wrapping; it took the arrival of skilled Huguenot paper-makers, fleeing France after the revocation of the Edict of Nantes (1685), to bring a surge of manufacturing skill capable of producing fine white paper.

Thus the history of paper is a sprawling, complicated story ranging across thousands of miles and thousands of years – but it is also a story of relative constancy, of the possibility of recognition across time. By the eighth century there were paper mills operating in Japan producing paper with no yellowing acid content: a sheet looks the same today as 1,200 years ago. The paper used by Gutenberg in the first printed Bible (around 1450), with its brilliantly clear bunch-of-grapes watermark, is of a time-defying quality unsurpassed by modern industrial processes. And even Ts'ai Lun, in the second century, spreading out watery mulberry pulp across a screen with his hands as court officials looked on, would – could he see 1,300 years ahead – have deduced much of what was going on in Jost Amman's woodcut from 1568. It's an image of paper-making in action, included in a German book of trades, and the oldest print of paper-making anywhere in the world.

Paper-making, from Hans Sachs, Eygentliche
Beschreibung aller Stände auff Erden *(1568).*

What are we looking at? We're inside a paper mill, somewhere
in sixteenth-century Germany, and although the scene is frozen,
and we can't hear the noise or smell the stench, there's a sense of
busy motion. We're watching the vatman, with implausibly large
forearms – he has been doing this for years, moving from mill
to mill – dip a metal mesh held within a frame into a tub, which
may be a huge repurposed wine cask, filled with water and pulp
(or 'stuff') made from mashed-up linen. If he's lucky, the water is
warm; otherwise, since he'll be doing this all day, his hands will
be freezing. A barefoot boy turns on his heels, carrying not a giant
slice of cake but a stack of sheets of paper. At the rear we can see
a screw-press, used for squeezing the paper dry, and on the left
a set of hammers beating the rags to release the cellulose fibres.

(Around the 1680s, these hammers would be replaced by the 'Hollander beater' which used metal blades to slice and cut the rags.) Through the two windows we glimpse two large waterwheels.

Amman's woodcut is, it seems to me, rather loving: there is something about the tilt of the vatman's head that suggests affection and care on the part of both worker and engraver. But it's not an exhaustive depiction: Amman is perhaps guarding paper-making's secrets, even as he celebrates the trade. If this woodcut scene could somehow spool on, the figures springing to life, we'd see the vatman lift the frame out, holding it horizontally, shaking the mould right to left, and forward and back – four or five seconds in all, a care in his movements, even as they are swift – as the water drains to leave a thin layer of evenly woven fibres, now knitted together. (Decades of working at the vat left some craftsmen suddenly unable to perform this 'shake' or 'stroke', afflicted by a kind of paralysis from hundreds of thousands of repetitions amid the damp and the gloom.) The scene widens to show the vatman's sidekick, a coucher, who inverts the mould and tips a sheet of paper onto a damp woollen blanket or 'felt', adding another damp felt, then another sheet of paper, and repeating to build up a pile or 'post'. The coucher hands the mould back to the vatman, who has meanwhile made another sheet using a near-identical mould and the same 'deckle' (the upper part of the mould-frame). Later, a third worker, the layer, removes the sheets of damp paper from between the felts, before the sheets are dried and the felts returned to the coucher for reuse. Then follows 'sizing' (applying that protective, anti-absorbent compound made from boiled-down hooves and other delights) and 'finishing' (rubbing with a smooth stone). In early modern Europe, this process of dipping, removing, and tipping (to use non-technical terms) took about twenty seconds. An efficient partnership of vatman and coucher might produce four reams (or 2,000 sheets) of paper a day. The word reveals paper-making's migratory origins: 'ream' – originally meaning 20 quires, or 480 sheets, and today meaning 500 sheets – comes from the Arabic *rizma*, 'bale' or 'bundle', the word entering Spain when paper-making reached Arabic-speaking Cordoba, and then other cities, in the eleventh and twelfth centuries, becoming Spanish *resma* and then, eventually, English 'ream'.

Why did paper spread so successfully? It had big advantages over its rival media. It was cheaper than parchment: when Gutenberg printed his thirty-five parchment copies of the Bible, the 641 leaves meant about 300 sheep for every book. Figured as a sheep-to-book ratio, these numbers don't look good, particularly for the sheep. His 200 paper copies, by contrast, had their origins in piles of unwanted rags. The very lowliness of this supply was a source of both wonder and embarrassment for paper-users. 'And may not dirty Socks, from off the feet,' wrote poet and Thames waterman John Taylor in *The Praise of Hemp-Seed* (1620), 'From thence be turnd to a *Crowne-paper* sheet?' And while papyrus leaves came from the Nile Valley, paper could find a source wherever there were people and clothes: faced with an infinitely nimble rival, papyrus production in Egypt ground to a halt in the eleventh century.

We can witness paper's capacity to insinuate itself into almost all social interactions – and to make itself essential – in the extraordinary documents discovered in the late nineteenth century in a small storeroom in the Ben Ezra Synagogue of ancient Fustat, Cairo. Since the word of God was sacred, Jews believed that written texts referencing God could not be thrown away; and sometimes, as here, this attitude developed into a broader aversion to discarding any Hebrew text. The 'Geniza' (from the Hebrew for 'hidden') is the room in a synagogue in which these papers are preserved: not necessarily learned or high-status texts, but documents of everyday life. In the Ben Ezra Synagogue, this means 300,000 fragments, mostly on paper, spanning the ninth to the nineteenth centuries, but particularly rich for the tenth to the thirteenth. There are fragments of wills, marriage contracts, writs of divorce, prayers, shop inventories, financial receipts, love letters, poems, astrological predictions, tax records – all written in Hebrew letters in languages including Aramaic, Greek, Hebrew,

Judeo-Arabic, Ladino (or Judeo-Spanish), Latin, Persian, and Yiddish. Collectively these documents constitute a chaotic, streaming history of the life of Jews in medieval Cairo: 'Almost every conceivable human relationship is represented,' writes historian Shelomo Dov Goitein, 'and they often read like local news told by a gifted reporter.' The Cairo Geniza also shows the crucial role of paper in forging and sustaining this world. Paper is embedded in every social interaction: it is the glue for a local community. But paper here is also expansively international: manuscript fragments reveal Egyptian paper being exported to Tunisia, Yemen, and India, and imports coming into Cairo from Spain, Damascus, and, in the fourteenth century, from Italy and France.

The capacity to both spread and preserve is part of paper's magic. We see this in the way paper quickly flourished as the medium of modern government, where it both dispensed a ruler's words throughout kingdoms, and also – and in delicate tension – centralised state authority. It scattered, and it gathered. This is what happens with the Abbasid Empire in the eighth century, and then across Europe from the thirteenth, most famously under King Philip II who, ruling Spain between 1556 and 1598, disdained travel and forged a kingship dependent on paper's capacity to move, flow, convey, connect, archive, command, and represent. In the words of Lothar Müller, paper is 'a dynamically energized medium for storage and circulation'. Philip was the *rey papelero*, the paper king: his written commands, conveyed on paper, marked his presence even when he wasn't there.

Nicolas-Louis Robert was a bright child, born in Paris in 1761 to an upper-middle-class family. He was nicknamed 'the philosopher' at school, although it's hard to know, at this historical distance, quite the balance of mockery, affection, and respect this moniker may have implied. His years after school had a meandering quality: Robert tried and failed to join the army (he was too slight), and endured some unhappy times toiling as a clerk, increasingly guilty that he was a profitless drain on his mother and father. But then Robert successfully enrolled in the regiment of the Grenoble Artillery in April 1780, and fifteen months later was sent with the Metz Artillery to Santo Domingo in what we now call the Dominican Republic, where he worked as a gun-layer – aiming the artillery – and acquired a reputation for calm and bravery during battle with the English in the American War of Independence. So far, none of this is very papery, but after the army, Robert obtained work as a proofreader for the celebrated printer and publisher Pierre-François Didot the younger (1731–93). His master soon noted Robert's capacities, and recommended him to his son, Saint-Léger Didot, who was running the family paper mill at Essonnes; the production of paper for *assignats*, or banknotes, was a dominant part of the business. Robert was put in charge of accounts. He flourished; married; had a daughter. These were happy years, and Robert's thus far only latent talent for invention began to find expression. As he walked the floor of the paper mill, Robert's imagination crunched down on a problem like the hammers stamping macerated rags. The problem he saw was the 300 workmen. In Robert's eyes, they constituted a labour force too aware of its desirable skills, who brought acrimony and argument and clogged up what might somehow – reimagined – be a leaner process of production. Robert started to envision a better version of the Essonnes paper mill without these irksome bodies. An environment of machines – one can almost hear the sighs-to-come of William Morris and Thomas Cobden-Sanderson who attempted to reverse an industrialised process of book-making (Chapter 9). This is an important point to stress: the seeds of the machine production of paper lay not in any ideal of democratising paper consumption and encouraging literacy or in any other kind of cultural enrichment; working in the Revolutionary context immediately after 1789, Robert's machine-vision had its origins in a kind of business misanthropy, in a desire to eliminate people.

If we look today at the magnificent illustrations that accompany Diderot and d'Alembert's account of pre-mechanisation paper mills in their 1751–66 *Encyclopédie* (see plate section), what strikes us first is the vision of sparsely peopled cleanliness and order. These workspaces are full of a quiet and entirely unrepresentative calm: there is almost no one around, and the workers that are present are silently at one with the process of production. At most, a gentle whistling. The figures are dwarfed by huge close-ups of the tools of paper-making: while the *Encyclopédie*'s images generate a sense of the documentary, encouraged by the careful labelling of parts and a visual rhetoric of exactness, the images are allegories of technological progress. It's easy to see how they might have encouraged Robert's frustrations with messy humans.

In a 1798 letter to the Minister of the Interior in pursuit of a patent, Robert explained his paper ambitions in these terms:

> It has been my dream to simplify the operation of making paper by forming it with infinitely less expense, and, above all, in making sheets of extraordinary length without the help of any worker, using only mechanical means. Through diligent work, by experience, and with considerable expense, I have been successful and a machine has been made that fulfils my expectancy. The machine makes for economy of time and expense and extraordinary paper, being 12 to 15 metres in length, if one wishes.

Robert's machine worked by forming paper on a continuous screen made of a fine wire mesh that circulated on rollers, and onto which the pulp was poured. Excess water drained through the wire meshes. Robert himself explained the process like this:

> At the end of the cloth wire extending on the vat there is a fly-wheel or cylinder, fitted with little buckets which plunge into the paper stock, or liquid pulp. This cylinder, by its rapid movement, raises the material and throws it into a shallow reservoir in the interior of the head, and from there the stock is poured, without

interruption, onto the endless wire cloth. As the material settles on the cloth it receives a side-to-side movement, causing the fibres to felt together. The water drains off the wire and back into the vat. A crank turns the machine and causes the wire cloth to advance, the sheet of newly formed paper finally running under a felt-covered roller. When the paper leaves the first felt roller it is no longer saturated with water, but can be removed from the machine, just as a sheet of handmade paper is taken from the felting after pressing in a press.

The relationship between the actions performed for centuries by workers in paper mills and Robert's machine is both intimate and alienated: the machine is a homage to hand-made work, sustaining many of its characteristics, while seeking simultaneously to eliminate that tradition. While the vatman or vatwoman dipped the metal mesh frame into the tub of stuff (hence, after years of this, a stooped back and thick, red arms), Robert's machine has 'little buckets' which plunge and then pour on the 'endless wire cloth'. And where the vatman or vatwoman, with a movement so often repeated that it became instinctual, shakes the frame forward-to-back and then left-to-right to make the fibres clasp together, Robert's machine performed a side-to-side shake. In fact, the four-way shake of handmade paper means the fibres entwine more tightly: machine paper, with its simpler side-to-side shake, throws fibres in one direction, creating a grain, and thus a paper more susceptible to tearing in one direction than the other. (UK books typically have a short (horizontal) grain whereas US books have a long (vertical) grain, which makes them feel different and helps the page to stay open better.)

The machine constituted a radical change, and the nature of the transformation is strikingly total. In 1800, all paper was made by hand. One hundred years later, over 99 per cent of paper was made on a machine. According to bibliographer Philip Gaskell, across this same period, output increased by about a hundredfold – factories ran their machines day and night, twenty-three hours a day – and prices dropped by a factor of ten. Handmade paper was produced in sheets the size of the mould, but Robert's machine entirely reworked the space of paper: it could produce a vast length, as wide as the machine, which could then be cut according to need. A skilled double act of vatman and coucher, working fairly heroically, might produce 2,000 sheets (or four reams) a day. On versions of Robert's machine – the operating of which 'can be done by children', Robert wrote with pride – paper was manufactured at between 10 and 50 metres per minute. (And machines today produce paper at about 70 miles per hour – or about 1,800 metres per minute.) This enabled a vastly expanded sense of format – which meant wallpaper and huge posters and, more generally, in this shift from sheet to ribbon, different ways of thinking about paper.

The new idea of the 'endlessness' of paper was intoxicating and a sense of the machine's magical transformative potential took hold: 'A person might throw in his shirt at one end,' noted a writer in *Burton's Gentleman's Magazine and American Monthly Review* in 1840, 'and see it come out *Robinson Crusoe* at the other.' Not quite, but the range of uses of paper increased hugely. Paper had always been used for much more than books: wrapping has been, for much of paper's history, its primary function, and old pieces of paper had always been used as toilet paper – what John Dryden referred to as 'Reliques of the Bum'. (The seventeenth-century essayist and courtier William Cornwallis kept what he called 'pamphlets and lying-stories and two-penny poets' in his privy, and not for reading.) But machine production increased this range. Modern commercially available toilet paper was introduced, in America, by Joseph Gayetty in 1857: 'Gayetty's medicated paper for the water-closet' sold as flat sheets of pure Manila hemp paper, $1 for a thousand, watermarked 'JC Gayetty NY'. Paper hats, kites, lanterns, fans, money, newspapers, blank forms, umbrellas, clothing: a newly papery world was imaginable, thanks to Robert.

One second-order consequence of this increased productivity was the rise of new kinds of literary writing and publications.

Lothar Müller suggests that Robert's machine led to the emergence of cheap periodicals that could not have developed in the world of handmade paper. The Society for the Diffusion of Useful Knowledge launched the *Penny Magazine* in 1820 and sales figures were astonishing: something like 200,000 each week. Publications like the *London Magazine* and *Blackwood's* led to the rise of the essay and short-form prose as newly dominant literary forms, eclipsing the (to twenty-first-century eyes) remarkable popularity of books of poetry in early nineteenth-century England.

But even as Robert's technology – revised and improved by others, certainly, but in its inception the work of one man – began to take over the paper-making world, his machine was slipping from his grasp. Robert's temperament was ill-suited to a moment of focused capitalisation. He became over-zealous. He quarrelled with Pierre-François Didot. He appeared in court when arguments with his former patron could not easily or flexibly be settled. Robert decided to sell the patent for as much as he could manage, but the 25,000 francs paid by Didot seems cheap in retrospect – and in any case, the money never made its way to Robert. John Gamble, Saint-Léger Didot's brother-in-law, was in Paris to negotiate the release of English prisoners captured during the French Revolutionary Wars. Understanding immediately from Didot the massive potential of the technology, he obtained a patent in London in 1801 and Robert's machine – which was already ceasing to be Robert's machine – was soon carried across the Channel, despite war continuing to rage between England and France. It landed in a London that, rapidly industrialising, was the perfect context for the reception and development of the machine. If looms had been mechanised on textile factories, then paper machines in mills seemed something like an inevitable development. In London, Gamble persuaded Henry and Sealy Fourdrinier, owners of a wholesale stationery firm, to invest in the machine: they poured in £60,000 (about £2.7 million today), and the paper machine to this day carries their name, although they never received the profit they anticipated. Engineer Bryan

Donkin refined the technology, widening the roll, and improving the side-to-side shaking – that ghostly presence of the vatman – to produce a device that is, essentially, the machine on which almost all modern paper is made.

These advances in machine paper production were taking place around the time of other technological innovations. In 1804 German Friedrich Koenig moved to London and developed a steam-powered printing press that could print 1,100 pages an hour and was quickly adopted for printing *The Times*. New Yorker Richard M. Hoe designed a rotary cylinder press which spat out millions of pages a day. The discovery of chlorine in 1774 by a German chemist working in Sweden, adopted by American Joseph Gilpin, meant coloured rags could be bleached, increasing supply. And not quite here yet, but around the corner in about 1840, was the discovery – after a long, digressive series of experiments with paper made from wasps' nests, moss, vines, hemp, bark, straw, cabbage stalks, thistles, turf, pine-cones, potatoes (both skins and insides), walnuts, and tulips – of large-scale wood-based paper sources as an alternative to linen, supplies of which were under strain given the vastly increased paper production rates.

In 1806, the first paper machines based on Robert's technology were operating in England, priced at between £715 and £1,040, and then in France in 1811 – by which time Robert was fifty, and bitter to the point of despair – Russia in 1814–15, America in 1817, and Germany in 1818.

We can see something of this changing paper landscape by looking at two paintings whose central subject is paper: in the world, working its magic. First is handmade paper, the paper of sheets, of pages fluttering, covering, bedecking a seventeenth-century Flemish village.

Peter Brueghel the Younger's 'The Village Lawyer' (c.1620).

In Peter Brueghel the Younger's *Village Lawyer* (c.1620), a lawyer sits behind his desk in his cap, his left hand trying to stem the quantities of paper spooling out from his bag like some involuntary magic trick. A clerk sits by the door, head down. The doorway itself is filled by a figure whose sidling presence suggests something isn't quite right. And a troop of villagers queue nervously, hats off, counting out eggs as payment to secure the lawyer's aid, or to pay an overdue bill. Paper here is the medium of the handwritten: apart from the printed almanac on the wall, this is a manuscript culture. This is also a hierarchical world, a world where fearful villagers stoop as they approach their betters. Paper seems not liberating, not democratising (much as we may like to cling to those associations): paper here is an instrument of class and power, a way of keeping people in their place. And paper is everywhere: Brueghel's scene is one of overflowing, of superabundance. In leather bags that function like filing cabinet drawers; pinned to the windows (we can only see the back); tacked to the wall, in the form of that almanac; slotted in a letter-rack; and piled high in string-tied bundles. Paper has a horizontal spread – there are sheets across the floor, torn into fragments by unaware feet – and it has a vertical presence, too, rising up from the ground, to the desks, to float above heads. Is this an image of order, or disorder? Of rule by law, or law's fragile contingency? Of a filing system, or its chaotic absence? It's hard to tell because paper, in Brueghel's painting, seems at once essential (the village's memory, the medium that ties lives together), and also excessive (there is simply too much). And while identifying the tone of the painting is tricky – is the lawyer, with his little hour-glass, satirised? – I think we can confidently feel Brueghel's fascination. Is love for paper too strong? Maybe: but we can hear (almost) his guffawing delight at the papery stuff-ness of seventeenth-century life. The painting struck a chord with contemporary viewers, capturing something that was clearly recognised: there are nineteen signed original versions of this work, and dozens of imitations and copies.

Forward, now, a little more than 200 years, to a time when Robert's machine had revolutionised paper, and production levels (according to Dard Hunter) had soared from 55 tons a year in 1805 to about 25,000 tons in 1835. John Orlando Parry's *A London Street Scene* (1835) captures this new world (see plate section).

We are outside in the city street, in London, and after Brueghel's boxed-in paper world, we can almost smell the air and feel the breeze. The sound now is of approaching voices and – just out of view – the clatter of coaches. People walk past, in and out of the picture, a mix of ranks and fortunes. In this scene, paper is not held in hands or placed on desks. Paper is the city: an environment like a cloud or the smell of roasting chestnuts. It's a bit like a stage, with the posters as a kind of dropped curtain, although the poster-bedecked street is not the background to the eleven people plus dog (a dog whose calm stare suggests he has seen it all before), but the focus itself. Paper is the life force of the painting: people are oddly displaced, positioned as readers or consumers of papery news, but secondary, and not themselves the driving force of events. In 1836, the year after Parry's painting, Charles

Dickens described London as 'a circus of poster and trade bill, a receptacle for the writings of Pears and Warren's until we can barely see ourselves underneath. Read this! Read that!'

Paper here isn't the rolled-up letters or bills of Brueghel's village, but posters – some of them vast – that advertise the city to itself. Here is what an urban world can offer you.

Musical Fun. Robert Macaire at the Adelphi. The Comet coach to Liverpool, departing every morning at 9. The Last Days of Pompeii. Parry was better known for his dramatic and musical performances than his paintings – he wrote popular ballads with titles such as *Wanted, a Governess* (1840) and *Anticipations of Switzerland* (1842) – and one of his own is advertised in the painting's centre: a farce titled *THE SHAM PRINCE*, with the advice 'COME VERY EARLY'. There is a lot of news, here: the walls are thick with the contemporary. Posters cover up other posters, meaning paper is both surface and substrate, and the consequence of this messy layering is a kind of interpretative challenge: how should we read this huge text? What has reading become in this culture of paper unleashed, in part, by Robert's machine, with expanded formats and text looming over us from on high? There is too much, and one of the paradoxical effects of too much is that there is not enough. *ON FRIDAY NEXT THERE WILL*—what? *THE PRINCIPLE CHARACTERS WILL BE PER*—what? *READ!!! GRE* . . . – what should we read? This is information displacing information.

The word 'palimpsest' comes from the Greek *palimpsestos*, meaning 'scraped again', and applies most literally to parchment, where to write meant scraping away what was already written on the dried animal skin and replacing it with new text, leaving those prior layers of writing just visible. Parry gives us an urban, machine-papered version of the palimpsest: not goat- or calf-skin, but city walls covered and re-covered, where the literal subtext is still fleetingly visible. The city has become a kind of giant, exploded book, full of text coming at us from all angles; writing is public; advertising is everywhere; entertainment is for sale; and paper announces today's events, pasted over the recent past. We feel the now-ness of the scene as, like the chimney sweep in the centre, we watch as the latest news is unfurled: a production of *Otello*, it seems, but we'll have to wait to read the details until the man has finished pasting and – in the few seconds that remain for ever just beyond the painting – steps back.

The near-effacement of Robert from the historical record, unjust as it may seem, is at least in one way fitting. Most scholars who have studied the history of the book as a physical form have had a curious blind spot about paper. Attention and description has been lavished on bindings, on typography, on marks of ownership and description, and on other material traits, but paper itself has been a kind of invisible presence: a necessary but also unseen component. Even the earliest founders of bibliography, moustachioed men like A. W. Pollard and W. W. Greg, whose work was in general characterised by a proudly exhaustive rigour, considered paper itself of little interest: 'knowledge of the processes by which paper is manufactured,' wrote Ronald McKerrow in 1927, 'and of the substances of which it is composed has never . . . been regarded as necessary to the bibliographer.' To these bibliographers, paper was a kind of blank: it was, we might say, intrinsically self-effacing, its bookish purpose to serve as a substrate or support for something else, like a discreet Edwardian butler. A 'mute vehicle', as paper historian John Bidwell put it, that carries forward meaning but is itself not meaningful. This very blankness has given paper some metaphorical power. In his *Essay Concerning Human Understanding* (1689), John Locke described the mind as 'white paper devoid of all characters, without any *Ideas*': assuming the blankness, the content-empty nature of white paper, was a way of figuring the *tabula rasa* of the child which is then filled with content as a result of '*Experience*', like writing across a page.

But despite the influence of Locke's metaphor, there is no such thing as a blank page – not only because claims of blankness miss the watermarks or the fibres or the chain-lines or the imperfections: presences which mean that writing is always an interruption of something already there, a disturbance in an existing order; it is never the beginning. But also because to insist on blankness is to erase the labour, and the history, etched into paper, a history of centuries of use, development, and refinement, in China, the Middle East, North Africa, Europe, and beyond. And as the poet and environmental activist Mandy Haggith reminds us, conceiving of paper as blankness means also forgetting the resources and the environmental costs on which paper depends: 'We need to unlearn our perception of a blank page as clean, safe and natural and see it for what it really is: chemically bleached tree-mash.' We need also to remember the ingenuity and work that lies behind, or within, or across, each page. As the print historian Jonathan Senchyne puts it, 'Every sheet of paper is an archive of human labor.' The story of Nicolas-Louis Robert – which is the story of someone being forgotten, of a presence fading to something like a watermark that can be glimpsed only with care, and in the right light – might serve as an enjoinder to look at, rather than through, paper.

7. EXTRA-ILLUSTRATION

Charlotte (1782–1852) and
Alexander (1753–1820) Sutherland

a somewhat intricate labyrinth

Preface to *Catalogue of the Sutherland Collection in two volumes*

(1837)

The subject of this chapter is a form of radical book modification that goes by the name of 'extra-illustration', or sometimes
'Grangerisation'. In its purest form, this meant the collection and
insertion of prints and other visual items, most commonly portraits, into a printed book – a process of augmenting performed
by a reader, not the original publisher, printer, or author. The
book was understood as a potential container for other things.
A committed Grangeriser – I'll come back to the sense of wilful
transgression that that phrase suggests – would typically acquire
a printed volume of history, disbind the book – cutting open the
binding to open up the pages – and would collect, often over
years and decades, portraits of the individuals discussed in the
text. These portraits would be inlaid onto blank sheets of thick
paper – inlaying, or 'welding', involved cutting a window in a
sheet and laying the print flat into this space – and these often
wide-margined sheets would be inserted into the book which,
once completed (although in fact extra-illustration had no end: it
was merely halted, or frozen) would be rebound with a new title
page. A page from an extra-illustrated volume might look something like this, below, where James Granger's *Biographical History of
England* (1769) has been augmented with images of the scandalous

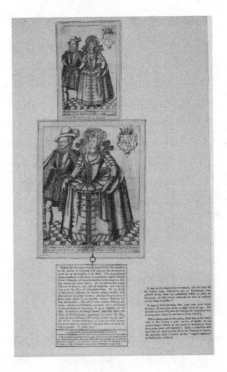

An extra-illustrated page from James Granger's
Biographical History of England *(1769)*.

Robert Carr and Lady Frances Howard – of whom more very soon.

Extra-illustration thus enacted at least two important transformations on the book. First, books got much, much bigger in ways that the original author, publisher, and printer did not anticipate. A single volume might be transformed by a reader-collector, via these sustained augmentations, into dozens and dozens of volumes. Richard Bull took four quarto volumes of Granger's *Biographical History of England* and, as a result of adding thousands of portraits and other prints, ended up with thirty-six large folio volumes, compiled over five years (1769–74) – hence the term 'Grangerisation'. The leaders in this strange field, and the actors in this chapter's drama, were Charlotte and Alexander Sutherland: a married couple who devoted much of their life to extra-illustration. The star of the pair was Charlotte – despite what commentators said, and despite her many self-effacing assertions – who continued and expanded the project after Alexander's death with a dedication one might normally expect from a religious cause. We don't have a portrait of Charlotte, but there is an anonymous watercolour in the Ashmolean Museum of Alexander, aged about fifty: his face rather strained, hardly an expression of joy, and his left hand curling the page of a large book, as if the tiresome job of being painted is distracting him from the real business of making progress through the pages.

The Sutherlands, as we will see, were bibliographical maximalists. This is the story of the book blown up, the book extrapolated into vastness – the conversion of something singular that might rest in our hands, into row upon row of publicly displayed, elegantly shelved expansions. And there's a second transformation: extra-illustration meant that a printed book which had been one of hundreds or thousands of identical copies in an edition became, as a result of these alterations, a bespoke, singular document of taste. In the bibliographer's language, it was now an 'association object': a book, or book-like object, linked to a particular person. And so if printing offered the prospect of many copies of the same text, of duplication and dissemination, then extra-illustration converted these identical copies into unique objects, turning print – against its own instincts – into a source for individual acts of curation.

Viewed in the long 500-year history of the printed book, extra-illustration was a way of remaking the book that returned to sixteenth- and seventeenth-century ideas of the book as incomplete and in flux, an object, like the cut-and-paste Gospels of Mary and Anna Collett, or the unbound sheets bought by readers from bookseller stalls in St Paul's Churchyard, to be marked, revised, augmented, and even physically dismantled. But extra-illustration also looked forward, too, to a twentieth- and twenty-first-century culture of the artist's book in which author-artists like Ed Ruscha,

Sol LeWitt or Dieter Roth produced self-conscious book-objects that challenged assumptions of the wholeness, linearity, and stability of the book – of which, more later.

The clergyman and print collector James Granger (1723–76) had little sense of the storm he was about to unleash from his vicarage in Dorset when he published his *Biographical History of England*. That book was an attempt to organise the past into a series of biographies, arranged into twelve classes, from first ('Kings, Queens, Princes, Princesses, &c.') to twelfth ('Persons of both Sexes, chiefly of the lowest Order of the People, remarkable from only one Circumstance in their Lives; namely, such as lived to a great Age, deformed Persons, Convicts, &c.'). Everyone had their place. 'Archbishops and Bishops' were class 4; 'Physicians, Poets, and other ingenious Professions' were class 9; 'Ladies, and others, of the Female Sex' were class 11.

Each named individual was described with a brief biography and, crucially, for what was to follow, a list of the known prints of that subject. Class 1 begins with Egbert, 'king of the West Saxons, first monarch of all England', and a note of 'a set of heads' by the antiquarian and engraver George Vertue; then comes King Alfred, his life briefly described alongside a list of five prints. By the time we get to Queen Elizabeth I or King James I, the number of prints has expanded to dozens and dozens. If monarchy isn't your thing, you can drop down to class 12 for 'the lowest Order of the People' who nonetheless achieved some kind of fame – like William Sommers, King Henry VIII's jester (one print), or Elynor Rummin, an ale seller from Leatherhead in Surrey, granted renown in a long and raucous poem by John Skelton on heavy drinking in the countryside, printed in 1550 with 'a wooden print' (a woodcut, rather than an engraving) of this 'old, ill-favoured woman, holding a black pot in her hand'.

Granger's book, then, was a catalogue of prints (without the prints themselves) of the historical figures from which history, as Granger saw it, should be composed: a map for finding the faces of the past. He was writing at a time when it seemed right to link facial features to character, and portraits to the formation of history. 'No invention has better answered the end of perpetuating the memory of illustrious men,' wrote Granger in his preface, 'than the modern art of engraving.' Writing exuberantly from 'the obscurity of the country,' Granger declared he would rather have a print than an Egyptian mummy, 'though I had a pyramid for its repository'. His book catalysed a fashion which became a craze and then a mania for Grangerising books, peaking between about 1770 and 1830 – often following Granger's prescriptions for portrait collection, but sometimes also including the addition of topographical scenes, cuttings from newspapers, and later, manuscript signatures and letters. County histories were a common kind of Grangerised text – their baggy structure and granular detail meant they were easy texts to augment – like the magnificently expanded *History and antiquities of the county of Somerset*, published in Bath in 1791 and now held at the Society of Antiquaries in London, and originally written by John Collinson, but expanded from three volumes to twelve through the insertion of maps, prints, and watercolours of the built and rural landscape.

It's probably fair at this point to include a portrait of Granger himself to grant him the perpetuity he associated with the medium, although we should note of course that attitudes to hair have shifted considerably since the 1770s.

Alexander Sutherland was born in St Petersburg, Russia, in 1753, the son of a Scotsman who built ships for the Russian fleet and who established a company of merchants trading with Britain, dealing in hemp, tallow, flax, wool, and sugar, among other commodities. The family for some time enjoyed great success: Alexander's eldest brother, Richard, became Court Banker to Catherine the Great, and when in the 1770s Alexander moved to London, the goods continued to flow smoothly back and forth. But things

James Granger, in a print of an engraving by Samuel Freeman (1803).

began to slide: Richard died under suspicious circumstances in Russia in 1792 and was found to have embezzled 2 million rubles, and back in London, his son's hedonistic lifestyle ended up bankrupting the Russian Sutherlands. A furious Alexander, writing with pride that he governed his own 'income with strict and great economy', refused to help his nephew with loans.

Alexander was careful to the point of pedantry – 'a most precise accountant', one family member recalled, and a man 'of great method & frugality' – and found it very hard to deal with people who were not. He began collecting prints and extra-illustrating in the mid-1790s, in his forties, and it's probably right to think of extra-illustration as a kind of retreat – perhaps a consolation – in which he could act with a calm and exactness impossible in his family business. When he was elected a Fellow of the Society of Antiquaries in 1809, he had transitioned from Russian merchant to (the Minute Book records) 'a Gentleman very conversant in the History and Antiquities of this Kingdom'.

In Charlotte, Alexander found a partner suited to this more temperate climate. Born in 1782, she was the eldest of twelve children of the Revd William Hussey and his wife Charlotte Twopeny of Sandhurst, Kent. We know nothing about her childhood or education, but in 1812, aged thirty, she married Alexander, a man nearly twice her age whose first wife Frances Beckwith had died three years before. Some sense of the marriage emerges from a letter written by Charlotte's brother William on 27 August 1852. William, who 'was continually . . . with both husband & wife during the concluding months' of Alexander's life, described a marriage of harmony. In his will Alexander left 'his whole estate', including the print and book collection, to Charlotte, asking that she continue to build and then complete the work.

Alexander prescribed that the collection 'should not be separated', but beyond this instruction Charlotte was given 'free will' to collect and expand the volumes in whatever way she thought best, 'fettered by no other condition'. That's why Charlotte's framing of her work as dutiful memorial to a deceased husband is only half the story: she also built the collection according to her own emerging interests as a single female collector, spending as much as her husband – £10,000 (£800,000 today) – on prints and books. The collection now resides in Oxford's Ashmolean Museum and Bodleian Library and runs to 216 volumes. The fact that Alexander and Charlotte had no children meant they enjoyed, William wrote, an 'independence', in terms of money and time, which enabled their extra-illustrating ambitions.

One darkening asterisk to this brief account. William wrote his letter in angry response to a bitter little article of 'imputations & insinuations' published by the *Quarterly Review* in June 1852, in which the print collector Richard Ford (1796–1858), writing anonymously, set out to shred Charlotte's reputation. Ford described an acrimonious marriage and a wife who responded to her husband's extra-illustrating with 'infinite . . . dissatisfaction'.

Alexander's final words were, Ford alleges, a threat to 'haunt' Charlotte if she failed to sustain the collection, and the project of Grangerising becomes not the stuff of happy domestic union, but a burden to be endured – a Sisyphusian toil. Charlotte was a figure 'before whom printsellers recoiled'.

Everything we know of Charlotte's deep investment in the collection suggests this isn't true: it's probably the case that Ford found it difficult to imagine a different kind of collector to the sort that he himself represented with such orthodoxy (male, born in Chelsea to an upper-class family, educated at Winchester and Oxford, then years of leisured travel and collecting in Spain). His invective represents the kind of misogyny Charlotte would have encountered frequently as she developed as a collector beyond the shadow of her husband. As the pioneering work of art historian Lucy Peltz has shown, Charlotte, a young widow, soon attended print auctions, despite the relative rarity of a female collector bidding competitively at these public events. We can see evidence of 'an informed and energetic collector' (Peltz's words) in her annotations in surviving sales catalogues from the 1820s. Charlotte was attracting renown, and also the kind of sexism articulated by Ford. She paid 80 guineas for a print of *James I and Queen Anne* from about 1610, the highest-ever price for such a work. Charlotte had it inlaid by the firm of W. Scott and incorporated it into her growing copy of Clarendon.

Extra-illustration often meant working on a copy of *The History of the Rebellion*, originally published in 1702 and 1704, by Edward Hyde, 1st Earl of Clarendon. This detailed, Royalist-inclined account of the English Civil War, written by a former advisor to both Charles I and II, was the starting core for many Grangerisers, alongside Bishop Gilbert Burnet's *History of his Own Time*, first published in 1724, an eyewitness, anecdote-rich description

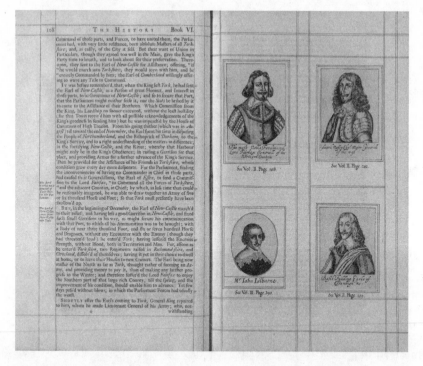

Edward Hyde, Earl of Clarendon, The history of the Rebellion and Civil Wars in England begun in the year 1641 *(1702–04), opening to page 108.*

of events from 1642 to 1713. The Sutherlands worked on both volumes. Alexander began clipping and slicing his way through Clarendon's *History* around 1795, aged forty-two, and the book became the focus of the Sutherlands' energies for decades to come. Pages were meticulously inlaid into larger thick-paper sheets – a window cut, the disbound printed page glued in – so that the type is now surrounded by a black frame and, beyond this, wide margins: the passage set off and dignified, as if displayed on a plinth.

Above is a page from an extra-illustrated copy of Clarendon's *History* now held at Yale – not the Sutherlands' work, but representative of the kind of text-and-image assembly that enthusiastic Grangerisers produced.

There's a portion of Clarendon's narrative which covers Court affairs in the 1610s and 1620s. And 'affairs' is the right word. Clarendon gives a condensed account of the favourites of James I, a king 'most delighted and taken with Handsome Persons, and with Fine Cloaths'. The details come thick and fast: the murder of King James I's favourite, George Villiers, the Duke of Buckingham ('his first introduction into Favour was purely from the Handsomness of his Person'), and, as a kind of shocking preface to this – the tangled events reduced to one sudden paragraph – the intrigue surrounding James's previous favourite and lover, Robert Carr, the Earl of Somerset. When Carr had an affair with the married Frances Howard, Countess of Essex, Carr's close friend, the essayist and poet Sir Thomas Overbury, opposed it as a disastrous political move, and wrote a poem called *A Wife* which took a predictable line on gender roles in marriage. The poem proved a hit with courtly readers, a culture of handwritten copying ensuring it spread quickly, like flames; but Howard took offence, reading the poem, probably correctly, as a censure of her alleged immodesty. Overbury died in April 1613. Howard obtained a divorce from Robert Devereux, the 3rd Earl of Essex, in the same year, on the grounds of impotence, and Howard and Carr married. But, this being the Jacobean court – its members brought up on Shakespeare's *Hamlet* and Thomas Middleton's *The Revenger's Tragedy* – rumours circulated about the cause of Overbury's death. After an infamous trial, Howard admitted her role in poisoning him with sulphuric acid: Clarendon describes her 'wickedness' in this 'horrible murder'. Howard and Carr were imprisoned in the Tower of London for six years until, in 1622 – aristocratic connections being what they were – they were pardoned. Four less well-connected accomplices were hanged.

History as a hand raised to an open mouth – as gossip and titillation. For Alexander and Charlotte, a narrative like this was a starting point: the page a base on which they could erect scaffolding to hang their swirl of prints. Each name meant the possibility of illustration, and so the text provided a logic, like an index, for the collecting and curating of prints. Facing Clarendon's text is a page, added by the Sutherlands, with four identical oval portraits of the doomed Sir Thomas Overbury. If this was not enough, there then follows another page, with four more portraits of Overbury. There then comes a page with three portraits of Lady Frances, Countess of Somerset, two of them from the same engraving. And the pages of prints continue: a page of Robert Carr and Frances Howard; another with two oval portraits of Carr; and a page of four portraits of George Villiers.

How are we supposed to read this thing? If we work our way through Clarendon's *History*, every named figure now leads us away from the text to pages and pages of inserted portraits. The experience of reading this book has become non-linear, a continual darting, despite the one-thing-after-another of the original narrative: our eyes like a ball in a pinball machine, our hands flipping pages back and forth in a gesture of ongoing evaluation.

The added prints are portraits, and while the Sutherlands also included maps and topographical scenes, the portrait is overwhelmingly their preferred form. The actors of history, in an extra-illustrated world, are individual men and women: the past is a series of faces staring back at us. Clarendon's text provides in effect a set of biographical headings – Carr, Howard, Overbury, Villiers – which Alexander and Charlotte use to organise their images. The book here has become a kind of archive or filing cabinet, a space and a method for ordering and holding the vast quantity of prints circulating at this moment. There is throughout a literalism to the Sutherlands' additions, as the mention of a name prompts the inclusion of a portrait: they aren't doing much that is obviously interpretative. But there are complexities at work here, most centrally in terms of the fine balance between creativity and destruction, between reverence and attack. Is this a homage to the book, or an all-out assault? A tribute (the text lavishly illustrated), or a parody (the book pulled apart)? Clarendon's original volumes have been disbound, sliced, inlaid, and

augmented to create something both impressive but also mon-
strous: the book vastly bloated, 'elephantine', as one critic puts
it, and 'vamped-up'. These volumes are both monumental works
of patient method, and also wild flights of individual fancy. And
as the scholar Luisa Calè has noted, extra-illustration is at once
iconophilic and iconoclastic – the Sutherland volumes are an
expression of an intense, meticulous, love for pictures, but those
pictures are often 'culled from other books'. The Sutherland Collection is an archive of images, but it is premised on the tatters it
leaves behind.

A sense of the book stretched and expanded – of rooms opening out onto other rooms – is evident on almost every page of
Clarendon's *History*. A passing mention of the minor Royalist diplomat and poet Endymion Porter prompts a facing page
with three states of the same portrait engraving (that is, prints of
the same plate with very minor variants). And when Clarendon's
narrative draws towards the 1649 execution of King Charles I,
a page summing up Charles's character ('if he had been of a
rougher and more imperious Nature, he would have found more
respect and duty') brings in sixty-one facing images of Charles,
several of them prints of the same plate in slightly different states.
This commitment to multiplicity, to many images of the same
person, and indeed many versions of the same image, is a signature trait, both of the Sutherlands' exhaustive work, and of
the logic of Grangerising. The effect of this is double-edged: on
the one hand, using many images generates a sense of play, of a
joyful piling up of print on print by the excited collector ('Look,
darling, I've found three more of the one with the horse!'); but it
also suggests an exhausting scholarly desire for completeness, for
the careful accumulation of every portrait, in the manner of an
editor tirelessly collating each version of a medieval poem surviving in dozens of manuscripts. The consequence of seeing so many
images of the same figure – sixty-one faces of Charles I – is dizzy-
ing. It results not, as we might expect, in an anchoring of history
in the body of a single individual, not in a sense of a real king

standing there before us as a still point in the world, but rather
the opposite: the teeming sea of representation, of image after
image floating out to the horizon with no end. This is a paradox
of the extra-illustrated book: the urge to gather so exhaustively is
a reaching for order, control, stability, and the book here is understood as something bound, as a mechanism for imposing limit;
but so much only points to so much more, a supplement without
end, and to loose sheets and scattered pages and the book as an
object-to-be-for-ever-expanded.

At Little Gidding in the 1630s, as we saw in Chapter 3, a particular
version of cut-and-paste book-making was performed by women.
The pious subject matter, the use of knives and scissors, and the
non-public domestic sphere of production enabled Mary and
Anna Collett to push through layers of misogyny to create their
miraculous bookish works. A loud man in the form of Nicholas
Ferrar constituted both an obscuring presence and also a justification: associated with Nicholas, the women's Harmony-making
was concealed but also enabled, and their books endure centuries
after Ferrar has gone. The Sutherlands' extra-illustration occupied a similar cultural space.

And here, below, are two sisters from a much later historical
period working in this tradition of female extra-illustration: Carrie
and Sophie Lawrence, professional inlayers at the start of the
twentieth century, slicing and cutting in their family workshop on
Nassau Street in New York City. The sisters took up the work seriously after the death of their extra-illustrating father. 'The whole
must be so daintily and deftly done,' said the elder sister, 'that,
when dried, the surface is perfectly smooth and only the most
skilled eye can detect where print begins and margin leaves off.'

Charlotte explained her agency as eternally submissive to her
husband's – even though that wasn't the whole picture, as Charlotte

Carrie and Sophie Lawrence, sisters extra-illustrating in their workshop in New York City, c.1902.

herself knew. In the preface to her *Catalogue of the Sutherland Collection in two volumes* (1837), Charlotte frames her motives for Grangerising Clarendon and Burnet in terms of a desire to repay 'the great confidence reposed in' her by her husband, who in his will granted that 'the Collection . . . was placed at her uncontrolled disposal'. ('Uncontrolled' is nicely ambiguous, suggesting 'without constraint', Alexander's intended meaning, even as it whispers 'disorder' or 'chaos'.) Charlotte's purpose is to achieve for the collection and for her husband the reputation they deserve: the volumes are a kind of memorial, a tomb without a body. As a result of its 'very magnitude', the Sutherland Collection 'may be said to be, in a manner, buried beneath its own grandeur', and Charlotte's catalogue is an attempt to make these catacombs navigable.

It's certainly the case that Charlotte writes with modesty about the limitations of her gender – 'A lady's pen, however, must claim the privilege of a lady's tongue, and crave excuse' – but these conventional tropes are upset by the activities they describe. We need to read this self-trivialising in a less literal way. When, 250 years before, the Elizabethan aristocrat and author Sir Philip Sidney dedicated his vast prose romance, the *Arcadia*, to his sister the Countess of Pembroke, he described an 'idle work' which '(like the Spiders webbe) will be thought fitter to be swept away, then worn to any other purpose'. He didn't believe anything of the kind, but it was the sort of thing a courtier should say. Sidney had to overcome the cultural stigma of an aristocrat labouring at a very long prose work in a culture that prized *sprezzatura* or effortlessness. In a similar way, Charlotte had to square forms of public display (of her books in a library; of herself at auctions) with her gender. Her expressions of modesty sit firmly in this tradition of paradoxical humility: self-effacement serving as a necessary preface to the ushering in of achievement.

Charlotte's sense of her abilities persists even in her assertions of the opposite. It would of course be preferable, she writes, for 'some more competent hand' to form the catalogue, but yet only someone with 'the necessary previous acquaintance with the prints', and the capacity to provide an 'unceasing and laboriously minute attention', could do the job. And that means Charlotte herself. When Alexander died aged sixty-seven on 21 May 1820, the Sutherland collection contained 10,160 works; when Charlotte finally handed over the collection to the Bodleian Library nineteen years later, it had 19,274 items, including 17,750 prints, and 1,460 drawings. And even while Charlotte was augmenting her husband's copies of Clarendon and Burnet, she was building her own, independent, post-Alexandrian collection of 8,000 prints and drawings inlaid within extra-illustrated volumes including Horace Walpole's *Royal and Noble Authors* and *Letters from Mrs Delany to Mrs Frances Hamilton*. The latter is the collected letters between two women, one of them the artist Mary Delany, known especially for her botanical works made from cut paper that she called 'paper mosaics'. Charlotte's Grangerised copy is a beautiful thing: small pages of text with facing images inlaid in large, thicker paper with gold fore-edges. Here is Queen Charlotte, and Windsor Castle, and Alexander Pope, and Longleat House. Here is St James's Church in Piccadilly. The wide margins and small blocks of text generate a sense of calm, and of a small book held within a larger structure, given dignity through this transformation. Charlotte donated these volumes to the Bodleian in 1843.

For Granger, print collecting served certain moral, conservative, ends. Not only did it do people good ('running over these portraits . . . will frequently excite the latent seeds of a martial, philosophic, poetic, or literary disposition'), but Granger also understood the ordered curation of prints of historical figures as part of a wider need for placement, rank, and apt distribution in the world. Granger's idea of history was deeply ideological, a shoring up of hierarchy to ensure that 'statesmen, heroes, patriots, divines, lawyers, poets, and celebrated artists, will occupy their respective stations'. There existed a deep correspondence between the carefully inlaid print of King James, correctly placed, and this stratified conception of society.

But despite all this, and with irony given Granger's enthusiasm for system, extra-illustration came soon to be seen by many as a kind of bibliographical vandalism, a frenzy or disease that gripped men and women and caused harm to books, prints, and libraries. 'A singularly perverted idea', as the bibliographer Holbrook Jackson rather magnificently put it.

Criticism in part focused on the physical damage inflicted on books when pages were cut or torn, and volumes were disbound and remade: the poet Robert Southey, writing in 1807, lamented that 'you rarely or never meet an old book . . . with the author's head in it; all are mutilated by the collectors'. Critics also castigated Grangerisers for inducing a kind of bibliographical hyperinflation in the form of the collector's desire for more and more.

Good collecting, these critics argued, was about acts of discrimination: *this print – but of course not that one – you can see the difference – look here, where I'm pointing.* Grangerising was contrastingly maximal: *this print, and that one, and also those two, and in fact give me the whole box.* What Lucy Peltz nicely calls the 'branding of collecting as an ailment' was a response to a sense that collecting was becoming a branch of consumerism, breaking out of a narrow aristocratic coterie and becoming the occupation for a broader slice of society, including women.

Many of these concerns are captured in *Bibliomania: or Book Madness* (1809), written when Grangerising was in full force, by the Anglican clergyman and prolific if erratic bibliographer Thomas Frognall Dibdin (1776–1847). Dibdin's joking-but-not-joking study anatomises the ways in which bibliophilia becomes disease – an uncontrolled passion for vellum sheets, or uncut pages, or that final variant print – and extra-illustration looms large as a particular variety. Dibdin blames Granger for having 'sounded the tocsin for a general rummage after, and plunder of, old prints'. ('Tocsin' – I had to look it up – is an archaic term for an alarm bell.) He calls them 'Grangerites', or 'Grangerian bibliomaniacs', and their process is described as a kind of 'attack' first on Clarendon, Shakespeare, and other luminaries, before their energies 'glanced off, in a variety of directions, to adorn the pages of humbler wights'. And it is the completist impulse of the extra-illustrator, the need to gather *everything,* that defines the sickness:

> To possess a series of well-executed portraits of illustrious men, at different periods of their lives, from blooming boyhood to phlegmatic old age, is sufficiently amusing; but to possess every portrait, bad, indifferent, and unlike, betrays such a dangerous and alarming symptom as to render the case almost incurable!

The theme was sustained in *The Anatomy of Bibliomania* (1930) by the British journalist and small-press publisher Holbrook Jackson.

Jackson's book is a wonderfully digressive celebration of books: he is particularly good on what he calls 'book eating' ('some books are tough, others tender; some green, others ripe') and also on the 'long but mostly unrecorded history' of 'reading during the ritual of the toilet[te], especially that part of it devoted to the coiffing'. (Do you read when you coif? Sometimes.) But in Part 28, 'Of Grangeritis', Jackson lays into 'impious biblioclasts, book-tearers, book-ghouls, collectomaniacs and dizzards' who 'look upon the printed word solely as the raw material of graphic interpretation', and who 'will acknowledge no standards of book-conduct outside their own':

> the patient is a sort of literary Attila or Genghis Khan, who has spread terror and ruin around him; and he pursues his obscene passion with a fiendish fascination: the moment [lawyer and Grangeriser] Irving Brown came into possession of a book, it was put under the rack to extort its capacity for illustration. Of one hundred books extended by the insertion of prints which were not made for them, ninety-nine are ruined; the hundredth book is no longer a book: it is a museum, or at best, a crazy-quilt made of patches cut out of gowns of queens and scullions.

Overleaf is a page from one of Irving Brown's Grangerised volumes, the images added directly to the page in a manner that fuses extra-illustration and scrapbooking.

We can see another manifestation of Holbrook Jackson's fears in the collected volumes now in the Huntington Library, California, that comprise the Kitto Bible (see plate section). The original (undated, but c.1850) three-volume royal octavo Bible, about 25 by 16 centimetres, had text from the 1611 King James translation and came with 'copious original notes, by J. Kitto, D.D.' These volumes were over several decades extended into sixty extra-large (or 'elephant') folio volumes, 56 by 38 centimetres each and bound in red morocco leather, holding more than 30,000 prints, inlaid

Irving Brown's Grangerising, New York, 1886.

or mounted, watercolour paintings, engravings, printed leaves
from various early Bibles, and other materials drawn from the
fifteenth to the nineteenth century, including woodcuts by Albre-
cht Dürer and engravings by William Blake. The whole thing
was assembled first by London bookbinder and print seller James
Gibbs (working *c.*1850–70) and then New York industrialist and
book collector Theodore Irwin (1827–1902). The Grangeriser's
enthusiasm for multiple representations of the same scene is evident here: the expulsion from Eden is illustrated with more than
fifty prints. This is all magnificent, in the original sense of 'making
great': it is the largest Bible in the world, and the Huntington
Library, who bought it from Irwin's son in 1919, calls it 'a verit-
able history of intaglio and woodcut religious art'. But it is also,
in Dibdin's terms, a kind of book madness. Holbrook Jackson
puts it like this: 'May the spectre of Thomas Frognall Dibdin
haunt the souls of these impious rascals, and torture them with

never-ceasing visions of unobtainable and rare portraits, non-existent autographs, and elusive engravings.'

&ele;

Madness, disease, fanaticism, mania. But there are other ways to think about Grangerising. One is as a form of stepping back from the world: no more the swirl of politics, or the storm of family financial scandal in Russia, but instead the sound of blades, mid-afternoon, cleanly cutting a paper window for an inlaid print. Richard Bull sat in the House of Commons as MP for the rotten borough of Newport, Cornwall, between 1756 and 1780, but his great energy in extra-illustration was premised on the almost total neglect of his parliamentary duties.

Bull seems never to have spoken in Parliament – he never voted against the government – and used Parliament as a base, alongside his London houses in Upper Brook Street and Stratton Street, and his mansion on the Isle of Wight, for coordinating his Grangerising ambitions, many of which, in fact, were practically enacted – rather than just dreamt up and chatted about – by his three daughters. Bull's letters full of questions about new prints and expanded bindings and rival collectors, lots of them sent to Granger himself, were often written from the House of Commons.

Perhaps the most spectacular instance of extra-illustration as a retirement from public life came in the person of Alexander Meyrick Broadley (1847–1916). Broadley was a lawyer, historian, and journalist who spent many of his working years in India, as a magistrate and defence lawyer, and Tunisia, as a special corres-pondent for *The Times*.

He became briefly famous as 'Broadley Pasha' as a result of his 1880s defence of Arabi Pasha, the leader of a failed Islam-ist uprising in Egypt. Back in London, Broadley's main job was being a prominent member of fashionable society. Described by contemporaries as 'abnormally clever' and as a character of 'Falstaffian proportions', Broadley was a kind of social fixer – the centre of everything – who enjoyed the excitement of new people: 'He had the faculty of attaching himself to and "running" whomsoever was the most amusing and useful person of the hour.' Remarkably, a phonograph recording survives at the Thomas Edison National Historical Park of Broadley giving a toast at a dinner on 5 October 1888: 'Gentlemen, the toast is Literature, coupled with the name of Mr Edmund Yates! Charge your glasses, gentlemen! Bumpers [raised], if you please!'

And Broadley got into trouble: as a gay man, scandal stalked him mercilessly. A warrant for his arrest for homosexual offences had led to Broadley absconding from India in 1872, and in 1889, back in London, he was at the heart of the notorious 'Cleveland Street Affair'. When police raided a gay brothel, a long list of eminent members of Victorian society was implicated – including the Prince of Wales's equerry, Lord Arthur Somerset; Henry James FitzRoy, Earl of Euston; and Prince Albert Victor, the eldest son of the Prince of Wales and the second in line to the throne. Broadley, in the midst of all this, was told to leave the country within twelve hours: he travelled ('fled' is more apt, such was the rage of the Prince of Wales, the future Edward VII) at first to Paris, then Brussels, and then for a time 'loafing' (according to the *Chicago Tribune*) in Tunis with Lord Arthur Somerset.

It is against this layered backdrop that in 1893 Broadley retired to a towered mansion called the Knapp in Bradpole, Dorset, where he sublimated his social energies into Grangerising books. Broadley not only extra-illustrated more than 130 books (creating some 600 volumes), but in *Granger, Grangerizing, and Grangerizers* (1903), he published a short but important guide to the subject. Writing in July 1903, Broadley noted that '[d]uring the last three years' he had extra-illustrated thirty titles, with five more in process. His book makes clear the extent to which the truly ambitious Grangeriser needed to draw on a range of professional services to help build these often huge, altered books. Broadley praises as essential for any serious Grangeriser the catalogues of British prints by W. V. Daniell of 53 Mortimer Street, and J. A. Breun of 4 Greek Street; the inlaying skills ('an almost ideal form of feminine occupation') performed 'by ladies' such as 'Miss M. E. Lone, of 121, Athanley Road, Nunhead, SE'; and printers such as 'Mr. W. Frost of Bridport' who could produce specially commissioned title pages 'which add materially to [the volumes'] completeness and general appearance'.

To his copy of Granger's *Biographical History of England*, which included *Letters to Mr. Granger*, Broadley added autograph letters, newspaper and magazine cuttings, prints, postcards, snippets about Granger's Shiplake vicarage, and original watercolour paintings, swelling the original book into twenty volumes. He had the whole bound with a new title page attributing authorship – or that version of authorship enacted by the Grangeriser – to 'A. M. Broadley', 1903, displacing Granger as the agent behind the book. The signature effect of the accumulated volumes is Broadley's showcasing of the process and labour of book-making: we are offered not only a book vastly expanded by thousands of historical and topographical illustrations, but also a book that shows how its own peculiar objectness came into being. We see it through time, growing and growing as a result of the intricacies not only of physical composition (the gathering, slicing, inlaying, binding), but also of social networks (the fellow collectors, the unending correspondence). We could call this bibliographical self-reflexivity, although Broadley, committed to the aesthetics of drawing-room amateurism, wouldn't have liked that. But he certainly creates the effect of a book gazing back on its own making, and of a craft aware of its past. He does this in part by including handwritten receipts for the various stages of production: 'Received from A. M. Broadley Esq the sum of £81.19.7 for providing and enlaying when necessary 1,230 portraits for Granger's Biographical History in addition to 300 portraits supplied by him . . . and arranging the whole into 20 uniform volumes / London Oct 17th 1903 / Walter V. Daniell.'

That sense of process is also produced by the huge number of autograph letters, many of these the originals printed in Granger's correspondence. These letters convey the excited mindset of the collector, so excited it becomes almost an acoustic, the bustle of exchange and enquiry and comparison and, infectiously, enthusiasm. Like the letter from antiquarian Richard Gough to Granger on 18 November 1774 which opens with thanks for 'the very obliging offer of a Print of Steeple Ashton church wch is quite new to me + which I shall be very glad to receive whenever you send a parcel to yr Bookseller Mr T. Davies who will keep it for me till call'd for, as I have at present no particular residence in London'. Or this one, from Richard Bull, tireless extra-illustrator and the world's worst MP, writing to Granger on 19 January 1774:

> The print inclosed in your letter to me is the identical Marquis of Hamilton I described; but the plate is so miserably worn, and so wretchedly touched up, that it hardly appears the same; I will add the writing to it, and return it to you the first opportunity I have.
>
> Being now convinced he is the father, I shall know where to place him; as also another no less valuable print of the same person, which I met with in Devonshire, and which I shall do right to describe to you for another occasion.

These busy letters mean Broadley, celebrating his new craft as a way to reinvent his life after scandal, makes extra-illustration its own subject. Gone is the exclusive focus on portraits of historical figures – here is Egbert, King of the West Saxons, first monarch of all England; and here is Canute the Dane; and here is Charles I. Instead Broadley builds a set of books – think of them as chambers, or drawing rooms where a community can gather – filled with Richard Gough and James Granger and Alexander Meyrick Broadley himself, eternally stooped over prints laid out on tables.

A bookbinder sews a book onto four cords with a gluepot at his feet; in the rear, his journeyman colleague beats pages flat with a hammer. From Christoph Weigels, *Ständebuch* (1698).

Little Gidding's chapel today.

The Whole Law of God, cover and title page. The gold tooling on the left was not yet finished when King Charles I examined the volume in 1642.

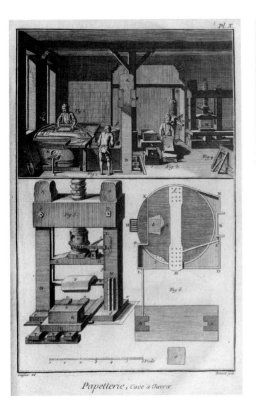

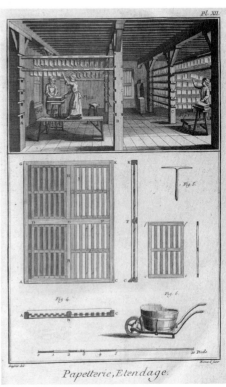

Paper-making at the Langlée factory, as represented in the
Encyclopédie (1751–66), featuring the vatwoman (*left*) and
the drying of sheets (*right*).

A letter-founder's work house, from the *Universal Magazine* (June 1750).

John Orlando Parry, 'A London Street Scene' (1835).

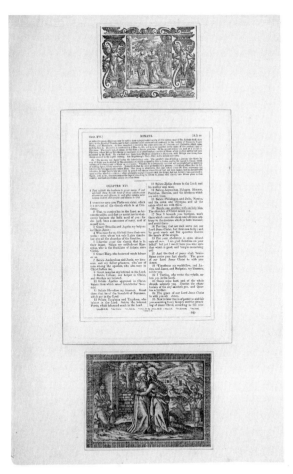

A page
from the
Kitto Bible.

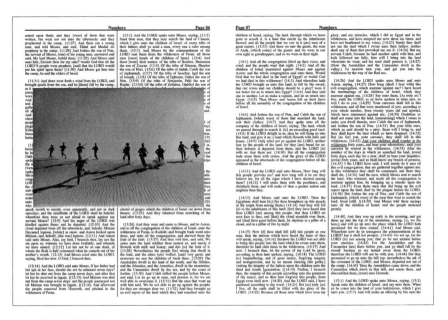

Holy Bible by Adam Broomberg and Oliver Chanarin (2013).

William Morris, *News from Nowhere, or, An epoch of rest: Being Some Chapters from a Utopian Romance* (1892).

The Doves Press edition of *The tragicall historie of Hamlet, Prince of Denmarke* (1909).

Doves Press type recovered from the Thames by Robert Green.

Calligrapher Edward Johnston in 1902.

Cunard and Henry Crowder in the Hours Press, 15 rue Guénégaud, Paris, 1930.

Savage Messiah issue 7.

Aspen number 4, opened up.

From BlackMass's *Trife Life* (2021).

For extra-illustrators like Broadley, and Charlotte and Alexander, straining always for maximal inclusivity, it was almost impossible to stop. The Sutherland Collection 'was every day receiving additions, and in which every print was immediately placed, as soon as purchased'. Why end now when there were more prints to collate? Many of the larger projects, like the Sutherlands' Clarendon and Burnet, and the Kitto Bible, were the work of collectors across generations because only death would cause the original compiler to slow down. Former MP Anthony Morris Storer (1746–99), famed for his collecting and his judicious taste and, not unrelatedly, rich on the inheritance from his father's Jamaican plantations, turned to extra-illustration as a response to 'the burden of having nothing to do'. He left several partially Grangerised volumes full of loose prints, the books frozen mid-process, suggesting not flagging enthusiasm but a pursuit that couldn't be finished within a lifetime.

The collection of documents held at the Bodleian Library as 'Bod MS Library Records c. 948' includes a lengthy series of letters relating to the donation of Alexander and Charlotte's Grangerised Clarendon and Burnet to the library. The letters begin in 1837 and their main business, as they ping to and fro between Guildford and Oxford – here is Charlotte taking the coach; here she is arriving at the Kings Arms 'but will leave Oxford very early on Friday morning' – is to establish the terms of the donation. These conditions were attempts to ensure the integrity, reputation and preservation of the books and included these clauses:

That the collection always be known as the Sutherland Collection
That it be neither taken from nor added to, and always be
    preserved distinct from other collections
That it be freely available to all those 'really interested' in its
    contents
That she be allowed free access to the collection and, should she
    so desire, to add items to it
That a portrait of her husband always be displayed next to the
    collection.

But the dominant refrain running throughout is Charlotte's inability to let go. The donation is imminent – is delayed – will soon happen – is delayed again. In the twenty-one months between the date of promised delivery and the actual deposit, Charlotte added 700 items to the collection, and removed about 200, as well as reordering the whole. Once the books are in the library, Charlotte returns and returns, making small changes to the catalogue. Here she is, writing from London in April 1838, to the Bodleian's librarian, Revd Bulkeley Bandinel, as she continues to work on the supplement to the catalogue:

> I am flattering myself that I can now at length, see something like a . . . termination of the apparently endless work of the Collection—I hope the Books will be in your hands before Midsummer & scarcely believe it possible that any thing will now occur to detain them . . . beyond the middle of June.

And here she is ten months later, writing to Bandinel on 13 February 1839:

> At length I have the <u>infinite</u> satisfaction of being able to announce that positively (humanly speaking) there will be no further postponement . . . [I have produced] the most perfect thing, <u>in its kind</u>, that the world can shew—and certainly as far as I ever saw or have been able to hear, the only Collection that <u>ever was really</u> complete—all others have been given or (more generally) left, in much the same state as Mr. Douce's—I may boast (if it be a boasting matter) of being the only Collector who . . . had courage to give up <u>accumulating</u>, to bestow attention on the final <u>arrangement</u> – in fact – to <u>finish</u>.

Mr Douce is Francis Douce (1757–1834), Keeper of Manuscripts at the British Museum and the author of one of history's best resignation letters – a bitter document from 1811 listing his thirteen reasons for leaving the British Museum. (Number 9: 'The want of society with the members, their habits wholly different & their manners far from fascinating & sometimes repulsive.') Charlotte's letter is important in part for the boasting (her word) confidence that she displays: an earned boasting, we might say, something she was entitled to after decades of labour, but an attitude that shows we shouldn't take literally her better-known statements of humility and ignorance. Charlotte knew she had done something major – 'the most perfect thing, <u>in its kind</u>, that the world can shew' – and recognised the proportions of her achievement. But finishing was, in Charlotte's words, a form of 'giv[ing] up', a letting go that took courage, and the accidental comedy of her assurances of the nearly-but-not-quite handover date – 'positively (humanly speaking) there will be no further postponement' – shows how powerful the finger-twitching urge was to add more. This is the librarian's nightmare: the donor who can't let go.

This wasn't only an expression of Charlotte's psychology. Extra-illustrating had an accumulating logic that meant it ran and ran, bursting the boundaries of the book even when the volume was rebound. In *Granger, Grangerizing, and Grangerizers* (1903), Broadley advised the inclusion of 'guards' within each volume: stubs of card in the gutter to act as spines for extra items that might be added at some point in the future, a way of making a book a continually expandable thing, 'without causing the "swelling" which so often disfigures grangerised books'.

The legacies of the Grangerised book are many but I'll finish this chapter by picking one of the most powerful, and disturbing, in the form of a work by the contemporary artists Adam Broomberg (b.1970) and Oliver Chanarin (b.1971). Broomberg and Chanarin's *Holy Bible* (2013) is an example of an artists' book. Artists' books are works of art that play out within the structures of the book: they take the physical form of the book and push it, challenge it, collapse it, in different ways. Artists' books are thus self-reflexive, in the sense that they are books that examine the form of the book, their purpose not discreetly to convey text – as a paperback novel might do, concealing its own mediation – but to challenge the assumptions we bring to the book, and the ways we read or navigate it.

Broomberg and Chanarin don't use the term, but their *Holy Bible* is in effect a contemporary response to the tradition of the Grangerised book: a direct, if unknowing, descendent of extra-illustrated volumes like the Kitto Bible. Broomberg and Chanarin's work appears, at first, to be a copy of the King James Bible, that text 'by His Majesty's special command appointed to be read in churches', complete with a spine title embossed in gold, cigarette-paper-thin pages, and a red silk bookmark: the kind of thing given as christening presents to godchildren. But the Bible has been altered. Images have been printed over the text in such a way as to look as though they have been not inlaid but glued on top of the page. As in eighteenth- and nineteenth-century extra-illustrated volumes, these additions have been made not by the original author, printer, or publisher, but by a later reader-user: the book that arrives in the hands of the compiler is understood as the basis for augmentation. Lines of printed text that correspond to the image have been underlined in red. So 'And your children shall wander in the wilderness' faces a photograph of soldiers running through a desert.

The relationship between underlining and image is sometimes, but not always, clear; and while some of the effects are surreal or even comic, and all are strange, in general the images work to draw out the various kinds of violence and suffering contained within the Bible. In the extra-illustrated volumes of Charlotte and Alexander Sutherland, names in the printed text served as sparks to draw in corresponding prints that were placed in a constellation around the original pages: George Villiers, Duke of Buckingham; Queen Anne of Denmark. In Broomberg and Chanarin, it is not names but clauses, possessed of an urgency ('And the LORD

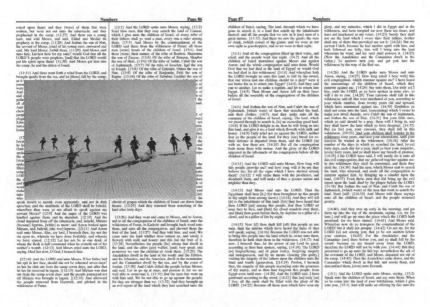

Holy Bible by Adam Broomberg and Oliver Chanarin, pp. 86–7.

came down in a cloud, and spake unto him, and took of the spirit that was upon him') that bring in the gathered pictures (see plate section). The pictures come from the Archive of Modern Conflict, a London archive founded in 1991 of found material, including photographs, relating to the history of war. Although in Broomberg and Chanarin's *Holy Bible* the images cover up portions of the text, the text to which the image responds always remains clear and legible and, like the Sutherlands' Grangerised pages, set in a relation of juxtaposition.

How strange, but also perhaps how familiar, this would have looked to James Granger, writing out his system of hierarchical historical biography from his country vicarage in Devon, and to Charlotte Sutherland, disbinding and expanding her books and wondering all the time how she could secure the proper legacy for this work.

8. CIRCULATION
Charles Edward Mudie (1818–90)

When it was proclaimed that the Library contained all books,
the first impression was one of extravagant happiness.

Jorge Luis Borges, 'The Library of Babel'

Let's start this chapter with a party.

On Monday 17 December 1860, the most talked-about event
in London took place not in an exclusive gentlemen's club on St
James's Street, or in a candlelit reception room on the fringes
of Court, but in a library. The location was 30–34 New Oxford
Street and the occasion was the opening of the new grand hall
of Mudie's Select Library. Forty-two-year-old Charles Edward
Mudie and his wife Mary 'received a vast number of literary and
artistic friends', according to the *Illustrated London News* – among
them, 'the venerable Mr. Tooke, the Rev. Dr. Cumming, [and]
Sir L. M'Clintock'. The crowd had 'representatives of all classes
of literature, science, and art'. There was a bookish buzz. More
than a buzz: a sense of something new happening. The handwritten list of 'Invitations accepted' survives today, along with lots of
Mudie papers, in the Rare Book and Manuscript Library of the
University of Illinois at Urbana-Champaign, and it conveys the
sense of both excitement and careful planning. Opposite is the
first page of three.

There were 530 guests in all. Some of the names we still recognise: George Cruickshank (Dickens's illustrator) was there, along
with philosopher and critic, and partner of George Eliot, George

Great Hall inauguration guest list, 17 December 1860.

Henry Lewes; the poet and social reformer Richard Monckton Milnes; and the publisher Charles Knight. So too was Anthony Trollope, who called the evening 'Mudie's great flare up'. The newly built neoclassical round hall was 45 feet high with white Ionic columns, stucco decorations, and a gallery, all designed by architect William Trehearne to echo the domed British Museum Reading Room less than five minutes' walk away, and so to suggest a kind of grand institutional history for this new building. Statues of Oliver Cromwell (a natural choice for the dissenting Mudie), Tancred and Clorinda (the Christian Crusader in love with, but battling, the warrior woman of the Saracen army), and Alfred Lord Tennyson stood in niches. The latter was by Thomas Woolner who finished it just hours before the event. Singers' voices rose above excited conversations. In the illustration accompanying the

217

'*Mr. Mudie's New Hall*', Illustrated London News.

article in the *Illustrated London News*, the bearded, balding Mudie stands at the centre of the scene, an inky point of condensed agency amid a swirl of young women in full white dresses, and older Victorian men all of whom look exactly the same. Sixty years later, in the 1920s, Wyndham Lewis described the still-running Mudie's Library as 'solid as roast beef', and 'about the only place in London where you could still find muttonchop whiskers, lorgnettes, tall hats from late-Victorian blocks, feathered and flowered toques'. Some of that frozen Victorianism is evident in this image from 1860.

Ambition, chatter, prospect, plans. Today what was then 30–34 New Oxford Street is an empty building seeking a business opportunity, and no one knows William Trehearne, but on that December evening the place was at the centre of a quiet revolution in book culture. Or perhaps not so quiet. Here is how one journalist saw it:

The whole book trade has become revolutionised. In a most important aspect we have undergone a vast social change. There are now, since the time of the last Reform Bill [of 1832], a dozen books published where there used to be one, and a hundred readers where there used to be a dozen. In fine old country libraries, where all used to be loneliness and stagnation, Mr. Mudie's books bring a fresh current of life, and remote provinces feel the ebb and flow of the London literary wave.

This is a chapter about one man's circulating library in the nineteenth century – a library that grew to become an institution, lending books out for a very low subscription charge to new kinds of reader, in London, throughout the British nation, and across the globe. The library revolutionised reading in terms of the range of titles it owned; in the sometimes ruthless professionalism it brought to the business of book-lending; in the scope of its readership; and in the extent of its tendrils reaching out across the map. In the process, its owner became a deeply controversial, yet also somewhat mysterious, figure.

Mudie's 'circulating' library changed a nation's attitudes to books, reading, and writing in profound ways, but Mudie himself was the subject of fierce and often rhetorically violent debates that played out in the papers of the day. We might not expect a librarian – even a businessman-librarian – to catalyse acrimony, but then 'librarian' doesn't quite capture the cultural influence that Mudie enjoyed. We see this when we read through the correspondence that survives: Mudie exchanged letters with illustrious figures such as Wilkie Collins, Florence Nightingale, Robert Browning, Alfred Lord Tennyson, Harriet Beecher Stowe, Thomas Carlyle, Charles Darwin, John Ruskin, and Charles Dickens. The letters describe his cultural centrality. Rarely before the times of Jeff Bezos has a single individual shaped a reading culture with such single-minded control. If you didn't like him – if you thought, like the editors of the *Literary Gazette*, that 'the whole tendency of this is most disastrous to the interests of the book world' – then Mudie was the 'Cato of New Oxford Street'. Cato was the conservative Roman senator and censor of the second century BCE who opposed Hellenisation, and who determined the literary landscape according to his own morality: Mudie (critics said) censored what was published, controlled publishers, and stunted literary creativity. 'The most dangerous public house in London is at the Corner of Oxford Street,' wrote George Bernard Shaw, 'and is kept by a gentleman named Mudie.' If you liked him – and lots did – Mudie found a very cheap way for hundreds of thousands of new readers, including women, including those far from London, including those, indeed, scattered across the globe, to have access to books they could otherwise not afford. Mudie distributed British book culture across the world. He also crucially supported the flowering of the dominant literary form of the time, the three-volume novel, which meant books by Trollope, Thomas Hardy, George Eliot, and others. Either way – love him, or really no thank you – Mudie's influence on literary culture was undeniable. Here is the *Literary Gazette*, two months before the opening of the new hall, lamenting his bookish monopoly: 'The great plague began in a corner. The great fire began in a corner. Mr. Mudie began in a corner. Like the contagion, and like the conflagration, Mr. Mudie has spread.'

It started small. 'Everybody who remembers anything,' wrote the editor of the *Literary Gazette* on 29 September 1860, 'will remember Mr. Mudie's little shop leading out of Holborn.' Mudie – the youngest son of Thomas Mudie, a Scottish bookseller and newspaper agent – was born in 1818 in Cheyne Walk, Chelsea. He worked for a time for his father before opening a shop at 28 Upper King Street (today's Southampton Row), where he sold newspapers and stationery. And while that was fine – people wanted the *Atlas* or the *Morning Chronicle* or the *Weekly Mail* – Mudie soon realised that loaning books offered a much more lucrative potential. He tended to stock progressive, even radical titles, like the works of American transcendentalists, and his shop was soon buzzing with students from nearby University College London. 'That little shop, in that little slum, was the beginning of the great monopolist.' By 1842, book loans – a penny a volume – had become his business.

Mudie's method was simplicity itself: he charged the strikingly low annual subscription fee of 1 guinea (£1 1s, or about £60 in today's money) for unlimited borrowing of fiction and non-fiction for 'Town' subscribers (but not more than one volume a day). 'Country' subscribers, who couldn't come in and relied on deliveries by train, were charged 2 guineas. This massively undercut other circulating libraries – Bull's Library charged 6 guineas; others varied between 5 and 10 guineas. Given the sky-high prices of books at this time – something that helped Mudie, and something that he sustained – this meant that a Mudie subscription for a year was less than the price of a three-volume novel. Mudie's margins were consequently tight, which meant, from the outset, and for all his rhetoric of the 'select', that he had to think in terms of huge numbers.

By 1852 he had more than 25,000 subscribers and needed new premises. He moved to 510 New Oxford Street. The sound of Mudie's book carts, providing free delivery, began to become part of the acoustic of this definitively bookish part of London: 'You have Mudie's, and you have the British Museum [opened to the public in 1759], and your path in Holborn or Oxford Street is almost lined with those bookstalls which are supposed to yield such delicious delights to spectacled bookworms.' Indeed:

> The Londoner who goes to Mudie's insists inexorably on the very latest new books, and Mr. Mudie will rain them down upon him as fast as he wants them. I feel disposed to believe that the summit of human felicity is attained by the man who has a reading ticket at the British Museum, and is also a subscriber to a liberal

proportion of books at Mudie's. He belongs equally to the past
and to the present.

Mudie started to advertise in newspapers and periodicals on a
scale unmatched by his rivals. Branch libraries opened across
London – at 281 Regent Street; and 2 King Street, Cheapside –
and offices were established on Cross Street, Manchester; and
New Street, Birmingham. A country department dealt with readers across the rest of the nation, and also the wider world. And
after that point, it becomes hard to measure with any precision
the cultural power of Mudie's operations.

How to quantify bookish influence? Here are the 2,500 copies
of Volumes 3 and 4 of Macaulay's *History of England* he ordered in
1855. That's 8 tons of Thomas Macaulay. Isn't that enough? Here
are the 1 million volumes Mudie claimed to have acquired by 1871.
'The famous Bodleian sinks into the shade,' said one giddy visitor
to New Oxford Street, 'and that of the Vatican becomes dwarf-
ish.' Here are the 7.5 million books owned by 1890. Here are the
8,000 letters, 3,000 English and foreign parcels, and 25,000 circulars posted each month. Here are the 1,000 letters and postcards
received *every day*.

Numbers created pressure for more and bigger buildings – 'The
guineas come in by thousands. Mr. Mudie wants more room. He
pulls down his near neighbour's house, and absorbs the areas' –
but we better catch a sense of Mudie's influence not by craning
our necks to look to the top of the domed hall but by closing our
eyes and thinking of all his books moving round the nation at any
one time, like aeroplanes too numerous to land all at once. 'Thousands are floating about the country,' wrote the essayist James
Hain Friswell in 1871, 'passing to and fro in the boxes, built almost
as strong as a railway-carriage.'

Mudie's books also travelled beyond the country: Mudie's
Library shipped books to readers abroad in tin trunks, holding
between ten and a hundred volumes each, by rail and sea, in
Egypt, Russia, Germany, South Africa, China, India, Mombasa

(Kenya), Zanzibar, Australia, Polynesia, and elsewhere. Many of these locations were parts of the British Empire and Mudie's Library became a powerful symbol of that colonial project, reaching readers directly or, more commonly, via local libraries and book clubs. Here was Britishness, arriving in tin cans: by the later nineteenth century, Mudie was sending out about 1,000 every week. The volumes with the yellow labels and the Pegasus symbol were spreading out across the world: soft power, alongside the soldiers and Oxbridge-educated administrators travelling out to subdue other nations. Mudie couldn't stop telling stories of tins dug up from the seabed, intact, after a shipwreck, the books still waiting for their Mudie readers.

Mudie's Library was a political beast not only through its centrifugal scattering of British cultural power; it was also political in its contribution to the rise of the idea of the 'common reader', that figure who read not the Classics but books of English literature that spoke to the contemporary and to the everyday. As Peter Katz has noted, Mudie's rise occurred at the same time as the rise of English literature as an academic subject. Oxford and Cambridge Universities were slow to show much interest in this new object of study – they only established English as a degree in 1894 and 1919, respectively – but the subject was beginning its institutional life in the London colleges during Mudie's youth. University College London, established in 1826 as London University by a coalition of Dissenters and Utilitarians, was the first university in England to admit students regardless of their religion, and was seen as a secular alternative to the Anglican worlds of Oxford and Cambridge. Its nickname was 'the Godless Institution of Gower Street'. It was also the first English university to introduce English literature as a subject, in 1828. A. J. Scott gave his inaugural lecture as Professor of English at UCL in 1848, and while his description of university education is wonderfully not of our time ('his studies should be chosen, therefore, with the purpose of preparing for the duties of manhood'), Scott grapples with the central objection to English literature as a subject that still pertains for some sceptics today: that writing in the student's own language is not sufficiently demanding as an object of study. Mudie faced parallel accusations that his library had a kind of populist thinness – that his books and his readers lacked depth. Scott argued that it was precisely this intimacy, this relative familiarity, in contrast to the study of Greek or Latin authors, which meant a deeper, more precise, knowledge was possible, and enabled the student of English literature to feel his subject's humanising influence: 'Instead of saying, it is easier to understand Shakespeare than Sophocles, say, a more full understanding of Shakespeare than of Sophocles is attainable for an Englishman; and propose to attain it.'

Scott argued that the study of literature could be a crucial bridge between university study and the wider world: 'As contrasted with science and with archaic learning, [English literature] stands as it were on the frontier of the university, to connect it with the world, and to prepare the passage between them.' Scott was making this case for (in the title of his published lecture) 'the Academical Study of a Vernacular Literature', just as thousands of new subscribers were flooding to Mudie's to borrow the latest English books. The students at UCL and the subscribers at Mudie's were part of a common enterprise, the creation of what has been called 'the literary public': what we could describe as the institutionally supported culture of borrowing, studying, and reading books in English by the non-elite. In 1925 Virginia Woolf published her account of what she called 'the common reader': the non-elite autodidact, the individual who doesn't know Greek, who doesn't have a private library, who, in being 'hasty, inaccurate, and superficial, snatching now this poem, now this scrap of old furniture', in many ways falls short of the critic and the scholar – but who nonetheless treads a path through English books. Mudie's Library, set amid a wider culture of the literary vernacular, was a crucial catalyst for the quiet heroism of this kind of reader.

But what was it like to walk through the doors? How did it feel to be inside? We can get a sense from accounts in publications like *London Society* – a magazine, the subtitle tells us, 'of light and amusing literature for the hours of relaxation' – written peak-Mudie. ' "Going to Mudie's" is an institution', we read, and it's busy. More than busy. Get there in the morning and there is already 'a swarm of early birds alighting by the counter side', exchanging books at the semicircular counters in the round hall. Readers don't browse shelves but order from catalogues and wait as attendants – one account calls them 'the supple young men below' – fetch volumes from shelves lining the two-storey walls.

There's a sense of modernity about the space: the lifts, the iron staircases, the workers communicating via speaking tubes. Light carts circulate from room to room, 'laden with books'. The impression is of busy efficiency:

> The arrangements at New Oxford Street are so good, and the clerks are so prompt, that no one need be long detained except the individual of feeble and indecisive mind, who has prepared no list, and is in a lamentable state of mental uncertainty and confusion. He generally collapses into an adjacent seat.

Buzzing past this collapsed figure is 'the constant stream of the passers out and in'; clerks from the Foreign Office; 'fresh, happy-looking girls' like 'Adelaide' who comes in for books 'while Laura [stays] in the carriage as company for her Italian greyhound'. There are the 'light pleasure-seekers'; the 'mere bookworms, who will sit down and pore over the catalogue'; the 'briefless barrister' who 'occupies himself with writing reviews'; the reader seeking travel books for their trip to Paris; the 'fast young man . . . who knows . . . he can hardly make his way out in society without a little help from Mudie'. And there is the author himself: a 'bookish-looking man, with an anxious face, asking for some volume, and inquiring if there is much demand for it'. Two thousand copies of George Eliot's *Felix Holt* – just arrived – are 'stacked and piled'. Bookcases hold coloured bindings: here is one case with the bright scarlet bindings of hundreds of copies of one recent novel; here is a case of 'the fashionable magenta'; another the 'black of graver works'. The bustle at the counters is as busy 'between five and six in the afternoon' as it was in the morning. Looking around, 'the spectator sees solid stacks of books piled about in odd places, just as he sees bricks stored near some rising building'. Outside, 'the carriages block up Museum Street and New Oxford Street' as 'powder-headed footmen carry to and fro the packages of books'. The impression is of a library growing itself larger all the time, and spilling out into London.

Largely because of this sense of bustle and business, Mudie readers were often mocked as foolish or poorly educated or, in particular, enamoured only of the modish. Here is 'J.D.' in the *Illustrated London News* in 1887 – anonymous, but clearly quite cross – lamenting the 'profound' ignorance of the 'reader who is satisfied with what Mudie's weekly cart brings'. That reader may have read 'Ouida's last novel' (pseudonym of the prolific English-French novelist Maria Louise Ramé) but 'probably does not know the chief characters in the *Waverley* novels, and has never read *The Ancient Mariner*'. Can you *imagine* such ignorance? Editors had a particular fondness for illustrations that ploughed the same furrow.

Others framed the idea of a library with wide doors in more positive terms. 'If an artist could photograph the eager faces that throng the long counters of this establishment,' wrote novelist Andrew Wynter in 1863, 'he would be enabled to give us a rare picture-gallery of intelligence.' In a how-to manual for library proprietors published in 1797 – half a century before Mudie's, and with a different price structure, but with many of the same commitments – the jostling mix of types is seen as precisely the virtue of a circulating library. In these 'depots of learning', as the pamphlet has it, all classes can borrow, read, and grow:

> The rich may subscribe for a year, and the subscription will not exceed one guinea, in many instances less. – The middling class, or where the residence is temporary, may subscribe for three months, at the expence of four shillings; and those whose means are not so good, but have leisure time, may indulge in the luxury of reading for a month, at the trifling expense of eighteen pence or two shillings, which probably will be more than doubly saved by thus employing it.

Mudie's Select Library was one important chapter in the long history of the library as an institution, and also as an idea. The story of the library is, as Andrew Pettegree and Arthur der Weduwen have recently described, a story characterised by cycles of creation, dispersal, and reconstruction. To think about the long story of libraries means usually to return to Alexandria, but if this is an origin story, it's also an unknowable beginning. Founded between 300 and 290 BCE on the northern coast of Egypt, close to the bustling harbour, in the city named after the Macedonian King Alexander the Great, the library was part of the Mouseion, a research institution dedicated to the Muses. The library, and, later, a second library built nearby at the temple of the god Seraphis, accumulated huge numbers of texts in the form of papyrus scrolls, stacked in alcoves, from Greece, Assyria, India, Egypt, Persia, and elsewhere. We can't know now exactly how many scrolls the library held – estimates range up to about 500,000, but no one is sure – but it is certainly the case that this was a library on a scale unsurpassed until the nineteenth century. In a letter by an Alexandrian courtier written in the second century BCE, the library's first director, Demetrios of Phaleron, is said to have 'received large sums of money to gather together, if possible, *all the books in the world*'. An impossible mission, but an irresistible idea. The scrolls covered literature (including works by Homer, Aeschylus, Sophocles, and Euripides), medicine, geography, physics, and mathematics. This was in no sense a public library, but a research centre for scholars, a restricted coterie, and in the second and third centuries BCE, the mathematicians Euclid and Archimedes, the geographer Strabo, the epic poet Apollonius of Rhodes, among other celebrated figures, came to work – walking in the gardens and the zoo, eating communally in the circular domed dining hall, between stints in the reading rooms and lecture halls. It was here that the poet and scholar Callimachus (310–240 BCE) compiled the *Pinakes*, the first library catalogue of authors and works, and a crucial document in the history of information. Like almost everything associated with the library, the original is now lost.

The reasons for the library's destruction are unclear. More probable than the traditional story of a raging fire accidentally spreading during Julius Caesar's civil war with his rival Pompey in 48 BCE, or of destruction by Muslim conquerors led by Caliph Omar in the seventh century CE, is a process of slow decline over several centuries during the Roman period – of damp spreading across the papyrus scrolls – until something like extinction is reached around 260 CE. A 'cautionary tale', as the Bodleian's librarian Richard Ovenden puts it, and a familiar one, of 'underfunding, low prioritisation and general disregard for the institutions that preserve and share knowledge'. Those stories of violent destruction are myths that serve to conceal an even bleaker truth: the manner in which vast institutions of great cultural significance can, unguarded, simply drift away. The library's importance for later centuries was to serve as a kind of double symbol, of both the vast accumulation and preservation of learning to the point of universality, on the one hand, and also its loss, on the other: an image, as one scholar puts it, 'of history consuming itself'.

This notion of Alexandria's universality – of a library holding every text – is an impossible but captivating ideal that resonates down the centuries and finds its most eloquent expression in the short fictions of the Argentinian writer Jorge Luis Borges (1899–1986). Borges was a librarian: first, as an assistant at the Buenos Aires Municipal Library, where he catalogued the collection (his co-workers told the industrious newcomer to slow down), and later, in 1955, at the time when Borges was losing his sight, as director of the Biblioteca Nacional. 'I speak of God's splendid irony,' Borges said in his acceptance speech, 'in granting me at one time eight hundred thousand books and darkness.' Borges's short fictions are like literary mobius strips – the impossible unfurls with seeming inevitability – and in 'The Library of Babel' (1941) he imagines 'a librarian of genius' turning over the notion of a universal library. The piece grew out of his essay 'La Biblioteca Total' ('The Total Library') and was written during his 'nine years of unhappiness' as a cataloguer.

> This philosopher observed that all the books, however different from one another they might be, consist of identical elements: the space, the period, the comma, and the twenty-two letters of the alphabet. He also posited a fact which all travellers have since confirmed: *In all the Library, there are no two identical books.* From those two incontrovertible premises the librarian deduced that the Library is 'total' – perfect, complete, and whole – and that its bookshelves contain all possible combinations of the twenty-two orthographic symbols (a number which, though unimaginably vast, is not infinite) – that is, all that is able to be expressed, in every language. *All* – the detailed history of the future, the autobiographies of the archangels, the faithful catalogue of the Library, thousands and thousands of false catalogues, the proof of the falsity of those false catalogues, a proof of the falsity of the *true* catalogue, the gnostic gospel of Basilides, the commentary on that gospel, the

commentary on the commentary on that gospel, the true story of your death, the translation of every book into every language, the interpolations of every book in all books . . .

When it was announced that the Library contained all books, the first reaction was unbounded joy.

Mudie's mind did not turn like Borges's: he saw not the *mise-en-abyme* of commentaries on commentaries, but sturdy iron staircases and carts rattling across cobbled streets and catalogues dispatched to provincial branches. Mudie's Library certainly advertised vastness, but it also, and paradoxically, stressed selection: Mudie offered the 'principal' new works of the 'higher class'. That selection meant Mudie proudly excluded certain works, just as he proudly advertised how many books he had acquired, and he grew adept, as Stephen Colclough has explored, at juggling the rhetoric of selection and availability. More than 1 million books available! But only for those seeking 'higher Literature'!

This selection was what angered Mudie's critics who condemned him as a censor who 'would mould all ideas to fit the narrow limits in which your own turn'. More than angered: Mudie's power of selection induced a kind of principled fury. When Mudie rejected George Moore's first novel, *A Modern Lover* (1883), Moore wasn't happy with Mudie's exclusion. The work is now seen as important for the way it turned from conventions of Victorian fiction to embrace French realist writers such as Balzac and Zola, but Mudie responded with a tart and straightforward appeal to the common reader: 'Two ladies from the country wrote to me objecting to that scene where the girl sat to the artist as a model for Venus. After that I naturally refused to circulate your book.' Moore's subsequent language was not temperate. Mudie's Library embodied a humanity that is 'headless, trunkless, limbless, and is converted into the pulseless, non-vertebrate, jelly-fish sort of thing which, securely packed in tin-cornered boxes, is sent from the London depot and scattered through the drawing-rooms of the United Kingdom'. Mudie excluded Moore's second novel, *A Mummer's Wife* (1885) – a book, according to the *Athenaeum*, 'remarkably free from the elements of uncleanness'. Because 'Mr. Mudie possesses a monopoly', Moore fumed in his pamphlet *Literature at Nurse, or Circulating Morals* (1885), he is 'a fetter about the ankles' of culture; he is 'the great purveyor of the worthless'. And 'although I am willing to laugh at you, Mr. Mudie', Moore ran on, 'to speak candidly, I hate you; and I love and am proud of my hate of you. It is the best thing about me.' We'll meet Moore again in the chapter on Nancy Cunard: let's see if he's calmed down by then.

While Moore saw Mudie's exclusions as moral decisions – 'would you or would you not give that book to your sister of sixteen to read?' – others understood his exclusions as expressions of his Dissenting beliefs: Mudie was perceived as a political agent working against the Established Church, a liberal in theology, and a radical in politics. This accounted for his progressive inclusions, too. So Charles Darwin's *Origin of Species* (1859) was in, as was *Essays and Reviews* (1860), a collection of seven essays deploying Darwin and the latest German biblical scholarship to refute accounts of miracles in the Bible, and which earned its liberal Anglican contributors the moniker 'The Seven Against Christ'. The High Church novel *Miriam May: A Romance of Real Life* (1860), by Arthur Robins, was out, and Robins complained this was a response to the novel's unflattering representation of an Evangelical minister who obtains a bishopric through fraud. Mudie denied the charges – he wrote in the *Manchester Guardian* that he would never circulate any novel that '*egregiously* misrepresents the views of any religious party' (my nagging italics) – but the *Literary Gazette* attacked 'Mr Mudie's Monopoly'. Its letters pages listed titles Mudie had apparently banned due to his Dissenting 'cause', including Marabel May's *Wedded and Winnowed . . . A Tale for the Divorce Court* (1860).

Whether Mudie's decisions were a result of moral concerns, or an expression of his Dissenting religious commitments, the power he wielded was maddening, not to say terrifying, for those authors and publishers who felt the door slam shut. For those on the inside, it was another matter – like novelist Amelia B. Edwards (1831–92), whose letter of 15 February 1865 to Mudie begins: 'I have for some time been wishing & intending to write to you, to offer my warm and hearty thanks for the marked kindness with which you put my name forward in all the published lists which I see of your library.'

'He is better known, perhaps, than any man in England,' said the *Literary Gazette*, but it is difficult for us today to draw close to Mudie. Perhaps all librarians have that instinct to curate the words of others rather than promote their own, to be, to quote one contemporary account of libraries, 'a polite misanthrope'. Wilkie Collins called Mudie 'an old fool' and an 'ignorant fanatic', but these were really responses to Mudie's gatekeeping power – his 'system of Mudie-ation', as one letter writer put it. The prude, if that's what he was, and the aggressive businessman, which is certainly what he was, seem in some ways at odds – the first has an instinct for cancellation, the second for accumulation – but Mudie may have combined the two. He was famous for saying that all books carried by his library had to be able to be shown to a respectable young woman without making her blush; but 'he walks about as a man would who can have his own way,' continued the *Literary Gazette*, 'and means to have it.'

His presence is loudest in the newspaper editorials and letter pages, where accusations of cultural gatekeeping fly back and forth. But Mudie was also a poet, and that gives us a route into his character. In 1872, at the height of his professional powers, he had printed for private circulation a collection of eighteen verses titled *Stray Leaves*. All but one of these are unknown today, but his lyric 'I lift my heart to thee' became a hugely popular hymn, and is still sung across the Christian globe. Here is the opening verse:

> I lift my heart to Thee,
> Saviour Divine,
> For Thou art all to me,
> And I am Thine.
> Is there on earth a closer bond than this
> That 'My Beloved's mine and I am His'?

The poems in *Stray Leaves* are dominated by religious belief, and in particular a sense of God's consolations in periods of adversity and struggle. ('So often in our hours of deepest sadness, / He fills our darkened hearts with holy gladness.') But there is a point of contact between this apparently conventional piety and Mudie's library work. Mudie's Dissenting faith rings loudly in verses that oppose the established Church:

> Thousands may gather where some Minster rears
> Its stately towers, observing every form
> Their Church appoints; – and yet each solemn creed,
> Each grave response, each plea liturgical,
> Though chanted to the organ's pealing note,
> May rise no higher than the gilded roof,
> And fetch no answer of more moment back
> Than its own echo. If Thou art not there,
> Each soul will go unblessed from the place . . .

Following a minister in chanting to a pealing organ doesn't, to Mudie, sound like religious conviction. He prefers less institutionalised forms of association:

Prayer finds a holy Temple anywhere;—
And Thy sweet Presence gives the humblest place
A greater glory than the highest skill
Of all earth's artists, with all tints of grace
And forms of beauty, ever furnished.

On the one hand, a passive and ineffective duty before traditional institutions; on the other, a sense of the life and potential in the anti-establishment, 'anywhere'. Mudie's bibliographical innovations can be understood as an expression of this Dissenting impulse: a library of new readers, from social classes previously excluded, reading books in English in places outside the traditional topography of literary caché, is a culture in which a reader, like a woman in prayer, can find a temple anywhere.

If you were turning the pages of the *Literary Gazette* and you came across an advertisement for Mudie's, you might like the promise of 'CASES SHIPPED AT LOWEST RATES TO ALL PARTS OF THE WORLD', or 'VILLAGE CLUBS SUPPLIED ON LIBERAL TERMS'. This sense of the expansively global and the cosily provincial coexisting in the Mudieverse at the same time was one of his characteristic rhetorical lines. But what were your other options? What was a library like circa 1860? What kind of access to books did you enjoy?

Mudie certainly had his rivals in terms of other circulating libraries. There were numerous smaller institutions which, lacking anything like the quantities of books at Mudie's, offered complementary services to attract subscribers. Lovejoy's Library in Reading in the 1880s, for example, also sold board games, leather goods, and maps, and provided bookbinding services. Others sold hats, tea, tobacco, snuff, perfume, and patent medicines. Some specialised in particular fields, like the Universal Circulating

Musical Library at 86 Newgate Street, London. Far from the capital, the Bala Circulating Library in 1865 had around 448 titles (330 in English, 118 in Welsh); subscription was a bargain at two shillings a year, but the library was only open on Mondays from 8 to 9 p.m.

These little institutions were small jewels, however, compared to the heaps of treasure accumulated by the Smaug-like Mudie. Of the more comparable beasts, the Library Company Limited, founded in 1862, tried to build itself as a direct rival, exploiting controversy around Mudie's acts of selection ('no work of general interest is, on any pretext whatever, excluded from the collection'), and halving Mudie's famous subscription rate to half a guinea per year. But the company was bankrupt within two years, thanks in part to Mudie's counter-attacks in the form of savvy advertisements. A more sustained challenge came from the leadership of a youthful William Henry Smith. W. H. Smith's had a history in the newspaper business, and operated a reading room in the Strand from 1820 where for a guinea and a half readers could browse 150 papers, magazines and reviews. In the 1850s, Smith's set up bookstalls in railway stations, at first selling newspapers and the paraphernalia a traveller might require (maps, rugs, candles), and then, under the title of the Subscription Library of W. H. Smith & Son, using these stalls to serve as 185 local branches within a subscription library. A commuter could borrow from one railway stall, read while the countryside flashed past, and, if they had a 'travelling subscription', return it to another. Smith's also experimented with new formats, most famously the cheap 'yellow back' reprints of popular fiction which sold for 1s, 2s or 2s 6d. In 1859 Smith's offered to work as agents for Mudie's, stocking Mudie titles in their railway stalls. Mudie declined – the money wasn't right – and so the two coexisted. Smith's reliance on the railway and a commuter market which favoured cheap one-volume reprints meant its library company, which survived until 1961, remained on a different track, literally and metaphorically, to Mudie and his triple-decker readers.

We might imagine that the local public library overlapped with Mudie's empire – an institution etched deeply into the British bibliographical psyche, in part because of the recent, twenty-first-century pressures it has faced, with the closures of a fifth of the branches (some 800) between 2010 and 2019. In fact, at the time of Mudie's emergence, the public library was a relatively novel, and still very uncertain, institution and not yet anything like a source of national pride. The 1850 Ewart Act – the work of pioneeringly progressive MP William Ewart, 'for enabling town councils to establish public libraries and Museums' – was the first British legislative attempt to establish free public libraries, and permitted (but did not require) larger boroughs to raise a levy of a halfpenny in the pound for this purpose. The money raised was to be used for staffing and maintenance: the building, and the books, would have to somehow come from elsewhere, via donations. The development was unsurprisingly slow and patchy, and it was not until the opening decades of the twentieth century, and the Public Libraries Act of 1919, that the library's potential as a source of free reading for the working classes blossomed into sustained reality, thanks in part to the philanthropy of the Scottish-American steel magnate Andrew Carnegie, and the Liverpudlian sugar merchant Henry Tate. This enthusiasm for public local libraries reached a peak in the 1930s. But this was in the future. By 1860, when Mudie's grand hall was opening, only twenty-eight library authorities had been established, and while these included some to-be-famous institutions such as the Manchester Free Public Library – opened in 1852 with a ceremony attended by Charles Dickens and William Thackeray – enthusiasm elsewhere, particularly outside of major cities, was low. In part this lack of support was a predictable resistance to tax increases (two-thirds of a borough's ratepayers were required to endorse the tax rise), but it also registered the popularity of alternative sources of books, such as the Mechanics' Institutes, important sources of working-class adult education, with significant libraries. The contrast between the starkly thin public provision, and the sense of prompt bounty offered by Mudie's, is striking. When, in 1860, Mudie was increasing his collection by 170,000 volumes a year, the entire stock of the (relatively major) Liverpool Free Library was still only 49,277 volumes. Set within this context of scattered provision, Mudie's Select Library flourished.

We have a sense of the vastness of Mudie's stock, but what kinds of books were available? In *The Use of Circulating Libraries Considered; with instructions for opening and conducting a library, either upon a large or small plan* (1797), the author proposes that a small circulating library of some 1,500 volumes should be organised as follows:

> 60 volumes of History
> 60 volumes of Divinity
> 30 volumes of Lives
> 20 volumes of Voyages
> 20 volumes of Travels
> 30 volumes of Poetry
> 20 volumes of Plays
> 1,050 volumes of Novels
> 130 of Romances
> 10 of Anecdotes
> 40 of Tales
> 30 of Arts and Sciences

This is a fascinating statement of literary commitments for the closing years of the eighteenth century. The dominance of novels is remarkable – a little more than two-thirds of the total – as is the relative marginality of poetry and plays (a figure which suggests the vitality of drama as performed theatre, rather than read literature). Some of these genres, like 'anecdotes' or 'tales', no longer really exist within our bookish culture, having migrated into other media. And the pamphlet makes it clear that curatorial acts of exclusion are as important as attempts at inclusion: 'The greatest care should be taken to exclude every book of a profane, immoral, or indelicate nature.'

We can get a closer sense of Mudie-world by looking at the circulars he published. *Mudie's Library Circular: A Monthly Register of Current Literature* began in April 1862 and purported to be something like an objective assessment of the latest titles ('the Purpose of the Editor precludes criticism'). In fact this document was a way for Mudie to curate the contemporary: its function was to promote the Library, and Mudie's market logic is proudly visible. ('The works in the above List will be added to the Library, when ready, in numbers fully proportioned to the demand.') Each circular offered 'Analysis of the Principal New Books'; 'Works of General Interest Announced for Early Publication' (some ninety soon-to-be-acquired titles, including books I wish I had read like 'Captain Clutterbuck's Champagne', 'Mountaineering in 1861, by John Tyndall', and 'A Cruise Upon Wheels, by Charles Alston Collins'); 'List of Surplus Copies of Recent Works Withdrawn from Circulation, and offered for sale at greatly reduced prices' ('Against Wind and Tide, by Holme Lee 3 vols. Published at 31s 6d Offered at 5s od'); and 'Advertisements' – the latter representing almost half the contents, with pitches by John Murray of Albemarle Street, Longman, and others. The 'Analysis of the Principal New Books' was intended, in the institutional voice of Mudie's, 'to epitomise the contents of the various works issued in the course of the past month, so as to facilitate the choice of books', and these potted critical summaries give a sharp sense of literary priorities, circa 1860. The issue for April 1862, for instance, contains critical summaries of seventy-four new books selected by Mudie: the subjects match reasonably accurately the outline in *The Use of Circulating Libraries Considered,* with a particular concentration on novels, histories (of Rome, modern music, the Church, the

United States, the West Indies), lives and memoirs (of Isambard Kingdom Brunel; of Queen Hortense, mother of Napoleon III), and travel – although there are also scientific works (metallurgy), and certain now-forgotten genres such as sermons. If you were a Mudie subscriber in 1862, your eyes might fall on this kind of breezy summary:

> *Beaten Paths, and those who trod them.* By THOMAS COLLEY GRATTAN. 2 vols. 8vo, pp. 346 and 388. London: Chapman and Hall.
>
> A collection of life incidents, the grave and the gay hurrying by in rapid contrast. Irish, Continental, Home, and military episodes succeed one another. English poets—Moore, Campbell, Coleridge, and Wordsworth—appear in the narrative; incidents and characters, political and historical, have their share: Young Italy and Mazzini; Louis Napoleon and France; Kemble, Dean, and other distinguished actors; and some of the more conspicuous American diplomatists.
>
> The purpose of the author seems to be to present not a connected narrative of what is essentially unconnected, but to make his reader share the experiences he went through, visiting the same places, and shaking hands with the same friends.

The colonial context is strong in many of these summaries, such as this overview of Henry Brown's *Victoria as I found it during five years of adventure, In Melbourne on the roads and the gold fields; with an account of quartz mining and the great rush to Mount Ararat and Pleasant Creek* (1862):

> A minute and elaborate account of five years of adventure in this colony . . . The writer appears to have aimed at photographing, as far as possible, his impressions and recollections of colonial life. Himself an emigrant, thrown into the centre of active work, and into the experience of inevitable hardships, he discards all impressions gathered from the writings of others, and aims at giving his own portrait of the place. Scattered through the pages

239

are sketches of various characters more or less peculiar to the place and life.

Would you want to read that? Maybe not: the promise of documentary-style veracity doesn't sit well, for us, today, alongside that fairly blatant imperial ideology. 'As I found it' catches a particular Victorian attitude, both acquisitive and complacent, to the world elsewhere. But for readers in 1862, it might offer a vicarious experience of colonial life: a way of seeing the world from your spoon-back chair. In 1871, Mudie's bought 3,350 copies of *Missionary Travels and Researches in South Africa* by Christian missionary David Livingstone, which meant, estimating conservatively, that more than 40,000 readers probably encountered this text via Mudie's. Here is Florence Nightingale, writing to Mudie on 20 November 1867, requesting that he 'send any lists of copies of books (for purchase) regarding <u>Australia</u> or the <u>Australian Colonies</u> – entertaining accounts of colonials – tales – or expeditions of discovery (<u>not</u> reports)'. (Nightingale had written to Mudie before, in March 1863, asking about second-hand books for sale – the 'object being . . . to fit out soldiers' libraries.')

But the form that is most closely associated with Mudie's is what was known as the triple-decker. Not everyone admired it. 'Anybody can write a three-volume novel,' Oscar Wilde wrote in 1890, 'it merely requires a complete ignorance of both life and literature.' The malign influence of the form is the quiet centre of *The Importance of Being Earnest* (1895). Everyone remembers poor baby Ernest, found in a handbag twenty-eight years before, but not 'the manuscript of a three-volume novel of more than usually revolting sentimentality' (Lady Bracknell's words), composed by Miss Prism during her 'few unoccupied hours' and left by her in the pram instead of the said 'baby of the male sex'.

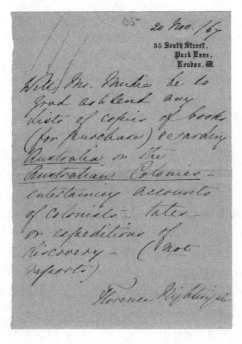

Florence Nightingale to Charles E. Mudie, 20 November 1867.

The three-volume novel predated Mudie: *Kenilworth*, Water Scott's hugely popular Elizabethan romance, published in 1821, was perhaps the founding instance, twenty years before Mudie's rise. But the triple-decker blossomed under Mudie's control (control is the right word), sustained not for artistic reasons but as a result of a tight circle of economic logic. Books were, by proportion of earnings, hugely expensive in the mid-nineteenth century, in part because of the French Revolutionary Wars and the subsequent economic depression. The three-volume novel was particularly, and artificially, costly: at a guinea and a half, it was about the same as a good working-class weekly income. It was also more than an annual subscription at Mudie's. Mudie pressured publishers to keep the price high to ensure readers could borrow, but not buy. The three-volume format meant three borrowings, rather than one, so it was good business. And when Mudie purchased multiple copies – like 2,000 copies of *Felix Holt* – publishers had a risk-free, guaranteed profit as he bought most of the first edition, even considering the discount rate he demanded (he paid 15s for a 31s 6d book). Authors got paid, and Mudie's subscriber base ticked up. There was profit, magically, for everyone, except for authors trying to write in different forms. Those writers were, George Moore lamented, 'crushed beneath the wheels of these implacable Juggernauts' – the Juggernauts being the circulating libraries. An author with the reputation of, say, Charles Dickens, did have the option of serial publication in magazines; but for almost all authors, if Mudie declined to take a novel, that work was, to all practical purposes, doomed. The spiky, worried letters from George Eliot to her publisher John Blackwood – 'Can you imagine why Mudie has almost always left [*Scenes of Clerical Life*] out of his advertised list, although he puts in very trashy and obscure books?' – show even this magnificent writer's deep concern for Mudie's estimation.

The need for authors to write in this fixed format often meant stretching material across three volumes, which led to what we might unhappily describe as the sagging middle of Victorian fiction. 'Three volumes mean, as a rule, the most reckless padding,' wrote the *Illustrated London News* in 1894, 'and padding is fatal to art.' 'Like a vast sarcophagus,' said Edmund Gosse, enjoying his words, 'in the manner of Bernini, with weeping angels blowing trumpets over tons of marble . . . a shapeless monster of a book.' If a book had to carry a 'cargo' of 250,000 words (Guinevere L. Griest's term), then the narrative almost certainly needed to digress, the subplots to rumble, the style to circumlocute. 'Twaddle in this shape is sent to clubs,' continued the *Illustrated London News*, 'chiefly to provoke the restful nap before dinner.' If the text still came in a little short, the publisher might step in, adding a preface or a table of contents, or ordering the print shop to fill space in more radical ways, by widening margins, for example, or increasing chapter breaks, or raising the size of the type, or adding extra lead between lines. 'I do protest against the "whited sepulchres" style of getting up the present day novels,' wrote a correspondent to the *Publishers' Circular* in 1894, 'with enormous margins, lines wide enough apart for a cyclist to drive between, and with "fat" enough to delight the compositor's heart.'

The three-volume novel had a long, but not endless life. When single-volume reprints started to appear at prices readers could afford, often 6 shillings or less, the triple-decker grew less attractive, and then unshiftable. Alongside the loaning of books, Mudie had always sold older copies in his second-hand department. But the inexpensive single-volume exploded this market, and old three-deckers were soon, as one commentator put it, 'stowed away in Mr. Mudie's capacious vaults', known as 'the Catacombs' – which as a publishing environment sounds sub-optimal. An example: Smith, Elder & Co. published Mary Augusta Ward's philosophical novel *Marcella* in three volumes in 1894. Mudie's – then run by Charles's second son, Arthur O. Mudie – bought 1,750 copies, which meant 5,250 volumes. But when a 6-shilling, one-volume reprint appeared just three months later, Mudie was left with mountains of unloanable, unsaleable, cumbrous books. Mudie's might have raised the subscription rate, but the 1 guinea charge was the library's defining trait. So Mudie's and its rival Smith's demanded from publishers a reduction in the price of novels, and also the assurance that publishers would wait a year before issuing cheaper editions. By reducing his expense on fiction, Mudie had in effect killed off the triple-decker, a form that could only survive in the artificial air that had circulated between Mudie's and publishers. Instead, he sought now to shift emphasis in the direction of one-volume novels, history, travel, and science. The triple-decker's eclipse was swift. In 1894, one hundred and eighty-four three-volumes had been published. In 1895, fifty-two. In 1896, twenty-five. In 1897, four. George Moore, whose loud voice has been a refrain across this chapter, congratulated himself on his role in the decline of Mudie's three-volume monopoly. 'The censorship of the libraries has come to an end, I said to myself, and I boasted that I had served the cause of humanity.'

The event that shaped, and in many ways ended, Mudie's life was the death of his eldest and beloved son Charles, aged twenty-eight, in 1879, of acute rheumatism and endocarditis. Charles spent the last eight years of his life working for his father, studying all aspects of the business in anticipation of a succession that never occurred. Very shortly after his death, Charles's sister Mary had printed for private circulation 'a memorial sketch' of her brother. But while she 'writes under the shadow of a deep and abiding sorrow', the memories are generalised and one-tone – Charles is 'vigorous and manly' and 'uniformly respectful' and his life is 'one unbroken record of love and care for others' – and the outline of the dead brother recedes even as it is being remembered. Better as an evocation are the Minutes of the Directors of Mudie's Library from 17 January 1879 which, despite the generic constraints of committee documentation, register that loss more powerfully:

> The Chairman reported the death on Monday, the 13th inst., of Mr. CHARLES HENRY MUDIE, the elder son of their colleague, at the early age of twenty-eight. In recording this sad event the Board desire to express their deep and tender sympathy with the bereaved wife; and with Mr. and Mrs. C. E. MUDIE and their afflicted family. Their loss is no ordinary one. Though young in years, his bright and generous nature had won for him the esteem of a large and loving circle, while his sagacity and diligence in business had given more than usual promise of a brilliant and successful future.

The death was intolerable for Mudie, who spent the next five years in a process of gradual retreat from life, uncoupling himself from everything, hook by hook. By 1884 Mudie's second son, Arthur, had taken over the business. Mudie died six years later at his home in Maresfield Gardens, Hampstead, but the 'Leviathan' of libraries ran on until it was finally closed by a court order on 12 July 1937 after declaring bankruptcy, a little short of a century since its inception. The obituary for Mudie ran in the *Illustrated London News* on 8 November 1890: in Mudie's Library, 'many families, and many lonely persons, have found more entertainment than in all the theatres, concert-rooms, and exhibitions of London'. *The Times* on 12 July 1937 described the cultural shock of this closure as 'the extinction of . . . a national institution'.

The Hammersmith Socialist Society (1892).

9. ANACHRONISTIC BOOKS

Thomas Cobden-Sanderson (1840–1922)

This marvellous photograph shows the Hammersmith Socialist Society in 1892: middle-aged men in white collars, young women holding babies, a very old seated figure with a shawl and cane, large banners like tapestries pulled from walls, and autumn leaves scattered on the ground. The dominant personality sits in the front row, left of centre, seemingly enlarged – but that's how he always looked – clutching white paper, with the intensity of Orson Welles, and the hair of Gandalf. This is William Morris (1834–96), revolutionary designer, artist, book-maker, socialist, author, someone for whom the word 'formidable' is unavoidable. 'A man of steel', in biographer Fiona MacCarthy's words, although that steel was tempered with eccentricity and friendship. But the focus of this chapter isn't Morris, although he's part of the story. Our man is second from the right on the middle row, shorter than his neighbours, his head tilted, his face a touch unfocused, a little lost in the crowd – although he, like Morris, would exert a huge influence on the bookish culture around him.

The rise of Thomas Cobden-Sanderson (1840–1922) to a position of eminence and also controversy within the book-making world came after a series of false starts and cul-de-sacs. At Cambridge University he lost his Christian faith and left without a degree, and, in the words of historian Alan Crawford, 'limped through the 1860s, not knowing what to do with his life'. He practised half-heartedly as a barrister; his health was faltering. He was saved by Annie Cobden (1853–1926): they met in 1881 outside the Duomo in Siena and married a year later. Annie was the daughter of the radical MP Richard Cobden but would have her own claims to political significance through her activities as a suffragette. She gave to Cobden-Sanderson her surname, a tidy inheritance, and even more importantly a sense of practical application – under her gaze he was less histrionic doom, more purposeful worldliness – and encouraged him to shift directions. In 1882 he joined the bookbinding workshop of Roger de Coverly where he trained for six months before setting up on his own, beginning a relationship with the physical book that would last until his death in 1922.

Cobden-Sanderson worked as a binder for about ten years and his books, many of which were sold to clients in America, were a major catalyst in firing a tradition of fine bookbinding in Britain that flourishes to this day. But soon his interest broadened into other aspects of the book. The man standing behind Cobden-Sanderson in the 1892 photograph, wearing a hat, is engraver, photographer, and printer Emery Walker (1851–1933). In 1900,

Cobden-Sanderson established the Doves Press in partnership with Walker, with premises at 1 Hammersmith Terrace, on the bank of the Thames. But to understand what Cobden-Sanderson was up to, and to grasp the ambitions of the Doves Press, we need for a moment to go back to that bearded giant and the private press he set up.

'I do not much believe in heroes, in leaders or examples,' wrote the great bibliographer Colin Franklin, 'yet Morris is a hero for me, with no great caveat or doubt.' The Kelmscott Press was just one, relatively late, expression of the philosophy of what we might call William Morris's political design. Ducking the path to holy orders that seemed inevitable as he went up to study at Exeter College, Oxford, Morris trained as an architect and established a close, complicated coterie of artists and poets, including the Pre-Raphaelites Dante Gabriel Rossetti and Edward Burne-Jones. Morris's interest in book-making came later in life and needs to be seen not only in relation to the history of the book, but also the wider sprawl of initiatives he set up and encouraged. Those initiatives included lectures to working men and women across the country, and pamphlets with titles such as 'Chants for Socialists', and 'Useful Work v. Useless Toil'; the design firm Morris, Marshall, Faulkner & Co., renamed Morris & Co. in 1875, which profoundly influenced the design of fabrics, furniture, wallpaper, stained glass, tiles, and tapestries; the Society for the Protection of Ancient Buildings, established by Morris, Webb, and others in 1887 to fight back against what they regarded as misconceived and intrusive ideas of Victorian restoration; and the country retreat at Kelmscott Manor, Oxfordshire, that served as a base for artistic activities and for meetings of the Hammersmith Socialist Society. The Kelmscott Press was founded by Morris in 1891 – the year before that Hammersmith photograph – as a purposeful anachronism: an attempt to print limited-edition books on a hand press, in an age of industrialised production, in forms that harked back to a medieval past. Or, we should say, that harked back to a late-nineteenth-century idea of the medieval past: a pastiche that was useful to Morris and his peers as a way to oppose mechanisation. The appearance of Kelmscott books evoked those very early days of print, and even earlier days of manuscript production: features like the clasps on Morris's books, for example, weren't strictly necessary – clasps were applied to medieval books made from vellum since vellum warps, but Morris's books were printed on paper—but they signalled an investment in that earlier time. More than an investment, we might say: these books were, in Colin Franklin's words, an attempt at 'obliterating time, returning to an imagined fourteenth-century bliss'. Morris's sense of the history of the book was the very opposite of a linear narrative of progress: for Morris, what came first was best, and the rest was a falling away, with a disastrous descent towards the mechanised in the second half of the nineteenth century. 'A born lover of the Middle Ages,' wrote J. W. Mackail of Morris in 1902, 'and a born hater of the ages which followed them.' In creating 'is backwards-looking aesthetic (Morris would reclaim 'backwards looking' as a positive), Morris sought to mount a powerful critique against cheapness, mass production, and waste, and he sought to put skilled human labour, performed by patient, careful men and women, at the heart of his culture. In this fundamental sense, his books were political interventions.

Kelmscott was a 'private press', meaning a small letterpress operation, producing a relatively low number of copies for a relatively limited market at a relatively high price, that rejected mechanised printing, despite its availability, and worked with traditional printing and binding methods. Private presses used high-quality materials, such as handmade paper and ink, and often specially designed type, and prioritised very high standards of craft, a sense of the book as a work of art, and the skilled and dignified work of book production.

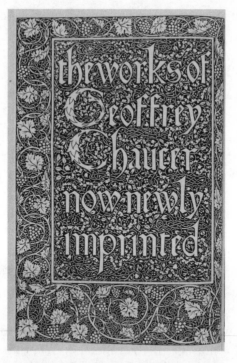

William Morris, The works of Geoffrey Chaucer,
now newly imprinted *(1896).*

Commercial imperatives often took second, or third, place to decisions about design and craft – 'More interested in making a good book,' wrote John Carter in 1961, 'than a fat profit' – although thoughts of money and income were certainly not absent. By working in this way, Morris was sustaining something like a concealed tradition, or a set of local instances, although those precedent private presses only began to be perceived as a movement after Kelmscott. This kind of prehistory of the English private presses might include Horace Walpole's eighteenth-century press at Strawberry Hill – the *Officina Arbuteana,* in Walpole's words – established in 1757; and the Daniel Press set up by Henry Daniel (1836–1919), fellow and later provost of Worcester College, Oxford, and run by Daniel, his wife Emily, and their daughters

Page proofs for the Kelmscott Chaucer *(1896),*
with Morris's autograph corrections and notes.

Rachel and Ruth, who printed, among others, the work of the
poets Robert Bridges and Richard Watson Dixon.

Kelmscott books were printed on Albion hand-printing
presses, using thick ink made from older recipes (Morris thought
nineteenth-century inks thin and grey), and handmade paper
based on samples held in Morris's own library; they were bound
not in the normal Victorian leather but in limp vellum or linen
and board. Morris himself designed the title pages and borders; illustrations were based on drawings by artists including
Walter Crane and Edward Burne-Jones. (These illustrations were
wood-engravings, the delicate and precise product of finer tools
than the v- or u-shaped gouges used for woodcuts.) The Kelmscott Press was also its own publisher, sidestepping what Morris
regarded as the inappropriately controlling, market-driven

contributions of London publishers. The press was located at 16 and then 14 Upper Mall, Hammersmith – on the banks of the Thames and just yards from where Cobden-Sanderson would set up his Doves Press. The Kelmscott Press printed fifty-three different titles (in total some twenty-two thousand copies) in its seven years.

The most famous and justly lauded was and is the Kelmscott *Chaucer*, the work of four years and the last book Morris saw through the press before his death in 1896. 'Like a pocket cathedral,' said Edward Burne-Jones, turning the pages. On the previous two pages you can see a finished title page, with all its density, and also a marked-up proof of page 63. To the pressman's polite enquiry on that proof, 'Please see if this page will do, & return', Morris thunders, 'This of course is the wrong measure what <u>is</u> the use of sending me things which are obviously wrong?'

The intertwining of lettering and design on the title page means that the letters seem simultaneously text and ornament. This is all before us, at once, a book, but also a beautiful, opened-up work of art. The care and, crucially, the *pleasure* in labour that this book gives body to is central to Morris's conception of work, performed with dignity and properly valued. 'My first sight of the Kelmscott Chaucer,' wrote Colin Franklin, remembering a schoolboy visit to the library of old deaf Mr Newman, in the village of Cotterstock, who had, years before, known Morris, 'lit such a spark as has never been quenched.'

The most important element of Cobden-Sanderson's Doves Press was not any single book or person or even Cobden-Sanderson himself: the centre was the font of metal type that Cobden-Sanderson commissioned, known as Doves Roman, or the Doves Press Fount of Type, or most commonly the Doves Type.

Printed by T. J. Cobden-Sanderson & Emery Walker at The Doves Press and finished 3 June 1902. Compositor: J. H. Mason. Pressmen: H. Gage-Cole, J. Ryan, T. Waller, A. Beaumont. Penmen: Edward Johnston, Grayley Hewitt. Sold at The Doves Press.

The Doves Press type, from the colophon to Paradise Lost, *which took inspiration from Jenson's type.*

Cobden-Sanderson took inspiration from two works of Venetian printing in the 1470s. After William Morris died in October 1896, and the Kelmscott Press closed in 1898, many of Morris's books were sold off in a Sotheby's sale in December that year. Cobden-Sanderson sent along Emery Walker and Sydney Cockerell, Morris's former private secretary, and the latter snapped up, for £7 5s, Morris's copy of Pliny's *Historia Naturalis*, printed in Venice by Nicolas Jenson in 1476 (see the image on p. 117 in Chapter Four). (Another copy of this book, illuminated by a Venetian artist for a patron, sold at Christie's in 2010 for £313,250.) Jenson's type provided the model for the Doves Press upper-case letters; the lower-case letters were based on Jacobus Rubeus's printing, also in Venice in 1476, of Aretinus's *Historia del Popolo Fiorentino*, also sold at the Morris Sotheby's sale.

Because what survived of Jenson's work was not the metal letters but the printed impressions, Walker and Cobden-Sanderson had to work back from the often over-inked pages to extract their understanding of the metal type. In designing his type in this way, Cobden-Sanderson was sustaining a tradition: Morris himself had worked in similar fashion to design his roman type, known as the Golden Type. But where Morris developed thicker letters that recalled medieval calligraphy, and produced denser, darker pages, Cobden-Sanderson sought a lighter, cleaner design.

Punch (left) *and matrix* (right).

The fifteenth-century Latin alphabet had no J, U, or W, so designer Percy Tiffin drew these letters anew, along with the Doves Press versions of the Venetian originals. Punctuation was based on Jenson and similar fifteenth-century precedents. Once Tiffin's drawings were transferred to photographs, the punches were cut by Edward Prince (1846–1923) in Edinburgh – a figure of considerable reputation, and also the last of a dying breed: on his death in 1923, Prince was the final living independent punch-cutter in England.

As we saw with John Baskerville's letter designs in Chapter 4, punch-cutting is the craft of creating punches on the end of a steel bar in the shape of a glyph (a letter, number, or punctuation mark), first by tracing the outline of the letter design to the end of the steel bar, and then by cutting; these punches are then stamped into soft copper to produce cavities, or matrices; and these matrices are then locked into a mould, and type metal (an alloy of lead, antimony, and tin) is poured into the matrix to cast the type and produce the desired letter, number, or symbol. This was exacting, meticulous work; each punch took on average about a day's labour. The earliest printers in the late-fifteenth century had often had prior careers in metalwork, developing skills in cutting that would transfer easily to type production: this was true of Nicolas Jenson, and also of Gutenberg himself. This fifteenth-century sense of printing operating within a broader craft context also chimed with Morris's Arts and Crafts movement, with its attention to printing books within a much broader conception of design.

This was the type that would find its way to the bottom of the Thames: but that's a story for the end of this chapter. For now what needs noting is the degree to which the clean and hyper-legible pages produced by the Doves Type stood in purposeful contrast to Morris's Kelmscott books. Edward Prince had cut the three types developed by Morris: Golden (a roman type), Troy (a gothic type, modelled on *The Recuyell of the Historyes of Troye*, Caxton's first printed book and the first book printed anywhere in English), and Chaucer (a smaller version of Troy).

We can get a clear sense of aesthetic difference by comparing a Morris edition to a Doves Press edition (see plate section). Which is for you? For me it's the difference between holding my breath, and breathing out. For British typographic designer Ruari McLean (1917–2006), the airy pages of the Doves Press books were the most devastating criticism possible of Morris's dense work. For historian Roderick Cave, Cobden-Sanderson's books are 'cold and sterile in their perfection; automata of the book world . . . We can admire, but it is impossible to love.' More extravagantly, and rather wonderfully, the poet and co-founder of the Nonesuch Press, Francis Meynell (1891–1975), thought Doves Press books 'lovely, impeccable, taut and silky like young muscles in play'. Maybe. But whatever our judgement, the two books show vividly how artistic expression proceeds in reaction to what has gone before: the Doves Press an answer to Kelmscott, and Kelmscott itself a pushing away from its industrial contemporary.

Cobden-Sanderson wanted the history of the Doves Press to be told through its books, not its personalities. He spent much of 1917 destroying old letters relating to the Press: 'I am determined that, as far as I am able to destroy, there shall be no debris left, no history of petty details, but only the books themselves.' The books themselves: the Doves Press produced forty editions between 1900 and 1916, each consisting of between 225 and 500 copies (300 was the standard run), with most printed on paper but a handful on vellum. Did a press ever kick off with a less commercially promising debut? Cobden-Sanderson's first was a work in Latin by a Roman historian, written about 98 CE, describing the life of Gnaeus Julius Agricola, governor of Britain in the first century: Publicus Cornelius Tacitus's *Agricola*, printed in October 1900. Click-bait it was not. The titles that followed were more conventionally canonical and signalled Cobden-Sanderson's ambition to give beautiful printed expression to what he saw as culture's most important works. 'So I should slowly build up the idea of monumental thought,' he wrote in his diary in 1908, 'and slowly would emerge the Vision . . . dedicated . . . to the majesty of the Universe, to man's part in its imaginative creation.' Cobden-Sanderson had a weakness for clauses like 'the majesty of the Universe', and on a certain level it's hard to know exactly what he's talking about, but we get a more focused sense of the Doves Press project through the list of titles: poetry by William Wordsworth, Robert Browning, Percy Bysshe Shelley, John Keats, and Alfred, Lord Tennyson; plays and poetry by Shakespeare; John Milton's *Paradise Lost*; the Bible. That sense of a canon stretched beyond England – Ralph Waldo Emerson's *Essays*; Goethe's *Faust* – and was augmented with books of more local, or personal, interest to Cobden-Sanderson, like John Ruskin's essay on political economy, *Unto This Last*, and his own work of bibliographical philosophy, *The Ideal Book or Book Beautiful* (1900) – of which, more later.

On 20 March 1901, Cobden-Sanderson invited calligrapher Edward Johnston for supper at 1 Hammersmith Terrace, and asked him to bring along his quills and reeds. He referred to Johnston as 'my dear scribe' in a manner which may well have been irritating. Cobden-Sanderson was not always good at reading what other people felt. He wanted to discuss the design of John Milton's *Paradise Lost*: the first major undertaking of the Doves Press, and a volume that Cobden-Sanderson hoped would establish the press's reputation.

Johnston (1872–1944) was a Uruguayan-born British designer who is often described as the father of modern calligraphy, most famous for the sans-serif typeface used for the London Underground until the 1980s – 'Johnston', or 'Johnston Sans' – and for the iconic roundel symbol still used today. In 1901, he was twenty-nine – over thirty years Cobden-Sanderson's junior – and had been teaching lettering at the Royal College of Art and the Central School of Arts and Crafts in Southampton Row, where his pupils included Eric Gill and briefly Cobden-Sanderson himself. Cobden-Sanderson said that observing a demonstration by Johnston 'is like watching some strange bird'. Many of Johnston's successes, including his formative handbook *Writing & Illuminating & Lettering* (1906) – a distillation of the evening classes he gave – and the London Underground commission (1913), were still before him, but Cobden-Sanderson relished the prospect of superb handwritten letters finding prominent place in his printed Doves Press books.

It took some time for Johnston to perfect the lettering that would open *Paradise Lost*: some thirty trial pages survive today in the Newberry Library in Chicago, and there are others scattered across libraries and archives. This slowness was in part an expression of his hyper-diligence and care ('It literally made Johnston feel ill to see work badly done,' wrote historian Marianne Tidcombe), but it was due also to Cobden-Sanderson's control-freakery. He couldn't stop hovering. 'The H's are very nice in colour,' worried Cobden-Sanderson in July 1902, 'blue & red, but are they not a little fat, or amorphous? But I will not carp. They *are* very nice & a great pleasure to my eyes wearied with looking at millions & millions of black l[ower] c[ase]!'

Each of the 300 paper copies of *Paradise Lost* that eventually emerged in November 1902, priced 3 guineas (about £85 today), was a small quarto, heavy in the hand, printed in black ink with red headings, with blue and red handwritten initials for the first word of each book, and bound in limp vellum with simple gold spine letters declaring 'PARADISE LOST'. As Cobden-Sanderson hoped, it would be celebrated. The great early twentieth-century bibliographer A. W. Pollard (1859–1944) called it 'the finest edition of Milton's *Paradise Lost* ever printed, or ever likely to be', and wrote, more expansively still, that 'I know no more perfect book in Roman type.'

The presence of Johnston's calligraphy connects his *Paradise Lost* back to traditions of medieval manuscripts (from the Latin *manu*, 'by hand' + *scriptus*, 'written'). Some of Johnston's letters were cut in wood by C. E. Keates and printed in red ink, but handwritten initials were added directly at the start of Books 2 to 12, alternating in blue and red. Across the total print run, almost 4,000 initials had to be added, and Johnston was aided by his former pupil, ex-barrister Graily Hewitt (whose name, with some irony, was misspelt in the printed colophon). The power of these initials lies in the way they are clearly the work of the hand, not the press. They are very slightly imperfect, but better for this, in terms both of vividly summoning a human presence, and also in that these aptly flawed letters seem to enact Milton's central theme of the fall of man. This is how Johnston put it in his *Writing & Illuminating & Lettering* (1906):

> The beauty and quality of Versal letters depends very much on their freedom; *touching-up* or trimming after they are made is apt to spoil them; and when good letters are made with a free hand, minute roughnesses, which are due to their quick construction, may be regarded as shewing a *good* rather than a bad form of *careless* workmanship.

Overleaf is the opening of Book 4, with a handwritten blue capital of 'minute roughness' alongside printed black verse and a red book number.

Even more spectacular are the three copies that were printed on vellum, rather than paper, with the first-page lettering of title, author, and the word 'OF' added by Graily Hewitt in raised, burnished gold. In the production of medieval manuscripts, gold lettering was a luxury with a purpose: a mechanism for lighting up – the literal meaning of 'illuminate' – the page. For scribes producing manuscripts between about 700 and 1200 CE, this gold was added either as leaf, beaten to the thinness of tissue, or as paint known as shell gold because it was often kept in a mussel shell. The gold was layered over a base of gesso (a plaster-of-Paris compound) which caused it to rise up from the surface, straining beyond the page and dazzling, particularly after burnishing with a smoothed stone or an animal tooth.

The Doves Press gold drags this medieval craft into the twentieth century to stand in defiance of a machine-led contemporary. It also announces a commitment to slowness, both in terms of how these books were made and how we read them. As our eyes trace the glittering letters – the interlocking 'R' and 'A' of 'PARADISE'; the reaching 'J' of 'JOHN'; the 'O' in the margin like a portal to somewhere else – we read gradually, lingeringly, and we wonder at the careful technical skill behind these letter forms. It was exactly

OFOR THAT WARNING VOICE, Book 4
WHICH HE WHO SAW
TH' APOCALYPS, HEARD CRY
IN HEAVEN ALOUD,
Then when the Dragon, put to second rout,
Came furious down to be reveng'd on men,
WO TO THE INHABITANTS ON EARTH! that now,
While time was, our first Parents had bin warnd
The coming of thir secret foe, and scap'd
Haply so scap'd his mortal snare; for now
Satan, now first inflam'd with rage, came down,
The Tempter ere th' Accuser of man-kind,
To wreck on innocent frail man his loss
Of that first Battel, and his flight to Hell:

The Doves Press Paradise Lost *Book 4.*

this kind of slowness, and the meditative reflection it enabled, that took over Cobden-Sanderson during periods of book-making when a kind of 'blessed quiet . . . enters into my soul'. Preparing a text, or checking sheets still wet from the press, is experienced by some book-makers as arduous, taxing, eye-straining work, but here he is, writing in his journal on 28 September 1902, 'at the Bindery, looking over the *Paradise Lost* sheets, preliminary to binding':

the sun, dear brilliancy, shining through the window on to the table and myself, making the moving water glisten, the west wind rustling the dry leaves, and gently shaking them, dead, from the living tree. O, world of wonder!

And then twelve years later, in November 1914, aged seventy-three, reflecting on the books he has printed:

How many moments in reading the proofs of the divine books it has been my privilege to print, have I paused to wander in the worlds of their creation, a world suspended as in vision, far seen and sunlit, and all quiet as a summer's eve or dawn.

Gutenberg's Biblia Latina, *42 lines (Mainz, 1454).*

That's an important idea for Cobden-Sanderson: that great books, as physical objects, have the capacity to *slow down time*. They do this partly because of the care that went into their production, that remains legible as we read; but this temporal warping is also a result of the way Doves Press books seem to exist at several moments at once. They are (Cobden-Sanderson would not have uttered the word) polytemporal objects. As a hybrid of the handwritten and the printed, this *Paradise Lost* recalls the very earliest printed books. Many copies of the Bible printed in metal type in Mainz in the 1450s by Gutenberg, Johann Fust, and Peter Schoeffer were also illuminated by hand-painted decorations. Above is the opening page of one of the forty-eight extant copies, this one now in the Beinecke Library at Yale, a wondrous mix of printed text and a hand-drawn natural world.

It's tempting to organise book history as a tidy progress through time, things getting better across a series of superseding moments and epochs, from manuscript to print to digital. But this version of history won't do. Gutenberg's earliest printed books, and the even earlier culture of medieval manuscripts, hover alongside the Doves Press *Paradise Lost* as both precedents and partners. The effect of Cobden-Sanderson's book is to summon up these earlier traditions as presences that are more substantial than ghosts, a mingling of 1455 Mainz and 1902 Hammersmith.

Cobden-Sanderson regarded the printing of the Doves Press five-volume edition of *The English Bible* as an inevitable but daunting bibliographical challenge. As it had been for John Baskerville, it was a key text for a printer to demonstrate their capacities. To produce such a thing required at first a certain amount of legal ground-preparation: he needed the permission of the Queen's printers, or the colleges of Eton or Winchester, or the university presses of Oxford and Cambridge. When Oxford said no, Cobden-Sanderson did that particularly English thing and invited the Secretary to the Syndics of Cambridge University round to lunch. We don't know what they ate, but Cambridge agreed, permitting the use of the Authorised Bible text as edited by the Revd F. H. Scrivener in 1873, providing that proofs would be read by someone at the university press.

The project took time – Volume 1 wasn't finished until the end of 1902; volume 5, the New Testament, in October 1904 – but it was a commercial success: all copies were sold before printing was completed, and with no expenses on advertisements or free review copies, Walker and Cobden-Sanderson shared £500 profit between them. The five-volume set in Trinity College, Oxford, contains three sheets tucked inside Volume 1 that recall the moment of this book's publication: a specimen page of the start of Genesis printed in 1901 that was sent to subscribers; a subscription flyer filled in by the lawyer and baronet C. E. H. Chadwyck-Healey (1845–1919), dated 27 March 1902; and a receipt for the purchase of the first volume at £3 3s 7d, including postage.

Each volume is heavy and large; each page measures 33.5 by 23.5 centimetres. Cobden-Sanderson had planned to print in folio format (that is, on paper folded once), but, realising how much time this would take – 'the estimate was eight years!' he wrote in his diary – switched to large quarto. Quarto meant each sheet was folded twice, and thus that a single pull of the press would print four pages, so if large paper was used, it would reduce the printing time for this massive volume. You need two hands to hold each volume, but the limp vellum cover means each book is pliable. That plain, limp vellum binding – 'THE ENGLISH BIBLE' in gold on the spine – is purposely anachronistic, recalling binding traditions from centuries ago, of the earliest printed books from the late fifteenth century, known as 'incunables' (from the Latin *incunabula*, 'cradle' or 'swaddling clothes', made by book-makers who had known a time when books were all in manuscript) and sixteenth- and some seventeenth-century books, before limp vellum fell out of fashion.

As he considered the challenge of printing a Doves Press Bible, Cobden-Sanderson saw himself working in a tradition established by William Tyndale (1494–1536), the first English translator of the Bible to see his works printed, and a scholar whose Protestant commitment to disseminating God's word in print led to his execution. Tyndale's translations were crucial precedent texts for the 1611 Authorised Bible, produced under King James I. Cobden-Sanderson's identification was thus not exactly self-effacing, and we get a sense of his grandeur of vision from a diary entry for 14 January 1902:

> My only fears should be that I may not live to accomplish it –
> Tyndale died to print his – or that the work itself may not be good
> enough.

Let me give all my thoughts to the work itself. Let it be my life's work.

Let me now live for it, and, if needs be, die for it. Never count the cost!

And so, with this new year, let me devote myself wholly to this great work. Let me desire for it the most beautiful frame possible for the Bible as a whole – that composite whole, wrought with tears and laughter in the olden times, wrought again in the paroxysm of a nation's reversion by the blood and tears of its first translators; and now set forth, not ornamentally for a collector's toy, but severely, plainly, monumentally, for a nation's masterpiece, for a nation's guidance, consolation, and hope.

Although it's hard to track exactly what Cobden-Sanderson is talking about, in part because of the romantic vagueness of what he calls 'the olden times', his ability to place himself in a tripartite historical sequence of the Bible's initial composition, its translation in the sixteenth century, and its printing now in Hammersmith in 1902, is remarkable. Did he really think the Doves Press volumes would be a nation's consolation?

Certainly Cobden-Sanderson never had a problem taking himself seriously. His diaries teeter precariously on the edge of the ridiculous, full of statements like 'in what glorious pageantry are we immersed'. There's a bit of the Malvolio about him, particularly when we imagine him in a smock. His former apprentice Douglas Cockerell said, 'Cobden-Sanderson's egotism was almost pathological . . . He lived in a world of his creation, swayed by emotional storms of great intensity, and I doubt if he was capable of true friendship.'

His disdain for what he calls the book as 'collector's toy', and his deep investment in the severe, the plain, and the monumental, is characteristic, too – and here at least Cobden-Sanderson was not over-reaching. The beauty that these Doves Press volumes possess is indeed of a stark, monumental kind: the beauty of the polished slab of marble, not the woven tapestry. The idea of the monumental appealed to Cobden-Sanderson because of its connotations of slowness of production (like the letters cut with chisels into stone that he used to illustrate his lectures on typography), and of permanence of reception (like the Roman statues he observed in the British Museum). In this sense, Doves Press books had definitively moved away from the busy typography and cluttered *mise-en-page* of Morris's Kelmscott volumes in favour of an aesthetic of *simplex munditiis*, 'simple elegance': 'a kind of architectural balance and just sense of proportion both in the type itself, closely modelled upon that of Jenson, and in the arrangement of the page.' These words came in a 'charming' article (Cobden-Sanderson's verdict) in the *Times Literary Supplement* for 12 April 1917 that noted the particular achievement of *The English Bible*:

> Perhaps of all the books *The English Bible* is the one at which criticism stops short, so perfect is it in the proportion of its page, the sparing and judicious use of the red, the admirable arrangement of the poetical portions. It is a noble book which will bear comparison with the great examples of typography of all time.

The opening page of the Doves Press Bible is one of the most famous pages in twentieth-century book design. The initial 'I' of 'IN THE BEGINNING' runs the length of the page: a sudden plummet, in red, as if joining (as Marianne Tidcombe suggests) heaven and earth.

This is Edward Johnston's calligraphic work translated into metal engraving. Recovering from an attack of sciatica at the Abbey Hotel, Malvern, Cobden-Sanderson wrote to Johnston: 'The Bible initial (In the Beginning) is magnificent.' Critics have agreed, like the *Daily Telegraph* reviewer who suggested that, despite 300 years of being in print, the Authorised English Bible 'until this day had never been worthily printed'.

Sixteenth- and seventeenth-century readers often marked the margins of their books with signs to denote passages of particular significance, as we saw with Wynkyn de Worde's books. Later

Doves Press Bible.

books were often annotated, too. Ben Jonson's copy of George Puttenham's *Arte of English Poesy* (1589), a handbook for writing verse, now in the British Library, is covered with Jonson's pointing fingers (or 'manicules'), flowers, underlinings, asterisks, and also vertical lines that, in their inclusive sweep down the page, suggest sustained passages of interest. In fact Jonson marks so much of this page – he's the GCSE pupil covering everything in yellow highlighter – that it's hard to distinguish significance from insignificance. The long red 'I' that runs down the Doves Press Bible recalls this tradition of marginal marking. There is also a nice paradox of placement here, since the 'I' is both the first letter of the Bible, and also a marginal mark outside that text: the 'I' is simultaneously inside and outside, constituting but also annotating the text.

Turning the pages of these five volumes, one is struck by the legibility of the typeface, and the uncluttered clarity of the page design. This clean typography is accompanied with a regular *mise-en-page*: page numbers at the foot, signature numbers bottom middle of each recto, running title in top left and top right of each page, chapter numbers in the margin. And after pages and pages of black text, with no illustrations and no breaks save the 'pilcrow' (or paragraph mark) indicating a new verse, the red initial of each new book represents a powerful visual break.

Cobden-Sanderson gave extended expression to this sense of proportion and of balance in *The Ideal Book or Book Beautiful: A Tract on Calligraphy, Printing and Illustration & on the Book Beautiful as a Whole*, printed by the Doves Press in 1900. Central to Cobden-Sanderson's philosophy is the idea of the book as a 'unity', 'The Book Beautiful . . . conceived of as a whole', by which he meant that the elements of production should form a harmonious composite, the unity 'higher than the art of each', with each art 'contributory . . . [but] in due subordination to the ideal which is the creation of all', and each art working towards 'something which is distinctly Not-Itself'. Elements of design which might in themselves be conspicuously beautiful were problematic for precisely those reasons: they interfered with the author's word, blocking its 'swiftness of apprehension and appreciation', and served only as 'a typographical impertinence'. This idea of balance and order drew heavily on Morris's conception of harmonious cooperation, described in his *Ideal Book* (1893). So important was this notion of balanced collaboration that Cobden-Sanderson characterised its opposite ('the self-assertion of any Art beyond the limits imposed by the conditions of its creation') as 'an Act of Treason'. The calligrapher who decorates letters too much is 'pressing his art too far. He was in danger . . . of subordinating his Text to himself.'

Crucially, typography should not distract from the author's text, but should rather 'win access for that communication by the clearness & beauty of the vehicle'. In 1930, Beatrice Warde, scholar of typography, published an influential essay titled 'The Crystal Goblet, or Printing Should be Invisible', in which she called for typography to serve as a clear glass serves wine: that is, to hold and reveal content, but to be itself clear, unobtrusive, transparent. Cobden-Sanderson was working with a similar aim and understood book design in fundamentally author-centric terms: that is, the

printer, designer, engraver, binder, and all the other agents of production should work to bring the author's conception to the world
with self-effacing clarity. 'The whole duty of Typography, as of
Calligraphy,' Cobden-Sanderson writes, 'is to communicate to
the imagination, without loss by the way, the thought or image
intended to be communicated by the Author.' (We note in passing a tension between this professed self-effacement, and what we
might indelicately call Cobden-Sanderson's massive ego.)

Good book design necessarily, through its sheer competence,
carries the threat of displacing the text itself: the potential for
antagonism is the flip-side of the skilled artist working in a collective, and collaborative work is the product of reining in, and
disciplining, the artistic assertion on which work depends. The
colophon to volume one of the Doves Press Bible is an expression
of this sense of individual agents working together, listing not only
what we might think of as the primary publishers – 'Printed by
T. J. Cobden-Sanderson and Emery Walker' – but a little community of makers: 'Compositors: J. H. Mason, J. Guttridge, C. F.
Greengrass. Pressmen: H. Gage-Cole, J. Ryan, T. Waller, A. Beaumont.' In this respect, Doves Press books were entirely unlike
the early modern publications on which they were in many ways
based. The agents behind those early books are usually effaced.
When the King James, or Authorised, version of the Bible was
printed in 1611, the colophon read only: 'Imprinted at London:
By Robert Barker, printer to the Kings most excellent Maiestie,
Anno Dom. 1611.' The little society of pressmen, proofreaders,
compositors, and more, was not listed.

The physical proximity of the numerous Doves Press workers, many of them clustered around Hammersmith Terrace, was
important to this vision of informed cooperation: it enabled,
Cobden-Sanderson hoped, a sense of a shared project, and of
intimacy with what others were doing. This version of the book
as beautiful and harmonious, 'without stress or strain', was a
means to express, and align with (the language gets cloudy here as
Cobden-Sanderson breaks out into capitals), 'that WHOLE OF

LIFE WHICH IS CONSTITUTED OF OURSELVES &
THE WORLD, THAT COMPLEX AND MARVELLOUS
WHOLE WHICH, AMID THE STRIFE OF COMPETI-
TIVE FORCES, SUPREMELY HOLDS ITS OWN'.

For Cobden-Sanderson the Doves was, as he wrote in his diary,
'the medium at hand wherein and wherewith to express my admiration for what I admire or for what I love', and we see this capacity of the book to take in and stand for the universe continually in
his writing. His diaries shift between precise, even myopic bookish detail and a sense of vast spiritual uplift. He worries about the
arrangement of the page for his edition of a speech by William
Morris at the Hammersmith Socialist Society – 'The first line to
be in red. The first words ("William Morris") of second division
to be in red, and first words, "The Times are strange and Evil", of
third division in red.' But then, in other entries, he breaks off into
reverie: 'Bind books, print books, think and write books; and do so
for ever with your eye on the goal – the kingdom of heaven.' And
in his *Credo* (1906) – a small, beautifully simple volume of just four
pages of text that perhaps of all Doves Press creations expresses
that ideal of calm harmony and material restraint – Cobden-
Sanderson voiced his philosophical beliefs by using the book as
the governing metaphor for everything:

> I believe and see that the brightly illumined to-day, or the shad-
> owed rest of to-night, is but as the turning of a page of the great
> Book, the Book of Life, and that to-morrow and to-morrow, other
> illumined pages, will be turned for other and other races & other
> & other generations of mankind . . .

The loud irony running through all Cobden-Sanderson's mus-
ings on harmony is the bitter hostility which defined the end of
the Doves Press – to which we must now turn.

After a strong commercial start, the Doves Press was experiencing money problems, despite Annie's financial support. Cobden-Sanderson's initial plan, characteristic in its totality, was to print all of Shakespeare's plays. This was then modified down to ten, and then to four. *Hamlet* was the first, published on 28 June 1909; editions followed of *Antony and Cleopatra* (1912), *Julius Caesar* (1913), *Coriolanus* (1914), with editions of the poetry, too: the *Sonnets* (1909), *Venus and Adonis* (1912), and *The Rape of Lucrece* (1915).

Producing an edition of *Hamlet* is complicated because the play survives in three early printed editions, each of which has differences from the other. These differing early editions are known as the First Quarto (or Q1), printed by 1603 with the title *The Tragicall Historie of Hamlet Prince of Denmarke*; the Second Quarto (or Q2), printed in 1604 and 1605; and the First Folio (or F1), printed in 1623 as *The Tragedie of Hamlet, Prince of Denmarke*, as one of the thirty-six plays included in this collected works. Each of these texts is recognisably the same play, but with significant differences. This is most radically the case with Q1, which is a little over half the length of Q2, and with significant textual differences in many common passages: where in Q2 Hamlet ponders his mortality with the most famous line in English literature – 'To be or not to be, that is the question' – the Hamlet of Q1 has a less equivocal 'To be, or not to be, I there's the point.'

What should an editor do? They could pick one text and work from that, using the other texts, when possible, to correct errors or to fill in gaps, but basing the edition around a single source. Q2, as the longest of the three, is often treated as this base or copy text, and the version of *Hamlet* known to culture today is largely a Q2 *Hamlet*. Or an editor could draw on all three editions and produce a conflated text, deciding at each moment which version is preferable. Worms pour forth from cans: does 'preferable' mean what Shakespeare intended (and if so, how can we be sure with no manuscript in his hand)? Or does 'preferable' mean the best line, dramatically or aesthetically (but by whose judgement)? The irony of a conflated text, like the in many ways magnificent edition produced by Harold Jenkins for the Arden Second Series in 1982, is that, even as it tries to organise itself into a best and most authentic version, it is certainly a text that Shakespeare never wrote: a patchwork of Q1, Q2, F1, and editorial speculations. The third route – and this is the path followed by the most recent Arden editors, Ann Thompson and Neil Taylor in their 2006 edition (revised in 2016) – is to present each edition as a distinct text, with its own integrity and claims on our interest. Suddenly we have three *Hamlet*s, not one – and each one a separate play. Is this a good thing? Have we expanded, or destroyed, the play we thought we knew? Is this richness, or superfluity? Expansion, or pedantry?

Cobden-Sanderson spent a lot of time in 1908 collating different editions and working out an editorial path for his edition of *Hamlet*. He took the advice of the great bearded philological sage F. J. Furnivall, who lived – as almost everyone seemed to, at this point – in Hammersmith, eighty-four years old, a co-founder of the *Oxford English Dictionary* and a huge figure within editorial studies. As Cobden-Sanderson buried himself in textual details, he felt his characteristic sense of philosophical expansion that put him in contact with all of the world. Here he is at 7 a.m. on Tuesday 29 September 1909, 'in bed', his diary records, and full of that sense of happy eternity that was his signature mode:

Windows open – pure delightful rain-washed faint blue heaven. Gentle wind, tree-kissing; benedictory sunlight shining on the leaves and houses, and filling and touching all things with peace now and to come; bell ringing, birds chirping, distant noise of passing train.

Sitting up in bed waiting for my little kettle to boil, my breakfast as usual at my side, I felt I wanted a fuller and a wider range of thought than I had been occupied with for some time past – something to be always going on whilst I occupied myself with the text of Hamlet . . . And how joy springs up in the presence of so full and so beautiful a world, man's past, the world and all the life to come.

This is vintage Cobden-Sanderson, a mix of the business-practical that is rooted in the now (the texts need to be fixed) with a spiralling reverie unmoored from time ('Earth is wonderful and divine').

He didn't show any interest in the short and, at that time, critically neglected Q1, which had only been discovered in 1823. Instead he tried to build his edition about Q2, while adding in portions of F1. His edition carried an appendix which supplied a rationale for his creation. At first he sought to stick to this method with complete integrity – as he put it with Hamletian quintessence, 'no more, no less' – but it soon became apparent he would have to make compromises. Not all of the supplementary F1 passages were included – he justified some exclusions rather cloudily in terms of 'metric & other considerations of fitness' – and to this hobbling but still full-bodied *Hamlet*, Cobden-Sanderson introduced a series of textual alterations in pursuit of clarity: 'elaborated punctuation' (the original punctuation is irregular to the point of chaos for twentieth-century eyes, but probably not for early-seventeenth-century readers), and a newly consistent and lucid presentation of speech prefixes; tidied-up stage directions, drawn from Q2 and F1; and the use of 'rubrication' (from the Latin *rubricare*, 'to colour red') for stage directions, act and scene numbers, and speech prefixes – in Johnston's words, 'a connecting link between plain writing and illumination proper'.

Cobden-Sanderson trod a fine line between innovating and maintaining: between keeping the text locked in the 1600s, and bringing it forward into the present day. And while he sought to eliminate the errors of the original printers, he wanted to keep 'something of the grit' of Shakespeare, lost in 'the slippery perfection of an adulterated text'. 'The plays of Shakespeare are not finished products,' he wrote in his diary on 9 February 1909. 'They are great, and almost as careless as they are great; and their carelessness is an attribute not to be glossed away.'

It is a paradox to carefully sustain historical carelessness, but the physical book produced by Cobden-Sanderson articulates this ambivalent relation to history. The Doves Press printed 250 copies on paper, as was typical, at 2 guineas each, and a further fifteen copies on vellum at 10 guineas. The books were bound in limp vellum with 'HAMLET' pressed in gold onto the spine, and possessed that characteristic stark simplicity. The book contains features that tug it back into the swirling streets of London in 1604. The title page is dated '(1604. 1623)', as though it sprang to life in those Jacobean years, and the pages feature not only conventional page numbers but also signatures: a series of letter-and-number marks designed to indicate the order of pages for the binder, typical of a book in the sixteenth and seventeenth centuries, but unnecessary in 1909, and serving here – like those clasps on Morris's paper books – to invoke a past order of book-making. The beautiful initial capital flourish by Edward Johnston – the 'W' of 'Whose there?' in flowing green ink – signals Cobden-Sanderson's investment in the skilled and patient work of the hand in 1909, and it also loops this *Hamlet* back into the world of the medieval scriptorium. In his *Writing & Illuminating & Lettering*, Johnston had advised students to look to pre-fourteenth-century calligraphy for the best models of versal letters, 'very simple and beautiful pen shapes . . . After the fourteenth century they were often fattened and vulgarized and overdone with ornament.'

But the context for this book-making was one of bubbling conflict. At the end of his 9 February diary entry in which he expresses his wish to sustain the 'grit' of Shakespeare's text, Cobden-Sanderson articulates another ambition:

> It is my wish that the Doves Press type shall never be subjected to the use of a machine other than the human hand, in composition, or to a press pulled otherwise than by the hand and arm of man or woman; and this I will see to in my Will, though, if I forget, I desire that this which I have written shall operate in its place.

He was not likely to forget. Cobden-Sanderson's determination to prevent the Doves Press from being used for machine printing consumed the final decade of his life. It was a manifestation

ENTER BARNARDO, AND FRANCISCO,
TWO CENTINELS.

Bar. WHOSE THERE?
Fran. Nay answere me. Stand & vnfolde your selfe.
Bar. Long liue the King.
Fran. Barnardo.
Bar. Hee.
Fran. You come most carefully vpon your houre.
Bar. Tis now strooke twelfe, get thee to bed Francisco.
Fran. For this reliefe much thanks, tis bitter cold,
And I am sick at hart.
Bar. Haue you had quiet guard?
Fran. Not a mouse stirring.
Bar. Well, good night;

The Doves Press Hamlet.

of a growing hostility between him and Emery Walker: Cobden-Sanderson thought Walker insufficiently engaged with work at the press; Walker was maddened by Cobden-Sanderson's habit of speaking of their collaborative venture as 'my press'. Beneath the irritation were two fundamentally different attitudes towards making books: 'I aimed at one thing,' wrote Cobden-Sanderson, 'Mr Emery Walker aimed at another.' Walker was a printer, type designer, teacher, and businessman deeply interested in not only hand-press printing but alternative technologies such as photo-engraving and lithography and in other forms the Doves Press might explore, like packaging, or newspapers, or commercial printing more generally. Walker saw an onwards life for the Doves Press that would take on modern forms. Cobden-Sanderson's blend of the spiritual and the controlling, and his commitment to pre-industrial technologies, was a wall that would not move: 'I am a Visionary and a Fanatic,' he wrote, 'and against a Visionary and a Fanatic he [Walker] will beat himself in vain.'

The original 1903 'Memorandum of Agreement' between the

two men, repeated in an indenture of 1909, stated that, if the Doves Press should cease, Walker would be entitled to a fount of the type, to be used in whatever way he wished. The idea of the potential machine use for the Doves type now haunted Cobden-Sanderson to the point of obsession. In 1908–9, as work on *Hamlet* was about to begin – that play about an older court order falling apart – relations grew colder and colder. Walker demanded his type; from December 1908, Cobden-Sanderson prevented him from entering the premises, and ignored Walker's proscriptions to stop printing. Communication started proceeding through solicitors, and in June 1909, Walker began an action against his former friend and partner at the High Court. Perhaps this was always the end point for a man who said things like 'the Partnership was not a business Partnership; it was a work of devotion . . . as I imagined'. There was little space for anyone else in Cobden-Sanderson's imagination; talk of devotion and the Book Beautiful descended into petty arguments: 'Mr. Cobden-Sanderson presents his compliments to Mr. Emery Walker and suggests that it would be an improvement if he were to clear up the waste-paper in his front garden.' Seeking to avoid a lengthy and costly court drama, Sydney Cockerell, the man who had snapped up that 1476 Jenson volume at the Sotheby's sale in 1898, and now Curator of the Fitzwilliam Museum, Cambridge, fashioned a compromise which both men eventually accepted: Cobden-Sanderson would have unlimited use of the type for his lifetime, and Walker would inherit the type, and do with it what he wanted, on Cobden-Sanderson's death.

But this image of the Doves type circulating in a modern, machine world, even after his death, was intolerable to Cobden-Sanderson, and in his diary for 11 June 1911, he described what he called 'My Last Will and Testament' in typically heightened terms – reprinting the text in the final *Catalogue Raisonné of Books Printed & Published by the Doves Press 1900–1916* (1916) for a public readership:

To the Bed of the River Thames, the river on whose banks I have printed all my printed books, I bequeath The Doves Press Fount of Type – the punches, the matrices, and the type in use at the time of my death, and may the river in its tides and flow pass over them to and from the great sea for ever and for ever, or until its tides and flow for ever cease; then may they share the fate of all the world, and pass from change to change for ever upon the Tides of Time, untouched of other use and all else.

Cobden-Sanderson carried the resolution to drop his beloved Doves type into the Thames unspoken in his head for two years, a coiled fury that gave him purpose, before beginning the 'Act of Dedication' (his words) in 1913:

I stood on the bridge at Hammersmith and, looking towards the Press and the sun setting, threw into the Thames below me the matrices from which had been cast the Doves Press Fount of Type, itself to be cast by me, I hope, into the same great river.

Three years later, on 31 August 1916, the seventy-six-year-old Cobden-Sanderson started on the type. At 'midnight', he wrote in his diary:

I threw three pages into the Thames from Hammersmith Bridge. I had gone for a stroll on the Mall, when it occurred to me that it was a suitable night and time; so I went indoors, and taking first one page and then two, succeeded in destroying three.

The process continued through 1916, and in total, Cobden-Sanderson made some 170 trips to Hammersmith Bridge. The type was heavy, and Cobden-Sanderson experimented with different methods of dispatch: 'linen bags, their own paper, loose in pocket, hand-bag'. Eventually he settled on 'a square wooden box with a sliding lid, used for keeping finishing tools in'. He called this 'my adventure, "bequeathing" the Doves type to the Thames':

Arrived at the bridge I cross to the other side, take a stealthy look round, and, if no one is in sight, I heave up the box to the parapet, release the sliding lid, and let the type fall into the river – the work of a moment . . . But what a weird business it is, beset with perils and panics! I have to see that no one is near or looking; then, over the parapet a box full, and then the audible and visible splash. One night I had nearly cast my type into a boat, another danger, which unexpectedly shot from under the bridge! And all nights I feared to be asked by a policeman, or other official guarding the bridge – and sometimes I come upon clusters of police – what I had got in my 'box'.

Cobden-Sanderson wrote an 'Apologia' in 1913, revised in 1919, to justify what he called the 'consecration' of the type, matrices, and punches. To 'consecrate' means to make something sacred and fit for religious use, and in this sense the destruction was a kind of elevation, a process at one with Cobden-Sanderson's spiritualised book-making and his fantasies of infinity, a means of making the Doves Press at 'one with the purpose of the Universe'. It also represented a way for Cobden-Sanderson to separate the Doves Press from the industrial present day in the most dramatic way possible. If that contemporary was built around ideas of profit, use, and economy, the secret melodrama of the tumbling type was a kind of maximal other: anti-worldly, anti-profit, extravagantly doomed. The 'Apologia' was never printed – it was eventually sold at Sotheby's in 1966 and now lives in the Bancroft Library at the University of California, Berkeley – but it is a document of a seriousness of intent, prefaced with quotes from Milton's *Lycidas*, Malory's *Morte d'Arthur*, Shakespeare's *The Tempest*, and (in Greek), the opening words of the *Iliad*: 'Singer of Anger, O Goddess'.

But the type was not lost for all time. It was the precision of Cobden-Sanderson's diary entries, and the published research of Marianne Tidcombe, that enabled graphic designer Robert Green to establish in 2014, within a 5-metre radius, where

Cobden-Sanderson had stood on the bankside on those evenings in 1916. At low tide, and with a mudlarker's licence, Green began to search for the type. Astonishingly, it took just twenty minutes for him to find three pieces: a lower-case 'v', 'i', and 'e'. On 10 November 2014, with the help of Port of London Authority divers, Green searched and quickly recovered a further 148 pieces (or 'sorts') of the original type lying at the bottom of the Thames (see plate section). It's unlikely more will be found, however: repairs to the bridge's foundations in 2000, after bombing by the Provisional IRA, probably means the other sorts are locked in concrete. Green produced a digital rendering of the typeface for contemporary usage, based on the recovered lead letters but with modifications for the contemporary, web-accustomed eye: it can be purchased today via Typespec.

The romance of the recovery would have pleased Cobden-Sanderson: he'd have liked that sense of collapsing time. But with his commitment to traditional design and his terror of mechanised (let alone of unimaginable digital) reproduction, Cobden-Sanderson would have been shocked at its dematerialised life today – to say nothing of his possessiveness. Walker, on the other hand, with his interest in new media forms, would have been delighted. Half of the type recovered in 2014 is now on permanent loan to the Emery Walker Trust, and on public display at 7 Hammersmith Terrace, Walker's former house – six doors down from where the Doves Press *Hamlet* was printed.

IO. SMALL PRESSES
Nancy Cunard (1896–1965)

Them were the days

Paris, June 1930. At 3.00 in the morning, Nancy Cunard quickly writes a letter to her friend Louise Morgan, American journalist and editor at *Everyman* magazine:

> We found a poem, a beauty, by a poet – so much so that it must be printed by itself. Irishman of 23, Ecole Normale here, that's all I know, but am seeing him tomorrow. Richard says many of the allusions are to Descartes. I shouldn't have known. Much in it none of us will ever know, and the whole thing so good it proves again the rest doesn't matter.
>
> Will you announce please that the Hours Press prize for best Time poem is awarded to Samuel Beckett.

'Richard' is Richard Aldington (1892–1962), novelist, poet, one-time husband of Hilda Doolittle (the poet 'H.D.'), and, in Nancy Cunard's words, a friend 'ever full of ideas for me to take up'. Aldington's most recent idea had been for a poetry competition for Cunard's Hours Press, a way to flush out unknown talent and so find a new author for a small, one-woman printing press that had until that point only published already well-known writers such as George Moore, Robert Graves, and Arthur Symons. 'Let us make it a poem on Time,' Aldington said, immediately decisive. 'On any aspect of Time.' One hundred lines maximum: much better an 'exquisite rhyming epigram' than something 'half the length of the *Iliad*'. The announcement of the competition was printed

quickly in red ink on small square cards which Cunard posted out
to literary journals in England and France:

> Nancy Cunard, Hours Press, in collaboration with Richard Ald-
> ington, offers £10 for the best poem up to 100 lines, in english or
> american on TIME (for or against).
> Entries up to June 15, 1930.

It's hard to think of many poems that aren't about time – perhaps
that was Aldington's canny point – and the 'for or against' clause
is odd, as if time was like fox hunting or the House of Lords.
When Cunard and Aldington read out loud to each other the
more than 100 entries they received, it looked until the very last
moment that the competition would be a disaster. This was mid-
summer in Normandy, in Cunard's farmhouse Le Puits Carré
(The Four-Cornered Well), in La Chapelle-Réanville. Cunard
and Aldington began reading with hope which became amuse-
ment but as the unread pile dwindled their voices transitioned
into a kind of panicked despair. 'God Almighty!' wrote Cunard
to Morgan. 'The things that come in.' The poems were bad ('one
about "two little toadstools"'), the relative peaks merely medi-
ocre, most of them taxingly handwritten, ranging, as Cunard
nicely put it, 'from doggerel to a kind of sham metaphysics', save
perhaps two or three – 'and not even those were good', according to Aldington. But back in Paris, in the early hours of 16 June
1930 – the competition deadline just passed – an unseen hand slid
a folder under Cunard's office door, the word 'Whoroscope' and
the name 'Samuel Beckett' handwritten on the outside. Neither
Cunard nor Aldington knew the name, but they realised four or
five lines in that they had a poem possessed of a strange, abra-
sive vitality, a poem that looked you dead in the eyes even as
it refused to explain. 'Mysterious, obscure in parts', as Cunard
put it, ninety-eight lines of erudite Renaissance scientific thought
mixed with jolting immediacy, and the whole voiced by a cantankerous René Descartes waiting to be served an egg that he insists

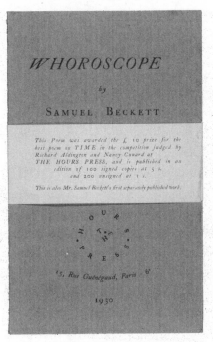

Cunard's printing of Samuel Beckett's Whoroscope *(1930),*
complete with wrapper.

(such was his penchant) must have been laid between eight and
ten days ago. Cunard said there needed to be notes. Beckett (only
twenty-three, and thrilled by the prospect of print and £10 in
cash) agreed, perhaps imagining his own sparse endnotes as a
parody of the (already parodic) notes at the conclusion of T. S.
Eliot's *The Waste Land* (1922), notes which open trapdoors as they
purport to lead us to the light.

'Whoroscope' was printed by Cunard on fine Vergé de Rives
paper in Caslon 11-point type, with smaller notes, and was bound
between dull scarlet covers: 100 signed and 200 unsigned copies
were advertised for sale at 1s and 5d respectively (the signed ones
go for £7,500 today). A white band wrapped around the pamphlet
declared this to be both a prizewinner and Beckett's 'first separately published work', and a copy of the poem was placed in the
window of Cunard's Hours Press shop in rue Guénégaud.

Beckett was in Paris studying at the École normale supérieure – deep in Descartes – and doing research work for James Joyce. Joyce gave him tasks like listing the names of all the rivers in Europe. This was twenty years before what Cunard called Beckett's 'spectacular and merited' rise to fame.

Beckett recalled the circumstances of his Hours Press publication in a letter to Cunard in 1959, remembering how he wrote the first half of the poem on the evening of 15 June

> before dinner, had a guzzle of salad and Chambertin at the Cochon de Lait [the Suckling Pig], went back to the École and finished it about three in the morning. Then walked down to the rue Guénégaud and put it in your box. That's how it was and them were the days.

I like the simple admiration of Beckett's biographer James Knowlson: 'It is a remarkable effort for anyone, no matter how clever, to have produced it in a matter of hours.' Remarkable, too, that Cunard so immediately perceived the unknown student's talent, and printed the poem herself – launching what would become Beckett's career.

Journalist and editor Samuel Putnam was only slightly exaggerating when he said that 'few persons have been more misunderstood than N.C.'. That misunderstanding is partly because Cunard's life seems to fall into contrasting, seemingly irreconcilable stages. Up until the late 1920s, her life in Paris and London looks like triviality on an aristocratic scale. 'First and instant impression,' remembered publisher and novelist Kenneth Macpherson, 'exciting, dotty tigress-dragonfly.' By the late 1920s, Cunard had (as Harold Acton wrote) 'dug through many layers of society to find only a crumbling foundation', and from the early 1930s, she began to live a fearless existence of leftist political commitment, risking her life and certainly (not that she cared) her reputation in pursuing the redress of political injustice in the form of black civil rights, and in the battle against Franco and Spanish fascism. 'In the middle ages,' wrote Acton, Cunard 'would have become a mystic', and there's absolutely something of the fourteenth-century Margery Kempe about her. Wynkyn de Worde would have printed her life, had chronology allowed. This phase was marked by Cunard's belief in the political power of the printed word: her anthology, *Negro* (Wishart & Co., 1934), published entirely at Cunard's expense (about £1,500), was an 800-page encyclopaedia of the African diaspora with 385 illustrations and essays on black history, culture, and politics by, among many others, Langston Hughes, Ezra Pound, Theodore Dreiser, and Zora Neale Hurston. Samuel Beckett provided translations of French contributions, and Cunard saw herself as the 'maker', a guiding hand of an international collective, working with a burning energy despite the hate letters. Cunard's *Authors Take Sides on the Spanish War* appeared as a special issue of *Left Review* in 1937, and documented the responses of 137 intellectuals to her question of their position on Spain, including black intellectuals Marcus Garvey, George Padmore, and C. L. R. James: 126 were for the republic, five were for Franco (Ezra Pound said, 'Spain is an emotional luxury to a gang of sap-headed dilettantes'), and six were neutral. Once again, Cunard worked on despite receiving replies like George Orwell's who, one imagines, would not have written this to a man:

> Will you please stop sending me this bloody rubbish . . . I am not one of your fashionable pansies like Auden or Spender, I was six months in Spain, most of the time fighting, I have a bullet-hole in me at present and I am not going to write blah about defending democracy or gallant little anybody.

Cunard's Hours Press in rural Réanville and then Paris between 1928 and 1931, where Cunard set type, hand-printed, packed and distributed what became an important canon of twenty-four modernist works, formed a crucial bridge between these two worlds of aristocratic dissolution and political commitment. The case for Cunard's importance to the history of the book rests with this press, both as an exceptional case study in itself, and as an enterprise that characterised the flowering of the small-press movement in the 1920s and 1930s more generally: a group of presses that drew some inspiration from the work of William Morris at Kelmscott, and Thomas Cobden-Sanderson at the Doves Press, and before them from Horace Walpole's Strawberry Hill Press, established in 1757. The 1920s and 1930s small-press movement, compared to these earlier experiments, placed less emphasis on the physical book as a fine art object, on early texts like Chaucer and Shakespeare, and on slow, even medieval models of craft – remember those 'late medieval' clasps on Morris's nineteenth-century books. This 1920s–30s iteration was more concerned with printing new modernist works, and included Laura Riding and Robert Graves's Seizin Press in London and Majorca; David Garnett and Francis Meynell's Nonesuch Press in London; Norman Douglas and Pino Orioli's Lungarno Press in Florence; the brief life of the Aquila Press in London, founded by Wyn Henderson, James Cleugh, and others; and Plain Editions in Paris, run by Gertrude Stein and Alice B. Toklas, and funded by the sale of one or perhaps two of their beloved Picassos. Cunard's Hours Press represented, and also advanced, this flourishing publishing movement.

Cunard died alone in the Hôpital Cochin in Paris on 17 March 1965, midway through the composition of an epic poem against war, carried to the hospital by police who found her ill and penniless and confused and bruised on the face, unable to recall her own name, and weighing only 26 kilos. Patrick McGuinness described 'the reverse Cinderella-arc of her fame and fortune' – but we need to add that Cunard's rejection of her affluent past was willed and political and not, ultimately, despite the pitiful drama of her last days, a story of something gone wrong. 'Never in her

Nancy Cunard, photographed by Barbara Ker-Seymer.

life, I believe,' wrote Raymond Mortimer, 'was she frightened of anything.'

She had been born into material luxury in 1896 in the sprawling halls of Nevill Holt, Leicestershire, now a Grade I listed building, dating back to before 1300, perched on a hilltop and set in vast grounds. Her mother was the American heiress Maud Alice ('Emerald') Burke, a beauty from San Francisco, twenty years her husband's junior, and while Virginia Woolf wasn't convinced ('ridiculous little parakeet faced woman ... coarse and usual and dull'), Lady Cunard became famed as a hostess of dazzling parties. At Nevill Holt and later in Cavendish Square, London, hereditary titles swaggered and artists glittered and politicians held forth (Lord Basil Blackwood, H. H. Asquith, pianist Ethel Leginska, the Prince of Wales (later Edward VIII), and Somerset Maugham). It was never quite clear where the romantic momentum was heading. Her father, Sir Bache Cunard, was the grandson of the founder of the Cunard transatlantic shipping line: hence the 13,000-acre country estate. But Sir Bache (pronounced, with a logic known only to the English upper classes, to rhyme with 'peach') declined the busy world of business and the clever chatter of his wife's friends, and retreated. He made metal weathercocks and intricate ostrich-egg holders in his workshop at Nevill Holt, 'carving', in Nancy's words, 'coconuts elaborately to mount them into cups'. Cunard's parents, from the start on different tracks, separated in 1911.

When Cunard recalled her earliest years later in life, she remembered a mix of ease and whirl:

> My picture of Holt is one of constant arrivals and departures during half the year, of elaborate long teas on the lawn with tennis and croquet going on, of great winter logs blazing all day in the Hall and Morning Room, with people playing bridge there for hours on end. Beautiful and exciting ladies move about in smart tailor mades . . . Summer-long in shot silk and striped taffeta they stroll laughing and chatting across the lawns.

Cunard's early reputation was as an exotic figure who seemed to stand for the 1920s in its most decadent form. She developed a reputation for a kind of militant idleness that, we see in retrospect, was itself a form of rebellious commitment. She travelled often between Paris and London, her social world dominated by writers and artists (Tristan Tzara, André Breton, Aldous Huxley, Ezra Pound, Wyndham Lewis), sexual affairs much chattered about, with days plotted around dinner at the Eiffel Tower restaurant in Soho, champagne, sudden 2 a.m. summonings of friends who on arrival Cunard had no memory of phoning. She was 'forever in a state of liquor' (that was a friend talking); she was (in Richard Aldington's words), an 'erotic Boa constrictor'. 'We responded like chameleons to every changing colour,' remembered her friend

Iris Tree, 'turning from Meredith to Proust to Dostoievsky, slightly tinged by the *Yellow Book*, an occasional absinthe left by Baudelaire and Wilde, flushed by Liberalism, sombered by nihilistic pessimism.' Brancusi sculpted her; Eugene McCown painted her; Man Ray and Cecil Beaton photographed her; Aldous Huxley and Michael Arlen put her in their novels. 'She looked famished,' wrote Harold Acton, 'and quenched her hunger with harsh white wine and gusty talk.' She was famed for what in French is called *son regard*: as Janet Flanner put it, her 'intense manner of looking at you, of seeing you and seizing you with her large jade-green eyes, always heavily outlined, top and bottom, with black makeup'. Her contemporaries describe beauty, rebellion, 'no façade, no carapace' (Leonard Woolf), an endless if flitting energy working in many directions at once. 'The clock did not exist for her,' Acton wrote, and

in town she dashed in and out of taxis clutching an attaché-case crammed with letters, manifestoes, estimates, circulars and her latest African bangle, and she was always several hours late for any appointment.

A nasty version of this reputation is caught in a passage in early drafts of Eliot's *Waste Land* – the third section of 'The Fire Sermon', written in 1921. Here Fresca, who sounds a lot like Cunard, or at least Eliot's idea of Cunard, brought up on Victorian sentiment and Russian literature, is described as a poet-manqué who reads eighteenth-century novels on the toilet. The description was sensibly deleted by Eliot on the advice of Ezra Pound, but it still conveys the misogyny awaiting someone like Cunard: a disgust that sneers equally at her body, her leisure, her circulation in public, and her poetic ambitions. Much better, because more variegated, is Virginia Woolf's diary entry on Cunard from 1 November 1924, when Cunard was twenty-eight. She had 'startled honest eyes,' Woolf wrote,

& she slipped into easy desperate-sounding chatter, as if she didn't mind saying everything – everything – had no shadows no secret places – lived like a lizard in the sun, & yet was by nature for the shade.

In fact, Cunard was a great admirer of Eliot's work and her own published verse constitutes a sustained engagement with his poetry. Cunard's two early collections – *Outlaws* (1921), published by Elkin Matthews, and *Sublunary* (1923), by Hodder & Stoughton – were followed by *Parallax* (1925), a long, major poem published by the Woolfs' Hogarth Press in an edition of 420, with covers designed by Eugene McCown and typeset by Virginia Woolf. 'Parallax', a term coined by seventeenth-century doctor and writer Thomas Browne, means an apparent movement in an object, 'some distance from their true and proper being', due to a shift in the viewer's perspective. This blend of observation and disorientation, or disorientation through observation, is the poem's signature mode as a 'poet-fool' walks the streets of London, France and Italy. Reviewers of Cunard's poems were frequently condescending: one, baffled by the difficulty of *Outlaws*, spent the majority of the piece discussing Cunard's hat, and F. R. Leavis dismissed *Parallax* as a 'simple imitation' of *The Waste Land*. But there were more perceptive critical voices ('the elusiveness that puzzles today will be tomorrow's delight') who paused to think about modernism's deep investment in literary repurposing, and an aesthetic of quotation, fragment, and echo, and who understood that Cunard's poetry, so overt in its relation to Eliot, is made more interesting – and not reduced – by its sustained entanglement with *The Waste Land*. The borrowings are the point.

Cunard's poem was admired by brilliant contemporaries like Virginia Woolf and her slightly less brilliant husband Leonard. If Janet Flanner was right, writing just after Cunard's death, that *Parallax* is 'so nearly forgotten that it is like a new poem today', then that newness – and the recent 2016 editorial efforts of Sandeep Parmar and Carcanet Press to bring Cunard's poetry back into the contemporary world – should be a source of delight. Perhaps the most honest response was Beckett's. In a letter to his friend Thomas MacGreevy, a month after winning Cunard's poetry prize, Beckett registered a careful uncertainty.

> I heard from Nancy from London. She has given me her Parallax that I asked her for, & lent me The Apes of God [by Wyndham Lewis] & some Pound Cantos. I read Parallax. I don't know what to say about it. There are some fine things.
>
> "By the Embankment I counted the grey gulls Nailed to the wind above a distorted tide."
>
> No . . . ? And then a lot of padding I am afraid. I don't know. Perhaps it's very good.

One crucial consequence of *Parallax* was that it introduced Cunard to the Woolfs' Hogarth Press, and, through that, to the flowering world of small presses, principally in Paris but in London and America, too. Cunard's Hours Press – the name 'not only pleasing to me', Cunard remarked, 'but suggestive of work' – was the result.

Over tea on Virginia's thirty-third birthday in 1915, Leonard and Virginia Woolf had made three resolutions: to buy Hogarth House in Richmond; to acquire a hand press; and to get a bulldog whom they would call John. With the precedent of William Morris's Kelmscott Press in mind, and also Cobden-Sanderson's Doves Press, the Woolfs spent £19 5s 5d on a Minerva Platen hand press and some Old Face type – and they got the house and the dog, too.

As the story of the Doves Press and Kelmscott has shown, this was a defining moment in the history of the small, independent press, organised around the commitment of a return to the hand press, a refusal of industrial modes of book production, an attempt (however imperfectly enacted) to uncouple publishing from the restrictions of the market and, for many later small presses, the belief in the importance of publishing radical literature that would otherwise stand no chance in print. Letterpress also allowed the possibility of experiments in typography that the Woolfs and later Cunard responded to. It's easy – and cynical, and not entirely accurate – to portray this movement as a project for the leisured rich: in a January 1930 letter to William Carlos Williams, Louis Zukofsky wrote that 'Nancy Cunard may be playing with the game but what else has she to do? Not a damned thing.' Cunard certainly had money, but the Woolfs didn't, at least not on any scale, and it's more generous and also truer to see individuals not idly playing but putting everything into the production of new writing. An early advertisement for the Woolfs announced the Hogarth Press's ambition:

> to publish at low prices short works of merit, in prose or poetry, which could not, because of their merits, appeal to a very large public. The whole process of printing and production . . . is done by ourselves, and the editions are necessarily extremely small, not exceeding 300 copies.

'We work like navvies at binding Morgan [E. M. Forster],' wrote Virginia in 1920, '& have no time for frivolity.' The Woolfs were not interested in what Cobden-Sanderson called 'the Book Beautiful': the refinements of fine printing and binding were 'too often a kind of fungoid growth,' wrote Leonard, 'which culture breeds upon art and literature.' Hogarth Press books were to look – in Leonard's winningly simple formulation – 'nice', but it was the contents, 'the immaterial side of a book', that mattered most. The flowering of modernism was a consequence: the Hogarth Press published Katherine Mansfield, T. S. Eliot, Gertrude Stein, E. M. Forster, Sigmund Freud, Christopher Isherwood, John Maynard Keynes, to note only the most starry names, in addition to a large number of translations, particularly from

Russian (Virginia and S. S. Koteliansky together translated Dosto-
evsky and Tolstoy). What is so striking – and this goes for Cunard's
list of authors, too, and many of the other small presses at this
time – is quite how unerringly good the taste was of the individuals running these presses. Time and again they printed unknown
works that, despite the low print runs and financial precarity, went
on to become masterpieces.

The Woolfs set up the press in the dining room of their home in
Hogarth House and in 1917 wrote, typeset, printed, stitched, and
bound 134 copies of their first publication, *Two Stories*, written by
themselves, with woodcuts by Dora Carrington. For the next few
years, they approached printing in the excited spirit of a hobby
('we get so absorbed we can't stop' – 'I should never do anything
else'), and the press hovered somewhere between a business and a
diversion – both a trip to the office, and a walk of the dog. Virginia
and Leonard drew no salary, and printing spilt out into everyday
life: 'I came in & set a page of Nancy [Cunard's *Parallax*]. Then
out to Ingersoll to get my watch mended.'

The Woolfs were far from perfect printers. They began, like
Cunard and many of the owners of small presses, with no direct
experience of hand printing, although Virginia had spent time
binding. In fact, they had been turned down for a course at St
Bride School of Printing because places were restricted to trade
union apprentices. Early Hogarth books are certainly no strangers
to error: in Hope Mirrlees's *Paris*, the title page has the wrong date
(1919 for 1920), and a handwritten 'St.' had to be added before
'John' on page 1. The first proof of Harold Nicolson's *Jeanne de
Hénaut* (1924) had the author's name misspelt, and in the opening section of Eliot's *The Waste Land*, Virginia inadvertently set
'A crowd flowed under London Bridge', rather than 'over'. Eliot
would correct this with his pen whenever he came across a Hogarth *Waste Land*. We're probably not then surprised to hear that
the Woolfs rejected Joyce's manuscript of *Ulysses* in part because
they considered it – as most mortals would – beyond their printing capacities. (Virginia also later described reading *Ulysses* as the

experience of growing 'puzzled, bored, irritated and disillusioned by a queasy undergraduate scratching his pimples'.)

Before long the Woolfs were besieged with orders. 'We came back from Asheham to find the table stacked, littered, with orders for *Kew Gardens*,' wrote Virginia. 'They strewed the sofa and we opened them intermittently through dinner.' The press transitioned into something more worldly: commercial machine printers were used for larger editions alongside small-run hand-press books; partnership offers from Heinemann (in 1922) were received and rejected ('we sniff at patronage'); and relations were established with other presses (in 1921, with Harcourt Brace in America). An early list dominated by literary works written by friends expanded to include books on politics, science, religion, and more, by authors far outside any misleading caricature of a bed-hopping Bloomsbury coterie, including working-class authors such as Welsh poet Huw Menai, and Birmingham Group novelist John Hampson. By 1925, Sylvia Beach was stocking Hogarth Press books in her Paris shop, Shakespeare and Company.

Most small presses, including Cunard's, were short-lived: a flowering for four or five years, with about five titles a year. A good idea that withered. But the Hogarth Press published 527 titles between 1917 and 1946 when, twenty-nine years after their first publication, and five years after Virginia's death, Leonard sold the press to the directors of Chatto & Windus. (The Hogarth Press still survives as an imprint within Penguin Random House: 'An adventurous new fiction list taking inspiration from the past.') The controlling and in some ways defiantly amateur presence of Leonard and Virginia – the sense of a book list formed in their own image, and a commitment to literary independence and freedom – remained crucial up until the 1940s.

Leonard described the Hogarth Press as a 'commercial hippograff'. This is a mythical creature with the body of a horse and the wings and head of an eagle: in publishing terms, a hybrid of the nimble freedom of the small press and the worldly clout of the prominent publisher. As the literary historian Helen Southworth puts it, 'What the Hogarth Press offered authors was precisely either a passage into or an alternative to the commercial press.'

When sixteen-year-old Richard Kennedy, fresh from educational failure at Marlborough College, went to work at the Hogarth Press as an assistant – 'more totem than fact' – he encountered an intoxicating blend of dynamism, disorganisation and artistic ambition. The Woolfs didn't function like normal employers: 'Mrs W said she was sure I had done enough work for the day and would I like to go to a lecture on Ibsen.' Kennedy's brief but captivating memoir, *A Boy at the Hogarth Press* (1972), describes spooling conversations ('LW and I have had long discussions about pornography on our walks round the Square'); Leonard's occasionally 'towering rage' ('Suddenly he gave a cry of vexation and tore out the pages of the [petty cash] book and threw them at me, shouting "This is totally inaccurate!" '); and also long periods of quiet productivity:

> In the printing room when Mrs W is setting type and I am machining we work in silence, unless, of course, she is in one of her happy moods – if she's going to a party or been walking round London, which she often does.

Since Gutenberg, printing could be stressful mayhem, a torrent of deadlines and technical difficulties and incompetent colleagues and type dropped off the bridge into the Thames; but it could also provide a meditative calm, a break from the pressures of work, even as it offered the consolations of steady productivity. 'You cannot think how exciting, soothing, ennobling and satisfying it is,' said Leonard. The practical experience of setting type, inking letters, and pulling sheets, also let Virginia's imagination run in new directions as she reflected anew on a writer's relationship to language, and her sense of the possibilities of letters on a page. In her 1926 lecture, 'How Should One Read a Book?', she provided a vision of a book that was powerfully shaped by her own experiences of printing.

Books are not turned out of moulds like bricks. Books are made of tiny little words, which a writer shapes, often with great difficulty, into sentences of different lengths, placing one on top of another, never taking his eye off them, sometimes building them quite quickly, at other times knocking them down in despair, and beginning all over again.

'I cannot think they actually wanted to dissuade me,' wrote Cunard of the Woolfs, 'yet I can still hear their cry: "Your hands will always be covered in ink!"' If the Woolfs were warning Cunard off, she chose not to take the hint, and in 1928, she bought a 200-year-old Belgian Mathieu hand press and some Caslon Old Face type, from American journalist and printer Bill Bird (1888–1963). She paid £300. Bird had run the small Three Mountains Press (named after the three mountains of Paris) in the 1920s from a tiny office tucked within the narrow streets of the Île Saint-Louis on the Seine, with space only for the press and the printer-editor. Bird started it 'simply to have a hobby' – 'most of my friends were golfers, but sports never interested me greatly' – but was soon producing small-run hand-press books of major literary significance, including William Carlos Williams's *The Great American Novel* (1923), Ernest Hemingway's *In Our Time* (1924), and Ezra Pound's *A Draft of XVI Cantos* (1925). Cunard noted that in Bird's books 'the pressure and inking (always a difficulty with hand presses) were sometimes irregular', but we get a feel for Bird's ambitions with Pound's description of his proposed *Cantos*:

It is to be one of the real bits of printing; modern book to be jacked up to somewhere near level of medieval mss. No Kelmscott mess of illegibility. Large clear type, but also large pages, and specially made capitals. Not for the Vulgus.

Bird's Three Mountains Press was one point in a network of small presses in Paris established by expatriate writers and literary entrepreneurs in the 1920s. Longest running turned out to be the Black Sun Press, set up by Harry (1898–1929) and Caresse (1892–1970) Crosby to publish small-run editions of hand-printed books, including their own poetry and the early works of modernists like Hart Crane and D. H. Lawrence. The press, and Caresse, endured the shock of Harry's much-publicised 1929 suicide pact with one of his numerous lovers, to flourish for almost thirty years with a long list of authors that included James Joyce, Dorothy Parker, William Faulkner, and Kay Boyle. Next to the Crosbys, perhaps the strongest publishing presence in Paris was American Robert McAlmon (1895–1956), known as 'McAlimony' because he used the money from his marriage to heiress Winifred Ellerman (better known as the novelist Bryher) to fund Contact Editions. McAlmon published the work of writers like H.D. (with whom Winifred was in a relationship), Mina Loy and Djuna Barnes – authors whom, Edwin Muir wrote, 'America . . . finds it hard to tolerate'. Manuscripts were submitted to McAlmon at Le Dôme Café in Montparnasse. Sylvia Beach said: 'He told me he discovered most of his writers at one café or another.' When McAlmon announced his plans in the first edition of Ford Maddox Ford's *Transatlantic Review* (January 1924), his ambitions matched almost exactly the early press release by the Woolfs:

> At intervals of two weeks to six months, or six years, we will bring out books by various writers who seem not likely to be published by other publishers, for commercial or legislative reasons . . . Three hundred only of each book will be printed. These books are published simply because they are written, and we like them well enough to get them out.

It's in this context that Cunard, with Bird's help, installed the 200-year-old dark green Mathieu hand press in the small stable in her

Nancy Cunard printing.

ramshackle Normandy farmhouse and started to learn how to print. She was helped by Maurice Lévy, 'a fat little Frenchman' (not his own words) and professional printer who tutored Cunard and, at the very start, Cunard's then-lover, the French poet and surrealist writer Louis Aragon (1897–1982). Lévy – fiercely committed to rules and customs like the ex-anarchist he was, and with a good line in deep disgruntlement – regarded Cunard and Aragon with extreme scepticism, as if they were aristocrats popping in to view the factory floor without taking off their stoles. When Lévy told them that in France a printer serves a seven-year apprenticeship – 'first of all you are made to sweep the floor and pick up fallen type' – Cunard and Aragon roared with laughter.

'Thank goodness there's none of that here, Monsieur Lévy!' exclaimed Cunard. 'We are going to forge ahead.' And then: 'Taste, Monsieur Lévy, taste!'

Cunard learnt fast – she proceeded by her own account 'sailless, mast-less, provision-less, uncompassed and abashed' – and found within herself both a natural aptitude and a love of work: 'It seemed to me that anyone who likes doing this at all must acquire the feel of it the first or certainly the second time he brings the *composteur* or printing-stick together with the letters.' (Aragon's experience as *aide-chirurgien* in the First World War, Cunard thought, with a lingering eroticism, explained the 'firm yet delicate touch of his hands in setting type'.) Not everyone was so immediately caught by the charms of printing. Richard Aldington visited Cunard at Réanville when she was operating, but in a letter of 1928 sounds like a tetchy teen: 'The hand-press is a bore. I set up a couple of lines of type, & helped pull off a few sheets of G.M. [George Moore] – & it takes ages.' But Cunard came quickly to like almost everything about it. She liked the business side of things: the fixing of author royalties at a generous 33 per cent after deducting costs of production (the average at the time was 10 to 15 per cent); the negotiations with bookshops in London (the Warren Gallery), New York (the Holiday Bookshop), Paris (Edward Titus), and Florence (Pino Orioli); the recording of costs in a 'large, black ledger'. She appreciated the sensory qualities of ink – 'the smell . . . pleased me greatly, as did the beautiful freshness of the glistening pigment' – and she even liked talking through the protocols of print hygiene:

> After a rinse in petrol and a good scrub with soap and hot water, my fingers again became perfectly presentable; the right thumb, however, began to acquire a slight ingrain of grey, due to the leaden composition. I soon learned that greasy black hands do not matter when one is at the proofing stage, but an immaculate touch is most important in handling the fair sheet when one has reached the pulling stage.

Cunard found, like Woolf, a meditative calm in the process. 'Distributing the type [back into cases] after printing four pages or so was pleasant and not the bore it is considered to be by printers.' Cunard began to think, too, like a typesetter, shifting her brain so that letters became important not as conveyors of verbal meaning but rather as pieces occupying space. Blank space was as meaningful as inked letters, and calculating the relation of the two was key to the pursuit of 'a good, or even a "noble" page':

> I began to learn that letters are one thing, and a mass of type something else to be thought over in relation to space to be printed and the unprinted space surrounding it . . . Vital too, I discovered, are the vertical spaces between words: the easy 6-point, 4-point, and 3-point, the more slender 2-point and the tenuous 1-point – even the tiny, copper hair-point space can make all the difference.

Along with the pleasure came what Cunard called the 'permanent fatigue' – 'back- breaking as well as wrist-breaking is typesetting'. Her rather stylish solution was to work sitting perched on a high bar-stool. Lévy was appalled – custom dictated that printers should stand for their eight hours a day – but Cunard found the work engrossing, and although she 'had never done regular working-hours before save as a child at day-classes . . . quite soon, it turned into a fourteen or fifteen hour day'.

The Hours Press's first book was *Peronnik the Fool*, a novella by the Anglo-Irish writer George Moore (1852–1933). We might remember Moore from his furious disagreements with Charles Mudie: Mudie deemed Moore's books unsuitable for his circulating library. Moore was the author of *Esther Waters* (1894), among many other novels, and was a major name in literary Europe, a friend of Mallarmé and Zola, and a patron of Manet and Degas, but he now occupies the margins of our sense of the canon. Moore was also an old friend of Cunard and of her mother, and there were typically Cunardian rumours that he, and not Sir Bache, may have been Nancy's father. Certainly, Moore had a quasi-paternal relationship to Cunard and gave her his text because, he said, 'I want to start your press off with a good *bang*!' No comment. Aragon was back in Paris and Lévy was temporarily away, and in a five-day stretch of solitary summer printing, 'working alone in a heat wave which made more tricky yet the right consistency of the paper that had to be dampened', Cunard began to feel herself become a real printer. By the time Christmas 1928 was approaching, and *Peronnik the Fool* was nearly finished, she had been joined by a new lover, the African-American jazz pianist Henry Crowder. Cunard had met Crowder in Venice in 1927, when he was playing in 'Eddie South's Alabamians' at the Hotel Luna. Cunard rather implausibly explained that Crowder's youthful experience in the US postal service made him particularly adept at packing and delivering her books – 'the string and paper flew through his expert hands' – but in fact he was 'invaluable to the Hours in a dozen ways'. Cunard's memories of these times have a winningly chaotic quality, a sense of an enterprise held together only by determination and wit. The length of Norman Douglas's *One Day* was such that Henry was dispatched to Paris to collect more type; he drove back with the heavy lead letters in the car, fearful the whole journey that the suspension would collapse.

In fact, Crowder was to play a more profound role in introducing Cunard to the politics of racial injustice and, in turn, catalysing her work towards her *Negro* anthology (she dedicated the volume to him). In his memoir *As Wonderful As All That?*, written in the 1930s but not published until 1987, Crowder wrote: 'I was amazed at Nancy's absolute ignorance about such matters. But she was interested and eager to learn.' Crowder also helped Cunard at the Hours Press. Among the texts he worked on, setting type, was Beckett's 'Whoroscope'. When not working at the press, or telling Cunard 'of Negro writers . . . [and] where she could get books on and by them', Crowder would practise the piano in the main house, 'and it was to the strains, now thundering and dramatic, now romantic and plangent, of Gershwin's *Rhapsody in Blue*, floating out of the window, that the first book of the Hours was finished'.

Peronnik the Fool was bound in Paris in blue pale cloth – Cunard was dissatisfied with the binders' work, disliking the gilt (gold) letters used for the title – and was finished in time for Christmas 1928: two hundred copies, all signed by Moore, with a further twenty-five printed for the author and reviewers.

Cover designs for Cunard's books were by Man Ray, Yves Tanguy, the New Zealand artist and film-maker Len Lye, Elliott Seabrooke, and others. Among the early titles are names from an older generation like Moore and Arthur Symons, but there were works too by celebrated contemporaries including Ezra Pound's *A Draft of XXX Cantos* (1930), in fact printed by commercial printers, due to the length of the text (142 pages); Norman Douglas's *One Day* (1929), an account of a day spent wandering Athens; Roy Campbell's *Poems* (1930); Robert Graves's *Ten Poems More* (1930); and Louis Aragon's French translation of Lewis Carroll's *The Hunting of the Snark, La Chasse au Snark* (1929). These jostled alongside newer voices, discovered or promoted by Cunard's own work as printer-publisher, including Walter Lowenfels, Harold Acton, Laura Riding, Samuel Beckett, and the Chilean artist Álvaro Guevara whose 'poem-fresco' *St. George at Silene* received typically Poundian praise: Ezra loved the poem for its 'simple ignorance of all criteria of English verse'. In their diversity, the last three books printed by the press caught, her admiring scholar-advocate Hugh Ford has noted, defining aspects of Cunard's personality: Bob Brown's *Words* as a radical experiment in the layout of poetry (Brown originally wanted his poems set not only in large 16-point but also in type so small they were impossible to read, but this 'microscopery' proved impossible); Havelock Ellis's *The Revaluation of Obscenity* as a work of resistance to censorship and hypocrisy; and George Moore's *The Talking Pine*, a two-page transcription of a dream fragment, brief, strange, and compelling.

Between 1928 and 1931, the Hours Press printed a total of twenty-four titles, all of them hand-set in runs of usually 150 or 200, the copies signed by the author, and usually offered for sale at £1 10s. Some were printed in rural Réanville; others were produced at 15 rue Guénégaud, Paris, close to the Galerie surréaliste, where Cunard moved the press in the winter of 1930, a small shop on a narrow street near the Seine in Montparnasse, with a black and white tiled floor, a leopard-skin divan, and a large Boulle desk that had belonged to Sir Bache. The whole was decorated with paintings by Miró and African sculptures. 'The shop had an hysterical atmosphere,' Harold Acton observed, 'the printing press seemed to work in paroxysms, and everything else seemed ready to lose control.'

The Woolfs' Hogarth Press was liberating because, like other small presses, it enabled the proprietors to print their own works: Virginia resented relying on her publisher half-brother Gerald Duckworth, who could not tell 'a book from a beehive'. In her diary on 22 September 1925, Woolf wrote, 'I am the only woman in England free to write what I like.' Cunard had no ambitions to publish her own books at the Hours, and yet the press was absolutely an expression of her personality and commitments: this was self-publishing, but not as that phrase is normally understood. We see this in terms of the friends and lovers Cunard printed, the literary-aesthetic freshness of many of her books (both in contents and appearance), and that desire she had, which took on different forms at different stages of her life, to help talented people find a voice. (A warped version of this impulse is caught in Richard Aldington's nasty portrayal of his former friend in his story 'Now Lies She There': 'She liked unread poets, painters who never sold a canvas, musicians who had to play in restaurants.') No publication embodies this more than *Henry-Music* (1930), a collection of poems set to jazz piano by Crowder, the music written during a trip Cunard and Crowder took to sun-scorched southwest France in August 1930 where they stayed in Creysse, a tiny rural village, in rooms 'that might not have been inhabited for fifty years'. The rent was £1 a month. To startled local onlookers, the small upright piano they hired from the nearby town of Martel arrived on an open farm-cart pulled by oxen, and Crowder began to improvise around poems by Cunard, Beckett, Richard Aldington, Walter Lowenfels, and Harold Acton. Beckett's poem was the only one written specifically for the occasion; the rest Crowder picked out from existing verses. This may be why on the cover Beckett's name appears squeezed in. He'd written 'From the Only Poet to a Shining Whore (For Henry Crowder to Sing)' on the terrace of Le Dôme Café in Montparnasse: 'one of Beckett's better jettisoned poems', says critic Lawrence Harvey, in a mix of dismissal and acclaim.

'The nights were velvet-dark and hot,' Cunard remembered, 'with an old village woman forever washing loads of linen in a great ancient copper [tank] outside . . . and Henry's hands going over his compositions as long as we thought permissible.' The politics of Cunard's poem 'Equatorial Way' – in her own words, 'a sort of battle hymn' – seem problematic to a reader today: 'The Negro says a fierce farewell to the United States, and heads for an Africa that should be his.' But even as they represent a rich white European telling a black American to return to Africa (Georgia-born Crowder used to say to Cunard, 'But I *ain't* African. I'm *American*'), they also voice Cunard's real – if, by our standards, clumsily articulated – interest in black lives that few of her contemporaries knew or cared about. Man Ray's black-and-white photomontage cover, designed to open flat front and back to make one large scene, presents similar ambiguities. Crowder's head is framed by Cunard's arms covered in West African ivory bracelets (Anthony Hobson remembered how Cunard's conversation 'was punctuated by the rhythmic clash of the rise and fall of her African ivory bracelets . . . worn seven or eight on each arm'). Is Crowder being held back, or pushed forward? Is this a celebration of Crowder, an advocation of his talents, or a representation of the patron who guides him?

Cunard ascribed the early success of the Hours Press to 'good authors (in several cases very famous ones), hard work, luck, and ignorance of the usual complexities in publishing'. The first year was financially prosperous, partly due, Cunard wrote, 'to my . . . doing as many things as possible myself'; by the third, that success had brought overheads and a need for management that never sat with Cunard's ambitions. By the winter of 1930, she moved

the press to Paris. She had grown tired of the erratic rural electricity, the terrible winter cold, the fumes given off by the stove
in the print shop that made her sleepy. She'd become frustrated,
too, that supplies had to be bought from Paris, and sheets sent to
the binders in Paris, Rouen or Evreux. But this move back to the
city was also a sign of Cunard's shifting attention. She gave daily
control of the press to her friend, the experienced small-press
publisher Wyn Henderson, and the printer and typographer John
Sibthorpe; but debts and then hostilities accumulated between
Cunard and Henderson (a 'shocking businesswoman'), and in
spring 1931, the Hours Press was closed. All of Cunard's time,
attention, and astonishing energy was now focused on research
towards what would become her *Negro* anthology. She sold the
shop in rue Guénégaud in 1934, shortly before *Negro* appeared.
The Hours Press, for all its importance, could only ever have been
a short-term institution. When the *Little Review* sent to artists and
writers living in Paris in 1929 a questionnaire, Cunard wrote that
she wanted to be 'impervious, egocentric, concentrated, secret,
unquestionable, and yet all things to all men.' What she feared
most was 'lack of change, repetition and similarity to the past.'

Cunard did undertake one further significant act of printing on
the Mathieu press, this time as part of her political work for the
Republican cause in the Spanish Civil War. She used the old
press to print six *plaquettes* of poetry, and sold them to raise funds
to support Republican relief in Paris and London. The authors
included Langston Hughes, Tristan Tzara, Pablo Neruda, and
W. H. Auden.

When Cunard returned to Réanville in March 1945, she found
that the remains of the press had been devastated by German
soldiers billeted there by the collaborationist local mayor: suspicions of a secret newspaper had been used to justify the plundering

and destruction of what had been the Hours Press. As if in a dream, Cunard wandered through the shell of her former home. There were holes in the roof of the print room, charred remains of furniture, gaps where doors and windows had been. Books were trampled into the ground. Nailed across an open window was the green vellum cover of John Rodker's Casanova Society edition of Ezra Pound's *Cantos*: according to Cunard, 'one of the finest looking volumes ever published'. On the floor of the living room, 'flung face down and horribly creased', was Cunard's 'lovely blue landscape by Tanguy . . . shot full of bullet holes'. The remains of a portrait of Cunard, painted by Eugene Mc-Cown in Paris in 1923, had had a bayonet thrust through it. Two paintings by Miró were mutilated. Under a tree, 'all mashed and earth-trodden', Cunard found a drawing by Wyndham Lewis. There were fragments of coral jewellery, hammered into pieces; thirty letters of Caslon type in an old tin cigarette box; and several fields away, villagers found ivory bracelets, scattered on the ground. The only object that remained undamaged in the face of Nazi looting was the great old Mathieu press which Cunard had acquired from Bill Bird, and which was still standing in the stable, preserved by its heaviness.

The physical bulk of hand presses means they have a capacity to persist through time, to keep going no matter what, passing from owner to owner, outspanning any individual age. Virginia Woolf gave the Minerva Platen hand press she and Leonard had bought for £19 5s 5d to Vita Sackville-West in 1930, a gift for her new home at Sissinghurst, where the press still stands today. The 1891 Albion used by William Morris at Kelmscott was shipped in 1924 to Marlborough, New York, where American type designer Frederic Goudy used it at his Village Press, from where it followed a path between several smaller American printers (Aries Press, Woolly Whale Press, Herity Press) before, in 2013, it was purchased by the Rochester Institute for Technology at a Christie's auction for $233,000. Another (this time 1835) Albion also used by Morris at Kelmscott had a similarly twisting journey: after

Morris's death, it was acquired by C. R. Ashbee for the Essex House Press, and then by A. H. Bullen at the Shakespeare Head Press in Stratford-upon-Avon, before passing into the hands of Sir Basil Blackwell, and then the Printing Department of the Oxford School of Technology, and then in 1972 – in a final return to the beginning – to the William Morris Society at Kelmscott House, Hammersmith. Wooden presses – predating the iron – can have even longer histories. The wooden (or 'common') press allegedly used by Benjamin Franklin in John Watts's shop in London in 1726, before he travelled back to Philadelphia, had a transatlantic trajectory before it found its place at the Smithsonian in Washington DC. After she had closed the Hours shop in Paris, Cunard sold her second press, a Minerva – bought with the proceeds of her profitable first year to speed up the printing on the mammoth Mathieu – to poet and printer Guy Lévis Mano (1904–80), founder of Éditions GLM. Mano used Cunard's old press to publish major works by surrealist authors and artists during the 1930s; in the 1950s, Cunard was delighted to hear that the press was still very much in service.

II. ZINES, DO-IT-YOURSELF, BOXES, ARTISTS' BOOKS

Laura Grace Ford (b.1973), Craig Atkinson (b.1977), Phyllis Johnson (1926–2001), George Maciunas (1931–78), and Yusuf Hassan (b.1987)

Laura Grace Ford (b.1973)
'the magic of the photocopier'

In 2005, around the time when London was awarded the role of hosting the Olympics in 2012, Laura Grace Ford (writing as Laura Oldfield Ford) began making a zine – for now let's take that term to mean a self-published, self-distributed, non-commercial little magazine – called *Savage Messiah*. Like most zines, Ford's was a product of photocopiers and informal hand-to-hand distribution. Rather as Mary and Anna Collett in the seventeenth century had sliced up Gospels to make Biblical Harmonies, Ford used scissors, knives, and glue to reorder the printed materials around her. And like her book-making forebears at Little Gidding, Ford's work was ideological, although it was leftist political activism, rather than Anglican piety, that her zines expressed. Across twelve editions, *Savage Messiah* recounts a series of walks or 'drifts' through London that stand in direct and confrontational opposition to what Ford saw as the destructive, neo-liberal modernising of the city, a process she associated with the Blairite government and, in particular, with the looming Olympics. Issue 2 ('Welcome to Elephant and Castle') has text juxtaposed with black-and-white photographs of ruined buildings: '"Young professionals" sit outside gently conversing in sympathetic tones. The translucent edifices of Starbucks and Costa become shimmering

306

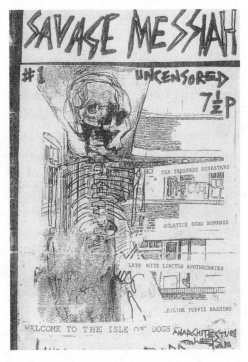

Savage Messiah *issue 1*.

promenades.' As issue 7 has it (see plate section): 'HANDS OFF
OUR ESTATES!!!!'

Different kinds of text collide in each issue within the descriptions of Ford's 'drifts' across the sites of demolished buildings, or
crumbling high streets, or along the routes of subterranean rivers:
drawings of places and people Ford has known; photographs of the
city's architecture (graffitied walls, tower blocks, stairwells, shop-
fronts); maps; advertisements from estate agents and flyers from
Reclaim the Streets; and diaristic accounts of drinking sessions
in pubs, fights, sex with strangers, of traveller sites and squatter
communities. Ford's zines are shot through with quotations from
authors and philosophers (J. G. Ballard, Italo Calvino, Samuel
Beckett, Thomas De Quincey, Charles Baudelaire, Walter Benjamin) who help Ford understand what is happening to London, the
displacement of working-class men and women amid corporate

land-grabs, and how the capital might be saved. Each edition takes in a different slice of the city – the Isle of Dogs; Elephant and Castle; Marylebone Flyover; the Lea Valley; Acton and Camden; Dalston and Hackney; King's Cross; Heathrow – and as Ford recounts her movements, her words and images also leap through time (it's 1973; it's 1981; it's 2006; it's 2012). Earlier moments of political rebellion or resistance are summoned up, or glimpsed like ghosts: 'a perambulation through the shadowscapes', Ford calls it. This combination of textual fracture – of pieces gathered and recombined – and a movement through space and time creates a warping, dream-like world where the reader simultaneously experiences different points in time. The effect is to release a sense of the city's radical possibility, to revive a politically resistant past, and to propose an alternative to a London that is, in Ford's conception, becoming gentrified, banal, and indifferent to its own actual history.

Ford produced eleven editions, and the zines were also later collected together in book form and published by Verso in 2011. In June 2018, after the fire at Grenfell Tower in June 2017, Ford produced a special single edition that returned to this area of London, placing the fire in a long history of middle-class gentrification and local government neglect of the working classes.

Part of the power of *Savage Messiah* as it appeared as a flimsy, Xeroxed zine was precisely its non-bookishness: it acquired mobility and political charge from its form. The vibrant presence of non-books is a vital strand running through the history of print, from the indulgences printed by Gutenberg in the 1450s through Franklin's jobbing print work. When I spoke to Laura Grace Ford, she described her decision to write serial zines, rather than a conventional book like a novel, as a consequence of her life at that time in 2005.

> I was living on a housing estate in Hackney – we were living in short-life housing. And we were being evicted. And so the zine was inextricably tied to that, really. So that sense of the ephemeral or

things being made quickly or that sort of transient quality of it – it actually was practical as well as aesthetic. Because my resources were limited. And I did photocopy things at work, because I used to work for Westminster Council teaching day centres and homeless shelters. And I used to just photocopy a few, a few zines in the office, and literally the first editions of them would be maybe twenty, thirty copies.

The zine format was an expression of Ford's sense of distance from any kind of cultural centre – 'It wasn't like I had a choice, it wasn't like I had access to the publishing world.' Ford had little sense of a wider readership: 'I was living on this estate, and my audience was my mates and fellow activists. I had absolutely no idea that it would ever be taken up by an academic publisher and turned into a tome. I would have been too frightened to write anything.' Ford organised nights at venues such as the Foundry in Shoreditch, a bar and space for art performances established by Bill Drummond of the band The KLF – 'it was quite anarchic and the activist element was always present' – and copies of *Savage Messiah* were sold there or handed out. Number 1 cost a parodic '7½p'; later editions were £2 or £3. The zine entered the world as one component of a wider celebration: DJs, and music, and drinks, and 'it would often involve a walk as well, or some sort of trespass'. It was a noisy birth. The printed text here was an event, or part of an event – a publication in the literal sense of being made public – and something is no doubt lost when, years later, the music has faded and the drinks have gone and we sit reading copies of *Savage Messiah* in special collection libraries or on silent screens.

By the time Ford started writing *Savage Messiah*, there was a long history of zine writing that found one origin in sci-fi fanzines of the 1930s such as the *Comet*; gained popularity in the punk scene of the 1970s with do-it-yourself, photocopied publications like *Sniffin' Glue*, *Search and Destroy*, and, slightly later, from 1982, *Maximumrocknroll*; and boomed in the early 1990s with feminist and queer zines, particularly those associated with the Riot Grrrl movement, such as *Bikini Kill*, with an accompanying band of the same name started in 1990 by Tobi Vail and Kathleen Hanna. As the zines scholar Jane Radway has written, the 'unifying thread' of zines 'is their outside-of-the-mainstream existence as independently written, produced, and distributed', and the potential they offer often marginalised communities to articulate or visualise their stories. Riot Grrrl zines like *Discharge* or *Wrecking Ball* defined themselves in opposition to a mainstream media dominated by a small number of global conglomerates and understood to be exclusionary, repressive, and technocratic. Of course, the tendency of capitalist culture to appropriate and commodify precisely the cultural forces that seek to oppose it complicates this idealism – as when, in Ford's words, in 2006 'you could go in a Topshop or somewhere like that, and there'd be T-shirts' designed with a post-punk aesthetic, neutered of any political intent. But the utopian energy of many zines is real, even if the effects in the world are more complicated, and compromised. The Riot Grrrl zines of the 1990s, for example, continue to inspire later publications, like the Oxford-based intersectional feminist zine *Cuntry Living* which has flourished since 2014. 'Like our sisters before us,' write the editorial collective in the first issue, 'we wanna talk about the problems women face in our society: endemic sexual abuse, economic discrimination, objectification and slut-shaming.'

As objects these zines are (Radway again) 'nothing if not motley', offering a patchwork of word and image; defying any ordered, linear reading; and possessed of 'a kind of uncontainable, ecstatic generativity'. The poet John Cooper Clarke catches things nicely when he writes of Mark Perry's *Sniffin' Glue* (1976–7): 'With its cheapskate house style and semi-literate enthusiasm . . . there was a piss-or-get-off-the-pot urgency about the whole production.' Zines often reprint and collage copyrighted images and play with format in a dance that is a continual mockery of the conventional bound book. Mark Todd and Esther Pearl Watson's *Whatcha Mean, What's a Zine?* (2006) presents instructions for zine formats they call standard half-page; no staples; quarter-page mini; accordion; stack-n-wrap; freebie; micro-mini; and French fold-n-bind. 'Break out of the format!' they urge, before listing 'Places to leave your zine' – bus stops, libraries, car wind-screens, concerts, copy stores, 'places where people sit', or 'any public place'. Zines make it clear how easy it can be to publish: on a fundamental level, that is their message – *you can do it, too!* – and this commitment to democratising, rather than mystifying, book-making is central to the zine as a form. In this sense, zines stand as polar opposites to the technical and aesthetic mastery of a book-maker like Thomas Cobden-Sanderson: remember the calligraphic flourishes of Edward Johnston, and Cobden-Sanderson's baffling way of talking about 'the Book of Life' (before things went pear-shaped and he dropped his type in the Thames). All of that might prompt admiration but to finish a Doves Press book is also to feel, *I could never do that* – and that was surely Cobden-Sanderson's aim. Zines encourage readers to become DIY makers, rather than stunning them into silent or baffled consumerism, or connoisseurship, or study; zines are a spiky riposte to a book-making culture that is seen as corporate, consumerist, profit-seeking, and commercial. In the age of the Internet, many zines became e-zines or webzines, but many did not, and persisted defiantly with older forms of book-making at the very moment when digital and online publication offered a more obvious route: rather than the blog, paper and pen, scissors and glue, staples and thread.

Ford has certainly always been conscious of this zine genealogy – 'I was aware that I was channelling this kind of post-punk aes-thetic' – although there were other cultural coordinates, too. The critic Mark Fisher saw a comparison between *Savage Mes-siah* and 1980s mix tapes – compilations of music from multiple sources produced by listeners on cassette, often with a contents list scrawled in biro – as works that proceed through the jolt of juxta-position. This link between zines and music is important for Ford, and she imagines reading *Savage Messiah* as a kind of listening.

You can't read it, like from start to finish the way you would a
novel. I don't think it really makes sense like that. I feel like, you
can zigzag across it, you know, in different routes. I remember in
the introduction to *A Thousand Plateaus* [(1980)], [Gilles] Deleuze
and [Félix] Guattari talk about how you should read that book,
like listening to a record. You know, you can like move between
tracks, some tracks that immediately resonate with you and some
that you don't like, and some are a slow burn. And you can, you
know, it doesn't have to be like, linear. I like that.

The physical quality of the zine is central to the achievement of
Savage Messiah, and it matters that this is a physical as opposed
to an online publication. In 2005, blogs were increasingly
popular – 'loads of people I knew were doing blogs' – but Ford felt
the urgency of the political context demanded a form of publication held in the hand, turned over, passed around: 'I felt because
of this encroachment on public and communal space, it was really
important to do a physical zine that could be a kind of catalyst
that would galvanise these collective moments.'

The DIY materiality of the zine – that sense that it is the product of the bedroom, not the office – is crucial for this sense of
animating different moments from London's past, for 'rupturing
the veneer', for feeling the power of glitches or gaps in the official history of London: 'being able to cut and paste these different elements, and juxtapose things that may be kind of jarring
to produce unexpected results'. *Savage Messiah* was a response to
Ford's sense that 'neoliberalism was imposing an official text of
what London was . . . that culminated around the Olympics', and
her zine's cheapness, ragged ephemerality, mobility, and immediacy meant 'it could just like pop up in the cracks . . . in these other
pockets that persisted, despite that onslaught'.

Ford was familiar with the cut-up techniques of William Burroughs and a wider tradition of modernist collage, although her
familiarity with these came first not through galleries or books but,
as a young teenager, via record sleeves. The Xerox machine is also

central to Ford's work, and in particular its capacity to bring together into a single flatness excerpts and pieces from diverse sources:

What I always loved was the magic of the photocopier. So you can have all these disparate elements and it's all messy and uneven, and the splotches of glue and wrinkles in the paper, and it's drawing on different temporal zones, but as soon as you photocopy it, it's all smoothed out, isn't it? . . . So you're kind of referencing those jarring moments, but the overall effect when you photocopy something's more that things coexist more seamlessly.

In 2005, Ford had little thought of literary posterity, or of the zines as collectible in the longer term. Today, she hasn't even got copies of all the editions herself: 'When Verso came to publish it as a book, I had to put a call out to see if people could lend me them back.' The sustained appeal of *Savage Messiah* beyond the small circle of friends and activists for whom Ford first wrote ('there's a lot of in-jokes and a lot of ludicrous stuff') is, she thinks, because the problem her zines attempted to address still pertains:

I think the reason *Savage Messiah* resonates with people is because you know, I feel like there's so many people that have been expelled and evicted from London that are no longer part of the discourse. Or like the contemporary discourse around art. I feel like there's a lot of voices that have been marginalised, geographically and, you know, on every other level as well, and that sort of discontent, I mean, it smoulders, doesn't it?

Craig Atkinson (b.1977)
'I publish a book every Thursday.'

At some point, being productive becomes being prolific, and Craig Atkinson has crossed that line. Atkinson has published something like 950 titles since 2005 – 'something like' because that number is increasing weekly. Based in Southport in North-West England,

Atkinson edits and publishes photobooks or zines under the title
of Café Royal Books. The publications have an elegant simplicity both conceptually and as physical objects. They are collections of black-and-white photographs from the recent past, one
image per page or sometimes one image spread across an opening. The books generally include very little or no text beyond the
colophon on the front. Each book focuses on a particular place at
a particular moment, often showing scenes of poverty, or protest,
or various kinds of alienation, but there is also a strong emphasis
on urban architecture, music, and fashion. A selection of titles
from 2019–22 includes Diane Bush's *London East End*; Brian Griffin's *The Broadgate Development*; Pete Davis's *Cardiff 1969–1977*; Paul
Glazier's *Vatersay 1985*; Trevor Ashby's *England 1970–1990 On the
Move*; and Janine Wiedel's *Port of Dover 1989–90*. Most of the
books ('books'? – we'll come back to that term) focus on specific areas within the UK, and constitute a kind of vernacular
documentary photography, but there are some that record more
distant events, like Mike Goldwater's *Bangladesh Floods 1999*. The
layout of the photographs, determined by Atkinson, is meticulous: there are often visual echoes and a sense of quiet sequence.
Some of the photographers are well known (Martin Parr, Homer
Sykes, John Claridge, Joni Sternbach), and the images come from
their personal archives; others are amateurs who shot one roll
of film but who happened to chance on something. The books
are staple-bound, a little under A5 in size, the paper thick and
sturdy – somewhere between paper and card – and each is usually
thirty-six pages long. The books are printed by a local family-run
firm, and are published weekly, in runs of about two hundred and
fifty. Most of the copies are sent out through the post. They are uni-
fied works in terms of form and content: the speed of production,
the anti-monumental physical form ('without fuss or decoration',
Atkinson puts it), and the political subject matter work together
to express a commitment to the book as a democratising form.

The uniformity of each volume means they are both individual zines and also components in an accumulating archive. The

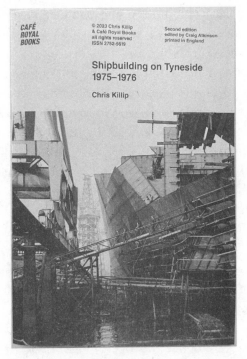

Café Royal's Shipbuilding on Tyneside 1975–76, *by Chris Killip.*

books constitute a long-form series of individual titles. Readers can buy a single edition for £6.50 (£5 in 2005) or take out a monthly or annual subscription for regular dispatches; museums, galleries, and libraries, with deeper pockets, can purchase a boxed set of 100 at a time. A complete run of 950 volumes, and growing, constitutes a major photographic collection of something in the region of 30,000 images that would otherwise be unknown – of *Southend on Sea 1972*, or *Fans and Clubbers 1978–1995*, or *Soho 1990*, or *Crufts 1974*, or *Greenham Common Women's Peace Camp 1983–1984*, or *Kentish Town 1975*.

When I spoke to Craig Atkinson about Café Royal Books, he described the mobility and lightness of these books as a direct reaction to the literal heaviness of his earlier work. Atkinson trained in Fine Art and his large abstract paintings could take eighteen months to make, and when finished posed constant problems of storage and display. Big, heavy, fixed. The works were immobile, or nearly so, and they also made particular demands of viewers: Atkinson didn't like 'the idea of putting something somewhere and then expecting people to come to see it', something that 'exists in one place at a time'. He liked art to move to people, rather than people to art. 'So as much as I love paint, still do, everything about it was kind of fighting against itself.' Books provided an alternative space for his art – initially drawings, and then, from 2012, photography. Books meant movement.

In using the slight, inexpensive book as a way to sidestep a more cumbersome culture of galleries, and to reach wide audiences who might not naturally be drawn to conventional art exhibitions, Atkinson is working in a tradition associated particularly with American artists in the 1960s who used the form of the book in nimble and inventive ways. Ed Ruscha's *Twentysix Gasoline Stations* (1963, but dated 1962) can stand as an example: although it is certainly not the first or only example of this conception of the book, its influence has been huge. *Twentysix Gasoline Stations* possesses at its heart a kind of flat literalism: it really is a book of black-and-white photographs of twenty-six different gasoline stations along the old Route 66 highway between Ruscha's Los Angeles home and his parents' house in Oklahoma City. The photographs possess a documentary quality: 'They are not "arty" in any sense of the word,' according to Ruscha, speaking with the breezy informality of the canonised artist; 'to me they are nothing more than snapshots.' The book first appeared in a print run of 400 copies; the printing was inexpensive and commercial; the format was small; and the pamphlet stitching suggested the opposite of a huge gallery wall. Copies were advertised for sale at $3 in 1964. As such, Ruscha's book stood as a bathetic answer to the kind of very grand artwork we might associate with a photographer like Ansel Adams, or the sort of luxury books we call *livres d'artistes*.

Critics have come to call this kind of book a 'democratic multiple': a work by an artist in which the idea of an 'original' is replaced by multiple identical copies that are inexpensive to buy, or are even given away for nothing; that are defiantly anti-grand as physical objects; that are available for readers who might not engage with gallery art; and that often convey a political or social message, either thematically or through their very everyday book form. The book form is itself crucial to the work: the book is not simply or neutrally a container for reproductions of works of art. In fact the very opposite: the work depends on the form of the book, with all its particular bookish features – of sequence, of page turns, of reading as a movement through time and through space, of double-spread openings, of linearity held in check by the possibility of reading back. In the words of the great scholar of artists' books, Clive Phillpot: 'The work is dependent on the book structure; it would not be effective flattened out on a wall.' Of course ideals break down – copies of Ruscha's book can sell today for a distinctly undemocratic £5,000, and a reader is more likely to encounter the volume behind a hushed glass case than in a teeming bookshop – but *Twentysix Gasoline Stations* helped establish a commitment to the book as a cheap and mobile form of art.

Atkinson describes Café Royal Books as something like a collision between this tradition of the democratic multiple and a National Trust pamphlet – 1963 Los Angeles meets the tea room at Chartwell. And while Atkinson had no prior experience in publishing ('You know, I knew how to fold a piece of paper and staple it, and that was all I needed'), the consequent straightforwardness of the books is central to their meaning: 'It's never been something that I want to create, you know, a cloth-bound, foil-backed, kind of hidden tail band with multicolours . . . I don't want to make that kind of thing.' (Wynkyn de Worde's eyes dart up, sensing a sympathetic book-maker.) Atkinson compares his books to brutalist architecture: 'There's no dressing it up, it's just there. And it works.' The books 'need to be simple, straightforward, functional'. The low price is important to Atkinson, too: there would be something perverse in a £120 hardback book of

Café Royal's Notting Hill Sound Systems, *by Brian David Stevens.*

images that represents *Allotments: Newcastle upon Tyne 1992*, or *The Post-Punk Years 1987–1990.* The cost to readers of new copies has only increased by £1.50 in nearly two decades. Of course, once released into a world of collectors, prices can balloon. At the time of writing, Martin Parr's *Abandoned Morris Minors of the West of Ireland* (2017) is on sale second-hand for £125 – not much less than the price of some actual Morris Minors on eBay. 'Which is ridiculous,' Atkinson says of this kind of increase, 'but good luck to the person who's selling it. And yeah, the person who's buying it, I suppose. It's nothing to do with me, those sales.'

When asked about online publication, and the decision to remain committed to the physical book at a time when the digital might offer a more predictable home for this kind of accumulating archive, Atkinson is clear.

Digital is great for some things, but I think most photographs, especially those from the time I publish, work better on paper. Screens are back-lit, reflective, rely on a power source, have no fold, no structure, texture, scent. Tablets, phones, computers are a catch-all, they do everything. A book is singular, it's 'just' a book. Physical books can be used anywhere, can be spread over a table amongst others, can be stored, shelved, looked after, don't rely on a power source ... Of course, books are fragile and can't be backed up in a like-for-like format ... but they come in multiples, so they are backed up already.

And are they books? Atkinson is interesting on this question:

I don't know. Yeah, books, zines, pamphlets. I mean, 'information pamphlets', I quite like calling them that. But, you know, who's going to buy an 'information pamphlet'? They started with that very DIY done-in-the-bedroom photocopied kind of ethos that zines have. But the paper is very considered. The position of the staples is very considered. Every aspect of it is very considered, which maybe takes it a bit away from that bedroom DIY thing. But maybe they're not heavy enough in some way to be a book. I don't know. I've never found a word that works for them, but I kind of like that as well. I've had a couple of complaints, literally a couple of complaints over the years [since 2005] to say something along the lines of, 'I purchased one of these publications and I was very disappointed. You call them a book, and it's certainly not a book.' But that's good as well.

Phyllis Johnson (1926–2001)
'we can put in all sorts of objects and things'

Aspen was a magazine founded by editor and journalist Phyllis Johnson in 1965, published by Roaring Fork Press in New York City. Johnson described it as 'the first three-dimensional magazine': each of the ten editions took the form of a box, and the box held a variety of inclusions – papery, and otherwise. In the words of an August 1966 advertisement – think *après ski*, and mid-'60s remake-it-all-optimism – Johnson wrote:

> Until now, every magazine was a bunch of pages stapled together. It arrived in your mailbox folded, mutilated, spindled—usually with more ads than editorial. Last year, a group of us enjoying the sun, skiing and unique cultural climate of Aspen Colorado, asked ourselves, 'Why?'

Read through a copy of *Aspen* and it still hums with this free-wheeling sense of possibility. Take Number 4, for example, from 1967 (see plate section). It's a hinged box, 24 by 32 by 2 centimetres, with a drawing of a circuit board and wraparound text. The whole is designed by Quentin Fiore and based around the work of Canadian media theorist Marshall McLuhan, whose aphorisms cover the surfaces of container and contents: 'all media work us over completely'; 'joy and revolution'; 'rite words in rote order'.

'The portfolio comprises many parts,' wrote Johnson, 'created and produced separately, in different media, by different processes; then combined, collated, and individually assembled and shipped.' Among Number 4's box-held parts are a fold-out poster of pages from McLuhan and Fiore's *The Medium is the Massage*; a colour poster of the Tribal Stomp at San Francisco's Avalon Ballroom; an essay on electronic music by Faubion Bowers and Daniel Kunin; a 'flexidisc' recording of early electronic music by Mario Davidovsky and Gordon Mumma ('for French Horn and Cybersonic Console' – obviously); a John Cage prose poem titled 'How to Improve the World (You Will Only Make Matters Worse)'; and a description of a nature trail for the blind. Even the advertisements follow this jostling-atoms format: a folder contains small booklets and sheets for very '60s brands like the Sierra Club, United Airlines, MGB autos, Rémy Martin, and others.

There are lots of stories here. One is about Phyllis Johnson, generally known outside of *Aspen* by her married name of Glick. Born and raised in Lincoln, Nebraska, Johnson worked as a reporter for the *Nebraska State Journal* and then, in New York City, as a reporter and editor for *Women's Wear Daily*, the *New York Times*, *Time Magazine*, *Advertising Age* and *American Home Magazine*. She also spent a lot of time travelling, skiing, and taking photographs. She worked for three years with the Navajo in the south-western United States, and wrote a guide to identifying and eating mushrooms. In 2001 her ashes were scattered in the sea off Hawaii.

Johnson combined this roaming intelligence with a sustained experiment in radical publishing. There's an exuberance to everything she writes – 'Who knows what the next issue will be!'; 'ASPEN gives you actual works of art!' – and by some criteria, Johnson's *Aspen* was astonishingly successful. Later editions feature pieces by Susan Sontag, Timothy Leary, Robert Rauschenberg, Samuel Beckett, Sol LeWitt, J. G. Ballard, Yoko Ono, and John Lennon. That is a line-up! *Aspen* 3 was designed by Andy Warhol (or, more likely, by studio assistant David Dalton, working as Warhol's delegate) and came in what looked like a package of Fab laundry detergent. *Aspen* 5+6 – the Minimalism issue – arrived in a two-piece white box with contributions by Marcel Duchamp, Merce Cunningham, William S. Burroughs, and Morton Feldman: 8-millimetre reels of film, essays, music scores, DIY miniature cardboard sculptures, and also Roland Barthes' extraordinarily influential essay 'The Death of the Author'. *Aspen* 9 – the Psychedelic Issue, subtitled 'Dreamweapon' – had the words 'Lucifer, Lucifer, Bringer of Light' printed on the back and included, inside, Benno Friedman's chemically stained frames from Western movies.

Johnson deserves a key place in that long history of female editors of journals who to a considerable extent shaped the literary and artistic landscape of the early to mid-twentieth century: a history that includes Harriet Shaw Weaver, whose *Egoist* serialised James Joyce's *A Portrait of the Artist as a Young Man* in 1914; Margaret

Anderson, whose *Little Review* (1914–29) did the same for Joyce's *Ulysses*; and Harriet Monroe, whose *Poetry* magazine from 1912 published early work by Wallace Stevens and H.D., was the first to publish T. S. Eliot's 'The Love Song of J. Alfred Prufrock' – and which, triumphantly, still exists today.

The other story is a material one. What happens when we imagine a book, or a magazine, as a box? There is a minor tradition of books produced not as bound codices but as boxes containing loose parts. One of the most compelling examples is *The Unfortunates* (1969), a novel of twenty-seven unbound sections, contained in a box, by the English experimental novelist, football journalist, and cantankerous man of letters, B. S. Johnson. *The Unfortunates* splices together a sportswriter's report on a football match with haunting memories of a friend who died of cancer. Johnson asked that readers reorder the unbound sections for each reading, to produce an almost infinite number of stories, different every time – and he did this as a way to represent the mind's non-linear, associative wanderings: 'A better solution to the problem of conveying the mind's randomness,' Johnson wrote, 'than the imposed order of a bound book.'

In her introductory letter to Edition 1 of *Aspen*, Phyllis Johnson wrote that by using the term 'magazine',

> we are harking back to the original meaning of the word as 'a storehouse, a cache, a ship laden with stores' [from the Arabic *makzin, makzan,* 'storehouse']. That's what we want each issue to be. Since it comes in a box, our magazine need not be restricted to a bunch of pages stapled together . . . [and we] can put in all sorts of objects and things to illustrate our articles.

A box enables a level of coherence – hence the themed issues – but, within this, an in-flux miscellaneity. Shake the box and the contents rattle. Empty the box and the parts fall in a random order. Remove an item and you can keep it apart. Place them back, one by one, as though you're packing a lunch. Add a component of your own. Close the lid knowing they'll still be there, waiting until next time.

The US Postal Service didn't like *Aspen*'s erratic publication schedule, and revoked the second-class mail licence granted to newspapers and magazines: without it, Johnson couldn't afford the postage costs and *Aspen* folded. In the judgment of 9 April 1971, Chief Hearing Examiner William A. Duvall declared *Aspen* to be 'nondescript' – in the sense of 'unclassifiable; belonging, or apparently belonging, to no particular class or kind' – and lacking qualities necessary to qualify as a 'periodical publication'. It was the very free-standing coherence of each edition that meant, according to Duvall, that *Aspen* couldn't be classed as a magazine.

Perhaps the most affecting item in Number 4 is the order form: it's a piece of ephemera that takes us back to the moment when *Aspen* was new, and Johnson had plans to run and run. It speaks of possibility. What would happen if we tick the box and fold the form ('No envelope required') and mail it in? 'We'll guarantee you,' writes Johnson,

> that our magazine is in fact as great as it sounds in concept. If you hate it, you can cancel at any time and get a pro-rata refund promptly. You have nothing to lose – and at the very least a conversation piece and collector's item to gain.
>
> Let's go.

George Maciunas (1931–78)

In 1964 a Lithuanian-American named George Maciunas published a sixteen-page book called *Flux Paper Events* (Fluxus Editions). It is a blank book in the sense that the pages carry no printed text. But things do happen. Each page is marked or manipulated in a different way: crumpled, stained, glued, torn, scored, stapled, paper-clipped, perforated, hole-punched, folded. What is going on?

'Fluxus' was the name of an international community of artists, architects, designers, and musicians, including, among others,
Joseph Beuys, Alison Knowles, Nam June Paik, George Brecht,
and Yoko Ono. It was founded, or gathered, or loosely coordinated, from about 1962 by Maciunas; Fluxus began in Germany
but soon found its home in New York. The word comes from the
Latin, meaning 'flow' or 'change'. It is also a pun: Flux Us – we
are in flux.

Fluxus was an unstructured, international movement which
produced art but not quite as you know it. The American poet
and visual artist Emmett Williams (1925–2007) described Maciunas as 'a clown and a gag man *par excellence*, and at the same time a
deadly serious revolutionary'. Maciunas was an impresario whose
stated goal was to make art 'unlimited, mass-produced, obtain-
able by all and eventually produced by all'; he liked performances
in which audience members became involved; he encouraged
mail art (a way to dispatch witty, subversive works into the world
in the post, without a reliance on galleries), and he printed manifestoes with words in bellowing capitals; he sought (as he wrote in
1964) the 'gradual elimination of fine arts (music, theater, poetry,
fiction, painting, sculpt- etc. etc.)' and the fostering of a 'collective
spirit, anonymity and ANTI-INDIVIDUALISM'; he delighted
in performances like *Piano Activities* (September 1962) in which he
and others pulled apart a grand piano with a saw and a sledge-
hammer in front of an increasingly furious audience; he encouraged the making of Fluxus objects like Robert Watts's *10-Hour Flux
Clock* (1969), an alarm clock with a ten-hour face, and Jock Reyn-
olds's *Potentially Dangerous Electrical Household Appliance* (1969), a plas-
tic box with a plug attached to each end of a wire; he sought to
'purge' (he liked the word) 'the world of bourgeois sickness, "intellectual," professional & commercialised culture'; he believed the
process of making art was the work of art, and he liked chance,
change, and projects that pulled down institutions; he believed in
the power of the joke (Eric Anderson performed a work in which
he bribed people to leave his performance), and his humour was

aimed (a friend said) 'at the entire cosmos'; he thought art could show us how to live more collaboratively; he organised housing for artists and started the first system of cooperative artists' lofts in Soho; he thought that Fluxus works might abolish the division between life and art (in Ono's 'Cut Piece' (1966), audience members were invited to take scissors and cut off pieces of the performer's clothing). There was something of Benjamin Franklin's total energy to Maciunas's book-making entrepreneurialism: had the two met to discuss ideas for new publications, something might have exploded.

Maciunas was sick all his life, 'clinging' (a friend remembered) 'to life with a large mountain of medicines' until his death from pancreatic cancer aged forty-six. He was a confirmed celibate until his final months; a narcissist who lived in austerity, eating cheap canned fish from Russia, putting almost all his money into Fluxus projects. He was (Emmett Williams again) 'a court jester in a tragic role'. He had a 'despotic way of silencing opposition'. More than anything, he made things happen: he brought into being things that weren't there before. He thought art was to be 'grasped by all peoples, not only critics, dilettantes and professionals', and that everyone could be a Fluxus artist. In Maciunas's last interview in Seattle in 1977, the year before he died, the interviewer asks, 'George, what is Fluxus?' We listen closely, leaning in, straining for a stable definition, thinking *finally* we will understand exactly what he has been up to, but all we can hear is the sound of strange, whirring, whistle-like noises.

Print was central to Fluxus. Maciunas printed posters, newsletters, flyers, and a Fluxus newspaper called *cc V TRE*. He experimented with the form of the book – testing its limits, pushing it to breaking point in order to make the familiar strange. Maciunas edited *Anthology 1* in New York in 1964: it's a wooden box, which doubles as the book's shipping crate, containing a book bound with three metal nuts and bolts, with pages in the form of manila envelopes. Each envelope contains a different object by a different artist – including a typewriter ribbon of his 'favourite story' by Joe Jones; a short story written on a long scroll by Emmett Williams; and Yoko Ono's 'self-portrait' in the form of a metal mirror. *Anthology 1* is typically Fluxus: an inventive format that encourages the active participation of the viewer with the work, and a collaborative project that makes use of everyday objects to create something extraordinary.

This is the context for Maciunas's *Flux Paper Events* (1964). Books had been made with purposeful blank pages before. In Volume 6 of Laurence Sterne's great comic novel *Tristram Shandy* (1759–67), the reader is invited to 'paint' their image of beauty on the facing blank page as a means to convey the intensity of Uncle Toby's love for Widow Wadman.

But perhaps it's wrong to talk of Maciunas's pages as blank, because they are all marked in different ways, although not with words. *Flux Paper Events* is a record of the everyday ways in which a page can be manipulated: it's a book of case studies of altered pages. The alterations are very familiar – we've all seen stapled or glued or folded or stained pages – and through this everydayness, *Flux Paper Events* closes the gap between art and life. But, organised in sequence, the book becomes strange. It's hard to say what this book 'means', and although there is a sequence there is no clear narrative or story. Perhaps it's wrong to think in these terms, of finding or concluding or extracting a meaning, in the way we would do when reading printed text. We could think of the pages instead as a series of events, or performances – and the book as something like a theatre or an exhibition space in which these performances take place. The book has become a gallery, and what is exhibited is the page. Here is one way a page can be. We turn it, as if we're walking through, as if we're involved in the artwork. Here is another way a page can be. We're aware of the specific ways a book works: how we turn the pages by hand; the way that moving through the book is a process that takes place both in space and in time. Are we reading? There is no printed text, but we do become finely attuned to the page: we read it closely, with our fingers as well as our eyes, noticing a tear or a fold or a stain or a staple where we might normally pass by. The habitual action of reading a book becomes more self-conscious, stranger, maybe even a bit wondrous, as if we are seeing it anew, as if – after 500 years of printed books – this is the very first time.

Yusuf Hassan (b.1987)
'zine making is a very rebellious practice,
if you want me to be completely blunt'

BlackMass Publishing was founded around 2019 in New York by Yusuf Hassan, collaborating with artist friends Kwamé Sorrell (b.1990), Devin B. Johnson (b.1992) and Jacob Mason-Macklin (b.1995). BlackMass publishes zines that are distinct, individual works, and that also cohere into a larger project of correcting what Hassan sees as the lack of representation of Black artists, writers and book-makers in contemporary publishing. Many of the publications combine photographs from archives with printed poetry and prose, meditating on aspects of African-American culture. Most of the zines are Xeroxed, staple- or sometimes sewn-bound, often about 29 by 21 centimetres, and relatively short – sixteen pages is the most common length. Edition sizes are very small – ten or fifteen or thirty. The decision about how many copies to print of each work is a practical question of resources. 'We find a lot of old paper,' Hassan said when I interviewed him, 'sometimes at flea markets,' and the edition size 'is based on how many sheets of paper we have. So sometimes we may have enough for just twenty books.' That sense of responding to resources connects with what Hassan calls the 'urgency' of BlackMass Publishing, and a commitment to speed and moving on to new work. Jazz is a topic running through many of the zines, and there's a connection between jazz as a subject, and jazz as a model for book-making, with its potential for improvisation, change, flow, and in-the-moment artistry.

We don't necessarily have time to keep printing over the same material, it's like on to the next because we're interacting with information so rapidly, and we're distributing information so rapidly, and . . . we are constantly, you know, on to the next topic on to the next subject. [The number of copies] . . . were made with that sense of urgency at that time at that particular moment . . . so if you were kind of around to be able to get one or you were in close proximity to get one, that's just what it was.

Hassan takes inspiration from the Black Arts Movement of the 1960s and 1970s and from artists who used 'flyers, and ephemera and poetry and zines and spoken word . . . I was very intrigued by that.' Writers Larry Paul Neal (1937–81) and Amiri Baraka (1934–2014 – also known as LeRoi Jones) are particular inspirations, and the name BlackMass Publishing came from Baraka's 1966 play *Black Mass*. For Hassan, the 'unfiltered' nature of zine publication – the fact that the author is also the maker, the publisher, and the distributor, and that the whole process of production can be swift and decisive – is key to its appeal. Hassan says the origins of BlackMass Publishing lay with 'me wanting to document my work through zines, and document what I was doing', and then distribute this to his peers, but soon expanded into something larger: 'I just wanted to have black people in a diaspora from all over the world working in close proximity with each other, through the lens of zines, and through the lens of self-publishing, and just being able to use this method to share information.'

The best way to get a sense of BlackMass Publishing is to witness the works themselves: short, mobile zines that come at you fast, possessed of both a direct and economical energy and a sense of an involvement in a larger project about the representation of black artists. *African Pottery Forming and Firing* (2021) is sewn-bound, Xeroxed, relatively long at eighty pages, and printed in an edition of ten. It offers a visual record of African ceramics, with images of pots and a title linking each to a people and area (Kassena people, Burkina Faso; Lela people, Burkina Faso; Yoruba people,

"I roped, threw, tied, bridled, saddled and mounted my mustang in exactly nine minutes from the crack of the gun."

BlackMass's "I roped, threw, tied, bridled, saddled . . ." *(2022)*

Nigeria). There are studies of architecture: Sorrell's *A study on Asante traditional buildings* (2022) is a small 14-centimetre book of images of buildings from Ghana; and Hassan's *Amaza Lee Meredith* (2022) has eight unnumbered pages of photographs of architect Meredith (1895–1984) and her work alongside text recounting her life and achievements.

"I roped, threw, tied, bridled, saddled and mounted my mustang in exactly nine minutes from the crack of the gun" (2022), at sixteen unnumbered pages, is a study of African-American cowboys – the title is a quotation from the autobiography of a former slave turned cowboy after the American Civil War, *The Life and Adventures of Nat Love* (1907). The zine offers a mix of photographs and poetry, song lyrics and short prose histories. This combination of archival photographs juxtaposed but not explained by text is a defining feature of BlackMass publications. We see it also in *The Zoot*

Suit & two Selected Poems (2020), a study of the 'zoot suit' popular with African-American men in Harlem, Chicago, and elsewhere, in the 1940s and 1950s, conveyed through photographs, pattern drawings, and prose history.

Kwamé Sorrell's *Fifteen Works by David Hammons* (2022) presents photographs of pieces by artist David Hammons (b.1943), with a loose print of one of the fifteen works also included in each zine. There are black-and-white images of racial violence: in *Come and Get me* (2021), a woman fighting back against a white policeman; in *Trife Life* (2021, see plate section) a photograph of the accused white men leaving a 1998 public inquiry into the UK's police handling of the case of the murder of Stephen Lawrence.

Hassan is interested in the challenge of how music might be conveyed in print. *Jazz Poems* (2019) features photographs (of bassist Edna Smith, for example) and poetry ('We Real Cool' by Gwendolyn Brooks, and 'Dear John, Dear Coltrane' by Michael S. Harper); Sorrell's *Jazz Glossary* (2022) is an A-to-Z list of terms from jazz, from 'a cappella' to 'woodshed'; and *Stay Close to Me* (2021) includes photographs of Black musicians juxtaposed with poetry. This method of juxtaposition is a BlackMass signature, a way of 'connecting dots':

> I'm inspired by Big L [1974–99], the American rapper, who I believe is a poet, and I put him in close proximity with Amiri Baraka, who's also a poet, one of the greatest, and I take Big L's lyrics, and I take Amiri Baraka's poetry, and I sit them side by side and know they are in conversation with each other.

A series of zines published in 2023 examines what Hassan calls 'the poetics of music' with editions focusing on images of and lyrics by Marvin Gaye, James Brown, Sade, Gil Scott-Heron, Curtis Mayfield, and Aretha Franklin.

Perhaps the most compelling BlackMass publication, and one of Hassan's favourites, is Sorrell's *Nigerian Pottery* (2022). This is a Xerox facsimile of much of a catalogue of Nigerian pottery, originally written and edited by Sylvia Leith-Ross and published in 1970 by Ibadan University Press, Nigeria. Leith-Ross's book provides images and descriptions of pottery, particularly domestic pottery in everyday use across Nigeria, based on holdings from the Jos Museum, Nigeria: lamps and incense burners, cooking pots, multiple-mouthed pots, and more. The original book is very hard to locate: this is a valuable work, in all senses, but one that is not circulating and being read. Sorrell was working in the studio of artist Simone Leigh and saw a copy of Leith-Ross's book. He borrowed it, and started to Xerox its pages. The result is BlackMass's *Nigerian Pottery* (2022): Leith-Ross's book, without some of the introductory essays, but Xeroxed, bound with string, stamped with a colophon 'BlackMass Publishing / P.O. Box 311277 / Jamaica, New York 11431', and relaunched into the world. Hassan talks about the effect of remaking this book in a different form, from non-circulating book to circulating Xerox zine, in these terms:

> the life of the book is still there, but what now you have is accessibility. And, you know, the idea was urgency, when producing something like that, because it was unavailable prior. And then, you know, he [Sorrell] did it in a format that was universal, and that everyone can now engage with, with this piece of material through the lens of a zine. So now it still holds the same material, but now it's presented as a zine. And that's one of my favourites, that was reproduced under this method, and under this format, which was very beautiful.

The informality of these BlackMass publications – quickly produced, bound with thread and string, and rapidly on the move – recalls a long history of printed pamphlet publication. Overleaf is an image of a play published 417 years before *Nigerian Pottery*. It's *The London Prodigall* (1605), published in London by Nathanial Butter, a swaggering city comedy falsely attributed on its title page to William Shakespeare. This is the final, time-battered

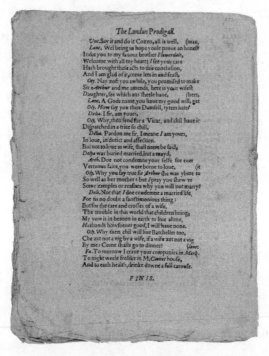

The London Prodigall *(1605)*.

page. Note the simple stab-stitched binding on the right: a single thread has passed though the whole text at three points, with no more elaborate binding or cover. This is speed, economy, light-ness, thrift, a desire for words to circulate out quickly to readers, in print form – a characterisitic mode of publication for early-seventeenth-century plays whose publishers saw some of the potentials that BlackMass's editors perceive.

We see something similar to *Nigerian Pottery*'s logic of repro-duction with BlackMass's *How Europe Underdeveloped Africa. Walter Rodney 1973: Chapter six. Colonialism as a system for underdeveloping Africa* (2021). Rodney's work describes the exploitation of Africa by European colonial regimes and BlackMass's book is a sixteen-page, staple-bound Xeroxed zine which reproduces Chapter 6, in which Rodney argues that Africa enabled Europe to develop at the same rate as Europe underdeveloped Africa, and that slavery and colonialism were crucially linked to international capitalism. This is zine publishing as excerption and transfer, a way of getting important texts quickly and nimbly out into the world. Hassan uses the word 'urgency' again to describe this publication.

> That chapter [by Rodney] still holds the same depth, it still holds the same sense of urgency. It still holds everything that it was presented to do, but now it's been kind of like abstracted from this hard cover, you know, this big book. And now it's just been Xeroxed on to computer paper. And it's a chapter that has now been transferred over into the zine . . . this is something that, you know, I want to just get out there, like, very quick, you know, the book has been around since the seventies. But now it's reproduced.

The physicality of these publications matters to Hassan – both the zine-materiality of cheap paper, unnumbered Xeroxed pages, staples, string bindings, stamped colophons, and also more fundamentally that sense that these works are objects for the hands. 'Online obviously exists,' says Hassan, 'it's the word of the day, it's taking place right now,' but central to BlackMass is 'tangibility': 'Being able to hold things in your hand and interact with them in this particular manner.' The process of zine-making for Hassan 'is still a very hands-on practice. We're involved in every aspect of the production . . . doing everything by hand. And this is what we're connected to.' And so: 'The soul of a zine is made to be experienced, physically, and we don't want to dilute that interaction, solely for the sake of what's taking place right now, which is the internet.' BlackMass's 'practice is rooted in the physical object to be experienced . . . It's a project and it's still in progress.'

Epilogue

A friend who teaches literature in New York told me that the historian Peter Lake told him that the historian of political thought J. G. A. Pocock told him that Conrad Russell told him that Bertrand Russell told him that Lord John Russell told him that his father the 6th Duke of Bedford told him that he had heard William Pitt the Younger speak in Parliament during the Napoleonic Wars, at the very beginning of the nineteenth century, and that Pitt had this curious way of talking, a particular mannerism – a kind of squeaky tone – that the 6th Duke of Bedford had imitated to Lord John Russell who imitated it to Bertrand Russell who imitated it to Conrad Russell who imitated it to J. G. A. Pocock, who could not imitate it to Peter Lake and so my friend never heard it. But all the way down to Pocock was a chain of people who in some sense had actually heard William Pitt the Younger's voice.

Or at least that's what I was told. There are alternative versions of this kind of cross-generational vaulting. A retired friend in Canada recalled that her now deceased Hungarian friend Dorothy told her that her mother had been walking in the park at the age of four with her mother when the Emperor Franz Joseph bowed to them from his carriage. 'In time,' Jorge Luis Borges wrote, 'there was a day that extinguished the last eyes to see Christ.'

One of the many things that books can do is articulate these kinds of temporal bridges: they can reach back, and back, and back, and in doing so, they can connect us with readers and makers from the past.

Overleaf is a copy of *Epistolae decretales summorum pontificum*, printed in Antwerp in 1570. Have you read it? Not quite finished it – I understand. Decretals are papal letters setting out decisions

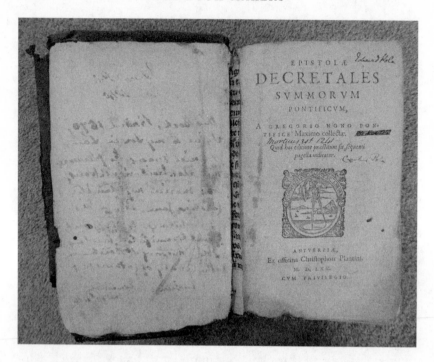

Epistolae decretales summorum pontificum *(Antwerp, 1570)*.

Fore-edge annotation.

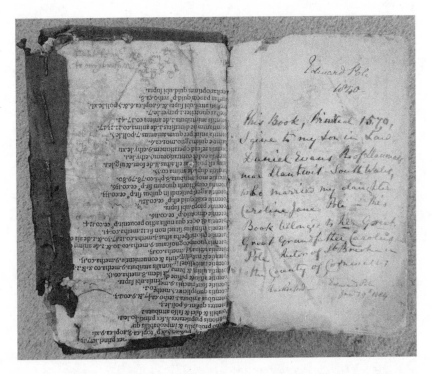

Provenance details inside the book.

in ecclesiastical law and were once hugely popular among law students. On this particular copy, the name 'Carolus [or Charles] Pole' is written across the fore-edge, and handwritten annotations have been added that describe a series of owners across several centuries.

On the flyleaf is written 'Edward Pole 1840', along with a detailed note in the same hand, dated January 1884 and recording:

> This Book, Printed 1570, I give to my son in law Daniel Evans R[ector] of Llanmaes near Llantwit South Wales, who married my daughter Caroline Jane Pole – this Book belonged to her Great, Great Grandfather Carolus Pole Rector of St Breock in the County of Cornwall.

What this collectively narrates is the movement of this book through time, and across owners: printed in Antwerp in 1570, and owned by, among others, Charles Pole (who graduated from New College, Oxford, in 1712); and then some time later his great-grandson Edward Pole (1805–90); and then, via his daughter Caroline Jane Pole, Daniel Evans, working in the small village of Llanmaes in Glamorgan near the market town of Llantwit Major. A loosely inserted leaf dated 1998 shows that the book continued to descend through members of that family.

This book is both the object that connects and, in those annotations, the document of its own migrations: annotated books carry their own accumulating histories with them. One of the things that lists of names like these suggest is the poverty of singular claims to ownership: books move on, passing out of one owner's clutches – however possessive those clutches might be – and moving on to meet the next generation. In this sense, the book always exceeds us, and the best we can do is feel it pass through our hands.

One of the reasons why books will endure is that they don't merely or straightforwardly convey text to readers. They are not only messengers, although they are that too. Books are themselves incredible objects whose beauty and complexity enriches the text being read. Peer closely at calligrapher Edward Johnson's curling green 'W' at the start of the Doves Press *Hamlet*, or the crystal-clear, immaculately spaced lettering of John Baskerville's *Paradise Lost*. These are works of art that contribute to the meaning of the whole. It is a different experience to read the first edition of Charles Dickens's *Great Expectations* (1861) in the three-volume door-stopper edition at Mudie's Circulating Library on New Oxford Street, compared to the form in which it originally came into the world: 'A new serial story', as advertisements in the magazine *All the Year Round* put it, 'to be continued from week to week until completed in about EIGHT MONTHS.' In much the same way, to read BlackMass Publishing's Xeroxed representations of out-of-print hardback books on Nigerian pottery is to feel the shaping presence of the material text: the opening-up power of the light, mobile, thread-bound pamphlet.

Not all of these material features are straightforwardly beautiful. The torn-up copies of Cicero that William Wildgoose used to bind Shakespeare's First Folio were not decorative, but they preserve a moment in the making of this book, when Wildgoose had a stack of volumes to bind and those plays in English were just one volume in the pile. In such moments, books tell their own material stories. 'Emprented in fletestrete,' shouts one 1506 volume, the exclamation marks implicit, 'by Wynkyn de Worde, dwellynge in the famous cyte of London his house in the same at the sygne of the sone.'

The story of the physical book is a story made by people, not algorithms, individuals with messy lives, and ideals, and talents, and non-infinite resources, and with other things to do. One of the things physical books do is carry something of the lives, or the personalities, of their makers, through their sheer weight-in-the-world presence. Books are expressive objects which themselves possess an emotional range and which convey, in their material forms, in ways that are sometimes legible, the texture of what it meant for a particular book-maker to be alive. The books printed by the Hours Press in France possess Nancy Cunard's velocity. Benjamin Franklin's cheap printed non-books flutter across North America on the wings of his ceaseless dynamism. Laura Grace Ford's attack on the historical amnesia of gentrification is enacted in the rough edges of her cut-and-glued-and-photocopied *Savage Messiah* zines. Even that million-selling paperback you keep seeing everywhere is the product of designers, editors, artists. Books inhabit the care or haste or defiance or anger or love that made them. They have the form they do because a particular person was alive at a particular moment and took a particular risk. All editions of *Great Expectations* may open with the words 'My father's family name being Pirrip, and my Christian name Philip', but they all differ as material propositions, and that difference – whether you call it a personality, or a supplement, or a meaning, or a residue – is the presence of the book-maker.

The Book-Makers is the story of the physical book and digital technology isn't its subject, but of course digital technology has the capacity to do wonders with the written word – wonders in terms of ease of production, and breadth of distribution, and also in terms of the magical effects that can be produced. A publisher like Visual Editions in London is testing the limits of what online works of literature can do. If you don't want to read *Great Expectations* as serial instalments in a magazine, or as a three-volume hardback from Mudie's, go online and survey your choices: scholarly editions, digital facsimiles of early printed editions, e-books (free, cheap, or pricey), pages and pages of vanilla text, even before we enter the world of interactive choose-your-own-adventures.

For anyone interested in the history of media, this is all fascinating and alive – as fascinating and alive as were the rolls of cine-film and flexidiscs and essays on electronic music included by Phyllis Johnson in her 1960s magazine-in-a-box, *Aspen*. But this isn't the end of anything – least of all the book – because a physical book is a different proposition to an electronic text. Print and digital need not be placed in an antagonistic relation to one another. The question 'Will the book endure?' or 'Is the book dead?' or 'Will the internet kill the book?' is mistaken because the five and a half centuries since Gutenberg show the book to be a form that has continually adapted to new people, ideas, contexts, and technologies, while all the time maintaining its identity as a physical support for text. We see newness in the most dramatic moments of that history – the extra-illustrated volumes of Charlotte and Alexander Sutherland, or the pious works of destruction-and-creativity sliced and glued by Mary and Anna Collett – but the similarity-with-difference of the story of the book is a refrain across the last eleven chapters.

Walt Whitman (1819–92) hasn't appeared in *The Book-Makers*, so let's squeeze him in as the final page closes on us. Whitman was a printer and a typesetter on Long Island, New York, long before his poetry collection *Leaves of Grass* (the first self-funded edition appeared in 1855) brought him fame and acclaim. Here is 'A

Font of Type'. The whole poem is only six lines, because its subject is the potential of small things.

> This latent mine—these unlaunch'd voices—passionate powers,
> Wrath, argument, or praise, or comic leer, or prayer devout,
> (Not nonpareil, brevier, bourgeois, long primer merely,)
> These ocean waves arousable to fury and to death,
> Or sooth'd to ease and sheeny sun and sleep,
> Within the pallid slivers slumbering.

Whitman's neat ordering of varieties of type shows, with slightly intrusive technical pride, his print-shop experience: nonpareil is 6 point; brevier 8; bourgeois 9; long primer 10. But this isn't a poem about taxonomies: we may give tidy names to these little metal letters, but what they offer, Whitman suggests, is potential – vast potential, the potential to body forth thoughts and ideas. Type, Whitman wrote elsewhere, 'rejects nothing'. Type represents possibility. The expression of Whitman's 'passionate powers' is latent 'within the pallid slivers slumbering'. The tidy font of type – and we can widen the category of 'type' to include all the materials of book-making – is potentiality itself: a way of bringing as yet 'unlaunch'd voices' into the world.

References

These references are not exhaustive but represent some important works that were helpful in the writing of each chapter.

Wynkyn de Worde

There are valuable and highly readable accounts of de Worde's career in James Moran, *Wynkyn de Worde: Father of Fleet Street* (London: Wynkyn de Worde Society, 1976), and Henry R. Plomer, *Wynkyn de Worde and his Contemporaries from the Death of Caxton to 1535* (London: Grafton and Co., 1925). For laser-targeted corrections to some details in these and other books, see Peter W. M. Blayney, *The Stationers' Company and the Printers of London, 1501–1557* (Oxford: Oxford University Press, 2013). On English printing's internationalism, I learnt much from David Rundle's 'English books and the continent', Chapter 13 of Daniel Wakelin and Alexandra Gillespie (eds), *The Production of Books in England 1350–1500* (Cambridge: Cambridge University Press, 2011). De Worde's pioneering experiments in Arabic printing are surveyed, a touch sniffily, by Geoffrey Roper in 'Arabic Printing and Publishing in England before 1820', in *Bulletin (British Society for Middle Eastern Studies)* 12.1 (1985), 12–32. For patronage and Margaret Beaufort, I recommend Susan Powell, 'Lady Margaret Beaufort and her books', *The Library*, 6th ser., 20 (1998), 197–240. On women and printing more broadly, see *Women's Labour and the History of the Book in Early Modern England*, edited by Valerie Wayne (London: Arden, Bloomsbury, 2020), particularly chapters by Alan Farmer and Sarah Neville. Helen Smith's *'Grossly Material Things': Women and Book Production in Early Modern England* (Oxford: Oxford University Press, 2012) is a groundbreaking study of women and the book trade in the period after de Worde's. For inventories, including the one from 1553, there is Tamara Atkin's 'Reading Late-Medieval Piety in Early Modern England' in *Medieval and Early Modern Religious Culture: Essays Honouring Vincent Gillespie on his 65th Birthday*, edited by Laura Ashe and Ralph Hannah (Suffolk: Boydell and Brewer, 2019), 209–41. For de Worde's marketing talents, a good start is A. S. G. Edwards and C. M. Meale, 'The marketing of printed books in late medieval English', *The Library*, 6th ser., 15 (1993), 95–124. And for repeating woodcuts, there is Seth Lerer, 'The Wiles of a Woodcut: Wynkyn De Worde and the Early Tudor Reader', in *The Huntington Library Quarterly* 59.4 (1997), 381–403. Prayer book deletions are discussed in Eamon Duffy, *Marking the Hours: English People and their Prayers, 1240–1570* (New Haven: Yale University Press, 2006). Margery Kempe in print is described in Sue Ellen Holbrook, 'Margery Kempe and Wynkyn de Worde' in *The Medieval Mystical Tradition in England* (Cambridge: D. S. Brewer, 1987), edited by Marion Glasscoe, 27–46. For title pages, I drew on Whitney Trettien's chapter in *Book Parts*, edited by Dennis Duncan and Adam Smyth (Oxford: Oxford University Press, 2019), Chapter 4. De Worde's will is treated in M. C. Erler, 'Wynkyn de Worde's will: legatees and bequests', *The Library*, 6th ser., 10 (1988), 107–21. And finally, that remarkable birth girdle is considered meticulously in Joseph J. Gwara and Mary Morse, 'A Birth Girdle Printed by Wynkyn de Worde', in *The Library* 13.1 (March 2012), 33–62.

William Wildgoose

For a brilliantly detailed account of Wildgoose's 1623 bindings, see Andrew Honey and Arthur Green, ' "Met by chance" – a group of ten books bound for the Bodleian Library in February 1624 by William Wildgoose of Oxford', available online: this has been crucial for my work. David Pearson is the essential authority on early modern English bookbinding: see in particular his *Oxford Bookbinding 1500–1640* (Oxford: Oxford Bibliographical Society, 2000), and *English Bookbinding Styles 1450–1800* (New Castle: Oak

Knoll Press, 2014). Three books by Strickland Gibson – the man who identified the Turbutt Folio in 1906 – are central to work in this field: *Early Oxford Bindings* (Oxford: Oxford University Press, 1903); *Abstracts from the wills and testamentary documents of binders printers and stationers of Oxford from 1493 to 1638* (Oxford: Oxford University Press, 1907); and *Some Oxford Libraries* (Oxford: Oxford University Press, 1914). See also Mirjam M. Foot, *Bookbinders at Work: Their Roles and Methods* (London and New Castle: British Library and Oak Knoll Press, 2006).

John Dorne's colourful life is described in Graham Pollard, 'John Dorne as an Oxford bookbinder', in Pearson, *Oxford Bookbinding*, 201–10. Dorne's day book is edited in Falconer Madan, 'The daily ledger of John Dorne, 1520', *Collectanea*, edited by C. R. L. Fletcher, Oxford Historical Society, 1st ser. (1885), 71–177. The life of the First Folio in the Bodleian is described by Falconer Madan and Gladwyn Turbutt, *The Original Bodleian Copy of the First Folio of Shakespeare (The Turbutt Shakespeare)* (Oxford: Clarendon Press, 1905), and in Emma Smith, *Shakespeare's First Folio: Four Centuries of an Iconic Book* (Oxford: Oxford University Press, 2016). For a digital facsimile of the Bodleian (or Wildgoose, or Turbutt – pick your choice) First Folio, see the Bodleian's https://firstfolio.bodleian.ox.ac.uk. Pepys's bibliographical world is carefully analysed in Kate Loveman, *Samuel Pepys and His Books* (Oxford: Oxford University Press, 2015).

Mary and Anna Collett
I discuss the cut-and-paste labours of Little Gidding in my *Material Texts in Early Modern England* (2018), and John Gibson in ' "Rend and teare in peeces": Textual Fragmentation in Seventeenth-Century England', in *The Seventeenth Century* 19 (2004), 36–52. For cutting texts more broadly, see the *Journal of Medieval and Early Modern Studies* 45.3 (September 2015), special edition on 'Renaissance Collage: Towards a New History of Reading', edited by Juliet Fleming, William Sherman and Adam Smyth. A number of important

articles have been written on Little Gidding's Harmonies over the last fifteen years: see, in particular, Joyce Ransome, 'Monotessaron: The Harmonies of Little Gidding,' in *The Seventeenth Century* 20 (2005), 22–52, and 'George Herbert, Nicholas Ferrar, and the "Pious Works" of Little Gidding', *George Herbert Journal*, 31 (2007–2008), 1–19; Paul Dyck, '"A New Kind of Printing": Cutting and Pasting a Book for a King at Little Gidding', in *The Library: The Transactions of the Bibliographical Society* 9 (2008), 306–33, and '"So Rare A Use": Hands and Minds on the Gospels at Little Gidding', in *George Herbert Journal* 27 (2006), 67–81. For the use of images, see George Henderson, 'Bible illustration in the Age of Laud', in *Transactions of the Cambridge Bibliographical Society* 8 (1982), 173–204. Two recent excellent books are essential, too: Michael Gaudio, *The Bible and the Printed Image in Early Modern England: Little Gidding and the Pursuit of Scriptural Harmony* (Abingdon: Routledge, 2017), on the Colletts' use of images, and Whitney Trettien, *Cut/Copy/Paste* (Minnesota: University of Minnesota Press, 2022), which locates Little Gidding within a broader account of book modification. Thomas Littleton's *Tenures* with those huge margins is discussed by Caroline Duroselle-Melish in *The Collation* (https://collation.folger.edu/2015/11/extravagantly-large-paper).

John Baskerville and Sarah Eaves

The most useful single volume for Baskerville is *John Baskerville: Art and Industry of the Enlightenment*, edited by Caroline Archer-Parré and Malcolm Dick (Liverpool: Liverpool University Press, 2017). I benefited greatly from this ranging and extensive treatment of Baskerville from multiple perspectives. Older but important surveys, of which there are several, include William Bennett, *John Baskerville, the Birmingham printer: his press, relations, and friends*, 2 vols. (Birmingham: City of Birmingham School of Printing, 1937–9), and Josiah H. Benton, *John Baskerville, Type-Founder and Printer, 1706–1775* (Boston, 1914, and Cambridge: Cambridge University Press, 2014). Caroline Archer-Parré has also written a series of excellent recent articles on Baskerville: 'Inhuming and Exhuming: John Baskerville's Death, Burial and Post-Mortem Life', in *Midland History* 47:3 (2022), 1–19; 'Places, Spaces and the Printing Press: Trade Interactions in Birmingham', in *Midland History*, 45:2 (2020), 145–60; and, with Ann-Marie Carey and Keith Adcock, 'The Baskerville Punches: Revelations of Craftsmanship', in *Midland History* 42:2 (2020), 176–89. Philip Gaskell's *A bibliography of John Baskerville* (Cambridge: Cambridge University Press, 1959) is a hyper-granular account of Baskerville's books and is essential for the specialist, but it's not a beach read. Beatrice Warde (sometimes writing under the name of Paul Beaujon), wrote important and very engaging articles on typography, Monotype, and Baskerville revived, including 'The Baskerville types: a critique', *Monotype Recorder*, 26 (221) (1927), 3–30, and *The Crystal Goblet: Sixteen essays on typography*, edited by Henry Jacob (London: Sylvan Press, 1955). For the history of the Baskerville punches, there is John Dreyfus, 'The Baskerville punches, 1750–1950', in *The Library*, 5th ser., 5 (1950), 26–48. On typography more generally, there is Stanley Morison's *A Tally of Types*, edited by Brooke Crutchley (Cambridge: Cambridge University Press, 1973) with an influential series of short essays on types, including Baskerville; and also Simon Garfield's fun and sprightly *Just My Type: A Book about Fonts* (New York, NY: Gotham Books, 2011).

Benjamin Franklin

Franklin's *Autobiography* exists in many editions: Joyce E. Chaplin's edition (New York: Norton, 2012) includes useful contextual materials. The best source for Franklin's printing is C. William Miller's *Benjamin Franklin's Philadelphia Printing 1728–1766: A Descriptive Bibliography* (Philadelphia: American Philosophical Society, 1974); also important is Peter Stallybrass and James N. Green, *Benjamin Franklin: Writer and Printer* (New Castle, Delaware: Oak Knoll Press & Library Company of Philadelphia & The British Library, 2006). The best biographical account is J. A. Leo Lemay, *The Life of Benjamin Franklin*, vol. 1 (Philadelphia: University of Philadelphia Press,

2005); Chapter 2 of Edwin S. Gaustad's *Benjamin Franklin* (Oxford: Oxford University Press, 2006) provides a brisk narrative of Franklin's career as a printer. Useful on Franklin's networking instincts is Ralph Frasca, *Benjamin Franklin's Printing Network: Disseminating Virtue in Early America* (University of Missouri Press, 2006). On job printing, there are excellent accounts in Peter Stallybrass, '"Little Jobs": Broadsides and the Printing Revolution', in Sabrina Baron Alcorn, Eric N. Lindquist, and Eleanor F. Shevlin (eds), *Agent of Change: Print Culture Studies after Elizabeth L. Eisenstein* (Amherst: University of Massachusetts Press, 2007), and Georgia B. Barnhill, 'Benjamin Franklin's Job Printing', in *Ephemera News or The Ephemera Journal* 8 (1998), 10–15. Franklin's London years are brilliantly analysed, bibliographically, in Hazel Wilkinson, 'Benjamin Franklin's London Printing 1725–26', in *PBSA* 110.2 (2016), 139–180. For Franklin's complicity in the slave trade through his newspaper, the most recent account is Jordan E. Taylor, 'Enquire of the Printer: Newspaper Advertising and the Moral Economy of the North American Slave Trade, 1704–1807', in *Early American Studies*, 18.3 (Summer 2020), 287–323.

Nicolas-Louis Robert

The best place to start is Dard Hunter, *Papermaking: The History and Technique of an Ancient Craft* (New York: Dover, 1943): rather old now, but still a wonderfully wide-ranging account that feels almost total in its scope. Jonathan Bloom, *Paper before Print: The History and Impact of Paper in the Islamic World* (New Haven: Yale University Press, 2001), is excellent on the Islamic context. Lothar Müller, *White Magic: The Age of Paper*, translated by Jessica Spengler (London: Polity, 2014) provides a history of paper with a sharp literary and philosophical emphasis. D. C. Coleman, *The British Paper Industry 1495–1820: A Study in Industrial Growth* (Oxford: Clarendon Press, 1958) is an economic historian's account of the domestic industry, big on numbers and statistics. Ian Sansom, *Paper: An Elegy* (London: Fourth Estate, 2012) is almost the exact opposite: playful, selective, imaginative, and literary. Caroline Fowler, *The Art of Paper: From the Holy Land to the Americas* (New Haven and London:

Yale University Press, 2019), provides an art historical focus. Jonathan Senchyne's *The Intimacy of Paper in Early and Nineteenth-Century American Literature* (Amherst: University of Massachusetts Press, 2020), considers the relationships between readers and paper, and situates paper studies within broader recent work on material texts. Mandy Haggith, *Paper Trails: From Tree to Trash – the True Cost of Paper* (London: Virgin Books, 2008) is excellent on the environmental consequences of paper use. R. H. Clapperton, *The Paper-Making Machine: Its Invention, Evolution and Development* (Oxford: Pergamon Press, 1967), gives a chronological account of the development of paper-making machines. If you want an exhaustive account of American mills, you need John Bidwell, *American Paper Mills, 1690–1832: A Directory of the Paper Trade with Notes on Products, Watermarks, Distribution Methods, and Manufacturing Techniques* (New Hampshire: Dartmouth College Press, 2012). The story of the Cairo Geniza is told, with a focus on the biographies of the central late-nineteenth- and early-twentieth-century players, in Adina Hoffman and Peter Cole, *Sacred Trash: The Lost and Found World of the Cairo Geniza* (New York: Random House, 2011).

Charlotte and Alexander Sutherland
Scholarship on extra-illustration isn't as extensive as the subject deserves, but Lucy Peltz's superb *Facing the Text: Extra-illustration, Print Culture, and Society in Britain, 1769–1840* (Pasadena: Huntington Library, Art Collections, and Botanical Gardens, 2017) has given the subject a definitive history from an art historian's perspective. There are a small number of shorter, excellent discussions that locate extra-illustration more explicitly in relation to the history of the book, particularly two articles by Luisa Calè – 'Extra-Illustration and Ephemera: Altered Books and the Alternative Forms of the Fugitive Page', in *Eighteenth-Century Life* 44.2 (April 2020), 111–35, and 'Dickens Extra-Illustrated: Heads and Scenes in Monthly Parts (The Case of *Nicholas Nickleby*),' in the *Yearbook of English Studies* 40 (2010), 8–32 – and Jason Scott-Warren, 'Reading on the Threshold', in *Thinking on Thresholds: The Poetics of*

Transitive Spaces, edited by Subha Mukherji (London: Anthem Press, 2012), 157–172. Also useful as introductions are Robert A. Shaddy, 'Grangerizing,' in *The Book Collector* 49.4 (Winter 2000), 535–46, and Robert R. Wark, 'The Gentle Pastime of Extra-Illustrating Books', in *Huntington Library Quarterly* 56.2 (Spring 1993), 151–65.

Charles Edward Mudie

The Charles E. Mudie Collection, 1816–1897, with papers relating to Mudie and his library, is kept at the Rare Book & Manuscript Library, University of Illinois at Urbana-Champaign, and is – wonderfully – digitised and freely available. The best single source on Mudie, and in particular on his library's relation with the three-volume novel, is Guinevere L. Griest's *Mudie's Circulating Library and the Victorian Novel* (Bloomington and London: Indiana University Press, 1970). There are some excellent historical accounts, including Stephen Colclough, 'New Innovations in Audience Control: The Select Library and Sensation', in *Reading and the Victorians*, edited by Juliet John and Matthew Bradley (Abingdon: Routledge, 2015), Chapter 2; Simon Eliot, 'Circulating libraries in the Victorian age and after', in A. Black P. Hoare (eds.), *The Cambridge History of Libraries in Britain and Ireland*. Vol 3 (Cambridge: Cambridge University Press, 2006), 125–46; and Daniel Allington, David A. Brewer, Stephen Colclough, Sian Echard, and Zachary Lesser, *The Book in Britain: A Historical Introduction* (Chichester: Wiley Blackwell, 2019). For the institutional history of English Literature as a subject, see D. J. Palmer, *The Rise of English Studies* (London and New York: Oxford University Press, 1965); for Mudie and the reading public, see Peter Katz, 'Redefining the Republic of Letters: The Literary Public and Mudie's Circulating Library', in *Journal of Victorian Culture*, 22.3 (2017), 399-417. Jorge Luis Borges's 'The Library of Babel' is in Borges, *Labyrinths: Selected Stories and Other Writings*, edited by Donald A. Yates and James E. Irby (New York: New Directions, 1964), 54–5. Andrew Pettegree and Arthur der Weduwen, *The Library: A Fragile History* (London: Profile, 2021) gives a down-the-centuries history of the library as an institution.

Thomas Cobden-Sanderson

Marianne Tidcombe's wonderful *The Doves Press* (London: British Library and Oak Knoll Press, 2002) gives a terrific overview and provides rich documentary testimony of all aspects of the press. Cobden-Sanderson's diaries are available in print and provide a fascinating, sometimes maddening, first-person perspective: *The Journals of Thomas James Cobden-Sanderson* (London: Richard Cobden-Sanderson, 1926), two volumes. There is a mass of other relevant publications. I found particularly helpful Colin Franklin, *Obsession and Confession of a Book Life* (London: Oak Knoll Press, 2012) – wonderfully written – and his *Emery Walker: Some Light on His Theories of Printing and on his Relations with William Morris and Cobden-Sanderson* (Cambridge: Privately Printed, 1973). The private press movement is assessed in Roderick Cave, *The Private Press* (New York and London: R. R. Bowker, 1983). Alan Crawford's *Oxford Dictionary of National Biography* entry for Cobden-Sanderson is unusually good. In a different key, but very helpful for *Hamlet*, is Sujata Iyengar, 'Intermediating the Book Beautiful: Shakespeare at the Doves Press', in *Shakespeare Quarterly*, 67.4 (2016), 481–502.

Nancy Cunard

Nancy Cunard's fascinating memoir – what we'd call today (but Cunard wouldn't) her bio-bibliography – is *These were the hours: Memories of my Hours Press, Réanville and Paris, 1928–1931*, edited by Hugh Ford (Carbondale; Edwardsville: Southern Illinois University Press, 1969). Hugh Ford (ed.), *Nancy Cunard: brave poet, indomitable rebel, 1896–1965* (Philadelphia: Chilton Book Company, 1968), is a collection of memories of Cunard by her friends and colleagues. Hugh Ford, *Published in Paris: A Literary Chronicle of Paris in the 1920s and 1930s* (New York: Collier Books, 1975) sets Cunard's Press in the context of *c.*1930 small publishing. Henry Crowder's memoir *As wonderful as all that?* (California: Wild Trees Press, 1987) gives a different perspective; for Crowder's life and also for audio recordings of his music, including the songs in *Henry-Music*, there is Anthony Barnett, *Listening for Henry Crowder: A Monograph on His Almost Lost Music* (Lewes: Allardyce Book, 2007).

The central biographical studies of Cunard are Anne Chisholm, *Nancy Cunard* (London: Sidgwick and Jackson, 1979), and Lois G. Gordon, *Nancy Cunard: Heiress, Muse, Political Idealist* (New York: Columbia University Press, 2007). See also Kris Somerville, 'Remembering the Hours: Nancy Cunard's Expatriate Press', in the *Missouri Review*, 33.4, Winter 2010, 67–78. Mercedes Aguirre, 'Publishing the Avant-Garde: Nancy Cunard's Hours Press', in *Publishing Modernist Fiction and Poetry*, edited by Lise Jaillant (Edinburgh: Edinburgh University Press, 2019), 135–53, is an excellent study of Cunard's press, particularly in terms of its links with surrealism. On Cunard's poetry, see her *Selected Poems*, edited by Sandeep Parmar (Manchester: Carcanet Press, 2016), reviewed by Patrick McGuinness, 'Their Mad Gallopade', *London Review of Books* 40.2 (25 January 2018). Woolf's Hogarth Press is well studied in Helen Southworth (ed.), *Leonard and Virginia Woolf: The Hogarth Press and the Networks of Modernism* (Edinburgh University Press: Edinburgh, 2010).

Laura Grace Ford, Craig Atkinson, Phyllis Johnson, George Maciunas, Yusuf Hassan

Digital scans of the contents of all ten editions of *Aspen* are available for free online at *Ubu Web* (www.ubu.com/aspen/aspen1). For zines, the most recent work is Gavin Hogg and Hamish Ironside, *We Peaked at Paper: An Oral History of British Zines* (London: Boatwhistle Books, 2022). Jane Radway has written some of the sharpest pieces on zines, including 'Zines then and now: what are they? What do you do with them? How do they work?', in A. Lang (ed.), *From codex to hypertext* (Amherst: University of Massachusetts Press, 2012), 27–47, and 'Girl Zine Networks, Underground Itineraries, and Riot Grrrl History: Making Sense of the Struggle for New Social Forms in the 1990s and Beyond', in *Journal of American Studies*, 50(1) (2016), 1–31. Helpful in terms of the punk history of zines is Kevin Dunn and May Summer Farnsworth, ' "We Are the Revolution": Riot Grrrl Press, Girl Empowerment, and DIY Self-Publishing', in *Women's Studies: An Interdisciplinary Journal* March 2012, 41.2, 136–57. On the need to address the whiteness of traditional zine studies, see Melanie Ramdarshan Bold, 'Why diverse zines matter: a case study of the People of Color Zines project', in *Publishing Research Quarterly* 33 (2017), 215–28. For Fluxus, there are many excellent introductions, including Jacquelyn Baas (ed.), *Fluxus and the Essential Questions of Life* (Chicago: University of Chicago Press, 2012). For a series of vignettes of Maciunas, there is Emmett Williams and Ann Noël, *Mr. Fluxus: A collective portrait of George Maciunas 1931– 1978* (London: Thames and Hudson, 1997).

Acknowledgements

The following people, arranged in democratising alphabetical order, have their inky fingers all over this book, and I thank them for it: Caroline Archer, Craig Atkinson, Mary Chamberlain, the late Stephen Colclough, Dennis Duncan, Laura Grace Ford, Alexandra Franklin, Robert Green, Yusuf Hassan, Jorg Hensgen, Ben Higgins, Chloë Houston, Richard Lawrence, Zachary Lesser, Jo Maddocks, Simon Morris, Rose Nordin, Julie Park, Gill Partington, David Pearson, Sarah Pyke, Laura Reeves, Emma Smith, Stephen Tabor, Siobhán Templeton, Tom Templeton, Whitney Trettien, Sarah Wheale, Abigail Williams, Stuart Williams, and Peter Willis. I am hugely grateful to my friend and agent Eleanor Birne for encouraging this book into being in the first place. More than thanks to Barnaby Smyth and Gill Smyth, and to Eliane Glaser, Ezra Glaser, and Anna Glaser-Smyth.

Image and Quotation Credits

Plate section

Grande danse macabre des hommes et des femmes (1499), f. 7r. Princeton University Library.

Christoph Weigels, *Ständebuch* (1698). Wikipedia.

Little Gidding's chapel. Author photograph.

The Whole Law of God, cover and title page. Royal Collection Trust / © His Majesty King Charles III 2023.

Two images of Denis Diderot and Jean le Rond d'Alembert, *Encyclopédie, ou dictionnaire raisonné des sciences, des arts et des métiers* (1751–66). Folger Shakespeare Library.

Universal Magazine (June 1750), reproduced in John Findlay McRae, *Two Centuries of Typefounding: Annals of the Letter Foundry Established by William Caslon* (London: George W. Jones, 1920).

John Orlando Parry, 'A London Street Scene' (1835). Photo 12/ Getty Images.

Kitto Bible, RB49000 vol58 p10557r2. The Huntington Library, Art Collections, and Botanical Gardens.

Holy Bible by Adam Broomberg and Oliver Chanarin published by MACK, 2013. ©Adam Broomberg and Oliver Chanarin 2013, courtesy MACK.

William Morris, *News from Nowhere, or, An epoch of rest: Being Some Chapters from a Utopian Romance* (1892), woodcut. Yale Center for British Art, Paul Mellon Collection.

The tragicall historie of Hamlet, Prince of Denmarke (Doves Press, 1909), pp. 80–81. Folger Shakespeare Library.

Calligrapher Edward Johnston, 1 January 1902. Wikipedia.

Doves Press type recovered from the Thames by Robert Green. Photograph by Matthew Williams-Ellis for Malcolm Russell's *Mudlark'd* (2022), copyright Thames & Hudson Ltd.

Cunard and Henry Crowder in the Hours Press, 15 rue Guénégaud, Paris, 1930. Keystone France/Getty Images.

Savage Messiah issue 7. Reproduced with permission of Laura Grace Ford.

Aspen number 4. Author photograph.

BlackMass's *Trife Life* (2021). Reproduced with permission of Yusuf Hassan.

Integrated images

Introduction

2: Margaret Cavendish's *Poems, and Phancies* (1664), p. 183. Bodleian Library Douce C subt. 17. The Bodleian Libraries, University of Oxford.

Chapter 1 Printing: Wynkyn de Worde (d.1534/5)

8: *A Lytyll Treatyse Called the Booke of Curtesye* (1492). Bodleian Library Douce Fragm. E. 4. The Bodleian Libraries, University of Oxford.

15: *Legenda aurea* (1507), final page. Folger Shakespeare Library.

24, 26 and 27: Three images of *The Ship of Fools* (1517), sigs. Aıv. Aii, O4. Bodleian Library B subst. 254. The Bodleian Libraries, University of Oxford.

31: John Fisher, *This sermon folowynge* (1509 or 1510), title page. Folger Shakespeare Library.

42: *The Descrypcyon of Englonde* (1502), Society of Antiquaries, Main Library Cab. Lib. C. Photograph by the author. Reproduced with the permission of the Society of Antiquaries of London.

Chapter 2 Binding: William Wildgoose (*fl.* 1617–26)

46: 'Deliured to William Wildgoose These books following to be bound 17 Febre. 1623'. Bodleian Library Records e. 528, fol. 45r. The Bodleian Libraries, University of Oxford.

59: Francisco Sánchez de Las Brozas, *In Ecclesiasten commentarium cum concordia Vulgatæ editionis, et Hebraici textus* (1619). Bodleian Library BB 12(1) Th. Bodleian Libraries, University of Oxford.

61: Hans Sachs, *Eygentliche Beschreibung aller Stände auff Erden* (1568), f. 22r. Beinecke Rare Book and Manuscript Library.

68: Shakespeare's First Folio, Bodleian Library Bodleian Arch. G c.7. The Bodleian Libraries, University of Oxford.

75: Wildgoose's signature in Bodleian Day Book, Bodleian Library Records e. 528, fol. 45r. The Bodleian Libraries, University of Oxford.

Chapter 3 Cut and Paste: Mary (1603–80) and Anna Collett (1605–39)

79: Genesis, chapter 1, from *The Whole Law of God*. Royal Collection Trust / © His Majesty King Charles III 2023.

84 and 85: Two images of Gospel Harmony (1635), British Library C.23.e.4, columns 37–38. © British Library Board.

91: 'The Last Judgement', after Marten de Vos of Antwerp. Ferrar Papers (prints) 213. By permission of the Pepys Library, Magdalene College, Cambridge.

100: Two images of John Gibson's commonplace book, BL Additional MS 37719, ff. 190v, 163. © British Library Board.

102 and 103: Two images of Harmony for Charles I (1635), BL C.23.e.4 © British Library Board.

Chapter 4 Typography: John Baskerville (1707–75) and Sarah Eaves (1708–88)

111: Baskerville's *Publii Virgilii Maronis Bucolica, Georgica, et Æneis* (1757). Beinecke Rare Book and Manuscript Library.

116: John Baskerville, *A Specimen*, four type sizes, Beinecke Rare Book and Manuscript Library.

117: *Historia naturale di Caio Plinio Secondo* (Venice, 1476), sig. 1r. Bodleian Library Arch. G b.6, sig. 1r. Photo: © Bodleian Libraries, University of Oxford.

118 and 119: Two images of John Baskerville, *A Specimen*, italic 'Q' and lower-case 'g'. Beinecke Rare Book and Manuscript Library.

120: Reproduction of Baskerville's slate made by the Library of Birmingham. Photograph by Caroline Archer.

Chapter 5 Non-Books: Benjamin Franklin (1706–90)

144: Franklin's Philadelphia lottery papers (1748). Beinecke Rare Book and Manuscript Library.

154: *Poor Richard, 1737. An almanack for the year of Christ 1737* (1736). Beinecke Rare Book and Manuscript Library.

162: Giuseppe Arcimboldo, 'The Librarian' (1566?). Skokloster Castle/SHM (PDM).

Chapter 6 Paper: Nicolas-Louis Robert (1761–1828)

173: Hans Sachs, *Eygentliche Beschreibung aller Stände auff Erden* (1568), f. 25r. Beinecke Rare Book and Manuscript Library.

183: Peter Brueghel the Younger's 'The Village Lawyer' (*c.*1620), Museum of Fine Arts Ghent.

Chapter 7 Extra-Illustration: Charlotte (1782–1852) and Alexander (1753–1820) Sutherland

189: James Granger, *Biographical History of England* (1769), RB283000 v4 p84a. The Huntington Library, Art Collections, and Botanical Gardens.

193: James Granger, print of engraving by Samuel Freeman (1803). Folger Shakespeare Library.

196: Edward Hyde, Earl of Clarendon, *The history of the Rebellion and Civil Wars in England begun in the year 1641* (1702–04), opening to page 108. Yale Center for British Art, Paul Mellon Collection.

201: Carrie and Sophie Lawrence, sisters extra-illustrating in their workshop in New York City, *circa* 1902, from *The Book-lover: a magazine of book lore*, Z1007_B712. The Huntington Library, Art Collections, and Botanical Gardens.

206: Irving Brown's Grangerised book, New York, 1886, RB108765_v2_p54. The Huntington Library, Art Collections, and Botanical Gardens.

215: *Holy Bible* by Adam Broomberg and Oliver Chanarin published by MACK, 2013. ©Adam Broomberg and Oliver Chanarin 2013, courtesy MACK.

Chapter 8 Circulation: Charles Edward Mudie (1818–90)

217: Mudie's Great Hall inauguration guest list, 17 December 1860. Rare Book and Manuscript Library, University of Illinois at Urbana-Champaign Library.

218: 'Mr. Mudie's New Hall', *Illustrated London News*. Wellcome Collection.

241: Florence Nightingale to Charles E. Mudie, 20 November 1867. Rare Book and Manuscript Library, University of Illinois at Urbana-Champaign Library.

Chapter 9 Anachronistic Books: Thomas Cobden-Sanderson (1840–1922)

246: The Hammersmith Socialist Society (1892). © National Portrait Gallery, London.

250: William Morris, *The works of Geoffrey Chaucer, now newly imprinted* (1896), Beinecke Rare Book and Manuscript Library.

251: Page proofs for the Kelmscott *Chaucer* (1896), p. 63, with Morris's autograph corrections and notes. Beinecke Rare Book and Manuscript Library.

253: *Paradise Lost* (Doves Press, 1902). Lady Margaret Hall, Oxford.

254: Punch and matrix, from Theodore Low De Vinne, *The Invention of Printing* (New York: F. Hart & Co., 1876), p. 55.

260: *Paradise Lost* Book 4 (Doves Press, 1902). Lady Margaret Hall, Oxford.

261: Gutenberg's *Biblia Latina,* 42 lines (Mainz, 1454). Beinecke Rare Book and Manuscript Library.

266: Bible (Doves Press, 1902–4). Trinity College, Oxford. By permission of the President and Fellows of Trinity College, Oxford.

274: *The tragicall historie of Hamlet, Prince of Denmarke* (Doves Press, 1909). Lady Margaret Hall, Oxford.

Chapter 10 Small Presses: Nancy Cunard (1896–1965)

281: Samuel Beckett, *Whoroscope* (1930). Bodleian Library Johnson d. 2052. The Bodleian Libraries, University of Oxford.

285: Nancy Cunard, photographed by Barbara Ker-Seymer. Tate Archive.

296: Nancy Cunard printing. Getty Images.

Chapter 11 Zines, Do-It-Yourself, Boxes, Artists' Books: Laura Grace Ford (b. 1973), Craig Atkinson (b. 1977), Phyllis Johnson (1926–2001), George Maciunas (1931–78), and Yusuf Hassan (b. 1987)

307: *Savage Messiah* issue 1. Reproduced with permission of Laura Grace Ford.

315: Café Royal's *Shipbuilding on Tyneside 1975–76,* by Chris Killip. Reproduced with permission of Craig Atkinson.

318: Café Royal's *Notting Hill Sound Systems,* by Brian David Stevens. Reproduced with permission of Craig Atkinson.

329: BlackMass's *"I roped, threw, tied, bridled, saddled . . ."* (2022). Reproduced with permission of Yusuf Hassan.

332: *The London Prodigall* (1605), sig. G4v. Folger Shakespeare Library Shelfmark STC 22333 Copy 2. Folger Shakespeare Library.

Epilogue

336 and 337: Three images of *Epistolae decretales summorum pontificum* (Antwerp, 1570). Copy owned by David Pearson; reproduced with his permission.

Quotations

vii: From Tom Phillips, 'Henri Matisse: The Cut-Outs', in *Times Literary Supplement*, 23 May 2014

82 and 105: Lines from T. S. Eliot's 'Little Gidding', from *Four Quartets* by T. S. Eliot. Copyright © 1936 by Houghton Mifflin Harcourt Publishing Company, renewed 1964 by T. S. Eliot. Copyright © 1940, 1941, 1942 by T. S. Eliot, renewed 1968, 1969, 1970 by Esme Valerie Eliot. Used by permission of Faber and Faber Ltd (UK) and HarperCollins Publishers (US).

216 and 229–30: From Jorge Luis Borges, 'The Library of Babel' (1941), translated by Andrew Hurley, published by Penguin Classics. © María Kodama, 1998. Translation © Penguin Putnam Inc., 1998. Reprinted by permission of Penguin Books Limited (UK), Viking Books / Penguin Random House LLC (US).

Index

Tacitus; *Agricola*, 256
Tangier, 55
Tanguy, Yves, 300
Tangye, Richard, 76
Tate, Henry, 236
Tate, John, 23, 172
Tate the Younger, John, 23
Taylor, John; *The Praise of Hemp-Seed*, 175
Taylor, Jordan E., 150–51
Taylor, Neil, 271
Ten Poems More (Graves), 300
Tennyson, Alfred, Lord, 219, 256
Tenures (Littleton), 101
Terence, 127, 137
Thackeray, William, 236
Theater of honour and knight-hood, The (Favyn), 52, 58
Theobald, Lewis, 71
Thompson, Ann, 271
Thorne, Joan, 49
Thorne, John, 48–50
Three Mountains Press, 294–5
three-volume novels, 240–44
Tidcombe, Marianne, 258, 265, 277
Tiffin, Percy, 254
Times, The, 168, 182, 245
Times Literary Supplement, 265
title pages, 28–30
Titus, Edward, 297
'To His Mistress Going to Bed' (Donne), 163
Todd, Mark, 310
Toklas, Alice B., 284
Tourner, John, 39
Towne, Humphrey, 39
'Tradition and the Individual Talent' (Eliot), 6
Transatlantic Review, 295
Travels (Mandeville), 11–12

Tree, Iris, 287
Trehearne, William, 217
Trinity College, Oxford, 262
Troilus and Criseyde (Chaucer), 27–8
Trollope, Anthony, 217, 220
Ts'ai Lun, 169, 172
Turbutt, Gladwyn Maurice Revell, 44, 72–4
Twain, Mark, 131
Twentysix Gasoline Stations (Ruscha), 316–17
Two Stories (Woolf and Woolf), 291
Tyndale, William, 263
typefaces, 35, 106–8, 126–7, 135, 257–9
 Baskerville, 115–19, *116, 118, 119*, 127–8
 Bell, 127
 Bembo, 127
 Caslon, 158
 Chaucer, 255
 Doves Type, 252–5, *253*, 274–8
 Fournier, 127
 Garamond, 127
 Golden Type, 253, 255
 Johnston Sans, 257
 Mrs Eaves, 128
 Poliphilus, 127
 Troy, 255
 see also typography
typography, 106–30, 253–5, 266–8
 definition of, 112
 fleurons, 157
 gold lettering, 259
 italic type, 35, 110, *118*
 machine setting, 126–7
 matrix, 35, 106–7, 156, *254*, 255
 roman type, 115
 type manufacture, 106–9, 122–3, 156–8

Credit: Eliane Glaser

Adam Smyth is Professor of English Literature and the History of the Book at Balliol College, Oxford University. He is a regular contributor to the *London Review of Books* and the *TLS*. He also runs the 39 Steps Press, a small printing press which he operates from a barn in Oxfordshire, England.